Acquisition.com Volume II

$100M Leads

How to Get Strangers To

Want To Buy Your Stuff

Alex Hormozi

Guiding Principles

Do more.

Thank Yous

To Trevor:

Thank you for your true friendship. Thank you for your tireless effort to extract the ideas out of my head. And, for your continued support in slaying the nihilism monster. People say you are lucky if you have one real friend in your entire life. Thank you for being the best friend a man could ask for.

To Leila:

Even though Lady Gaga said it first, it doesn't make it any less true.

"You found the light in me that I couldn't find.

The part of me that's you will never die."

Table of Contents

Section I: Start Here

"It's hard to be poor with leads bangin' down your door" - Hormozi family jingle

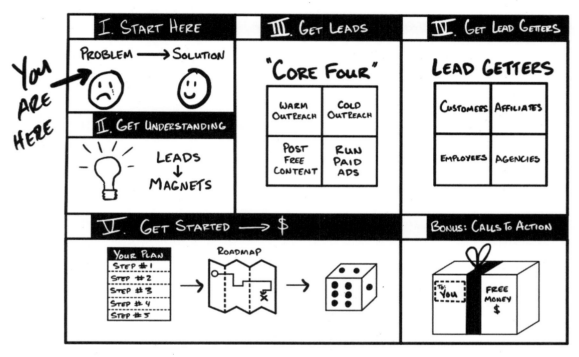

You have to sell stuff to make money. It seems simple enough, but everyone tries to skip to the 'make money' part. It doesn't work. I tried. You need *all* the pieces. You need the stuff to sell - an offer. You need people to sell it to - leads. Then you gotta get those people to buy it - sales. Once you put all those in place, *then* you can make money.

My first book, *$100M Offers,* covers the first step and gives you the *stuff.* It answers the age old question *"What should I sell?."* Answer - an offer so good people feel stupid saying no. But strangers can only buy your stuff if they know you exist. This takes leads. "Leads" mean a lot of different things to a lot of different people. But most agree that they're the first step to getting more customers. In simpler terms, it means they've got the problem to solve and the money to spend.

If you're reading this book, you already know leads don't magically appear. You need to go get them. More precisely, you need to help them find you so they can buy your stuff! And the best part is, you don't have to wait…you can *force* them to find you. You do that through advertising. **Advertising**, *the process of making known*, lets strangers know about the stuff you sell. If more people know about the stuff you sell, then you sell more stuff. If you sell more stuff, then you make more money. *Having lots of leads makes it hard to be poor.*

Advertising lets you have a terrible product... and still make money. It lets you be terrible at sales…and still make money. It lets you make a ton of mistakes and *still. make. money.* In short, having this skill gives you endless chances to *get it right.*

And in the unforgiving world of business, second chances are hard to come by. So you might as well load up. *Advertising is a skill worth having.*

And this book, *$100M Leads*, shows you *exactly* how to do it.

***

$100M Leads sits atop the foundation of my first book, *$100M Offers*. It assumes you already have a *Grand Slam Offer* to sell - the stuff. Once you have an offer to sell, it creates the next problem–*Who do I sell it to?* This book is my answer to that question. Leads. Lots of leads.

And before you know how to get leads, life *sucks.* You don't know where your next customer will come from. You scramble to cover rent and pay bills. You worry about laying people off, putting food on your table and… *going under.* You work your hardest to succeed, and others laugh at you for trying. It feels like death. I've been there. I get it. This book puts you in a better situation. One where you've got more leads than you can handle and more money than you can spend.

Here's How:

First, it explains how advertising works.

Second, it reveals the four core ways to get leads.

Third, it shows you how to get other people to do it for you.

Finally, it wraps up with a one-page advertising plan you can use to grow your business *today.*

***

Once you know how to get leads, life gets easier.

As for why you should blindly listen to me about getting more leads - don't. Make up your own darn mind! But, in the spirit of "walking the talk," here's my track record:

I advertise in a variety of industries through my holding company Acquisition.com. Our portfolio includes software, e-commerce, business services, consumer services, brick & mortar chains, digital products, and plenty of others. Together, they make $250,000,000+ in annual revenue. And they do it by getting 20,000+ leads per day selling offers from $1 to $1,000,000+.

On the personal side, I have a lifetime average return on advertising of 36:1. That means for every $1 I spend on advertising, I get $36 back. A return of 3600%. Some people built their wealth in the stock market. Others in real estate. I built mine advertising.

This year I surpassed $100,000,000 in net worth at age 32. And if you're from the future, that's in 2022 US Dollars. Which, much to my dismay, came with no flyers. No awards. No parades. I'm still 2000x poorer than the richest man in the world. My life is pretty much the same. I'm still the same height, married to the same woman, and graying faster than when I was poor.

In these pages, I share the skills responsible for the bulk of my material success. I did it all using the advertising methods in this book. I left nothing out. This isn't a book of theories or armchair analysis. This book is built on what worked for me. And I wrote it hoping it'll work even better for you.

To answer a question I got after releasing my first book: "Why do your books look like they're written for kids?" The answer is simple: my books must be books I would read. And I have a short attention span. As such, I liken my reading preferences to that of a child: short in length, simple in words, and with lots of pictures. These books are my attempt to do that.

$100M Leads is about getting strangers to show interest in the stuff you sell. And once I transfer that skill to you, it's your turn to use it.

With that out of the way…let's get rich, shall we?

Pro Tip: Faster, Deeper Learning By Reading & Listening At Same Time

Here's a life hack I stumbled on years ago. If you listen to an audiobook and read the physical book or ebook at the same time, you read faster and remember more. You store the contents in more places in your brain. Nifty stuff. This is how I read books worth reading.

I also do both because I struggle to stay focused. If I listen to the audio while reading it helps me avoid zoning out. It took me two days to record this book out loud. I did it so if you struggle like me, you don't have to anymore.

If you want to give it a try, go ahead and grab the audio version and see for yourself. I've made my books as cheap as the platforms let me, so this isn't a ploy to make some extra coin - I promise. I hope you find it as valuable as I have.

I figured I'd put this "hack" early on. This way you'd have a chance to do it if you found the first chapter valuable enough to earn your attention.

Pro Tip: Hack For Finishing Books

I get distracted easily. So I need little tricks to keep my attention. This one helps me a lot: Finish chapters. Don't stop in the middle. Completing a chapter gives you positive reinforcement. It keeps you going. So, if you meet a tough chapter, finish it so you can start fresh on the next one.

How I Got Here

"Hope is being able to see the light despite all the darkness" - Desmond Tutu

March 2017.

I felt hurried taps on my shoulder while working at my desk. It was Leila, my (then) girlfriend and business partner.

"What's up? You alright?"

"We have a problem." She said.

What now? I thought.

"Look at this." She shoved a stack of books out of the way to make room for her laptop.

"What am I looking at?" I squinted.

"A disaster."

She ran her finger down the screen to direct my gaze.

-$99… -$499…-$499… -$299…-$399… -$499…-$499…

Every other number was more than my rent.

"What are these?"

She started scrolling. "Refunds. All of them. From the two gyms we launched last month."

"Wait. How? Why?"

She scrolled more. "I got lots of weird texts last night from the members we sold at the Kentucky gym. I guess the owner stood up on a chair and told everyone to refund and go home. He didn't want to deal with all the new customers."

"That's insane," I said.

She was still scrolling. "Yeah, and the other gym owner told his new customers he would take them for half price if they asked for refunds from us and paid him instead."

"Wait what? They can't do that." I said.

"Well, they did." *She scrolled faster, the numbers blurred.*

"Have you called them? That's not allowed in the agreement." I said.

"Yea. I know. They're ignoring my calls."

I put my hand on hers. The refund waterfall froze in place. Hundreds of droplet-size reminders of how much I sucked.

"How bad is this? How many refunds? Just cutting profits? Or enough to go negative and owe money?" I tried to keep my voice steady. I failed.

Leila paused before answering. "It's a hundred and fifty grand." The number hung in the air. "...we won't be able to pay my friends."

Their faces flashed through my mind, and the little hope I had drained from my chest. A month earlier, I got her friends to quit their jobs for this. Now I had to tell them I didn't have the money to pay them.

She continued. "We can't sell our way out of this either. It'll just create more refunds to deal with. And we're out of money." Her eyes met mine, looking for the answers she deserved. I had nothing.

I felt sick.

A year earlier-

I was good at getting leads for my gyms. I scaled to five locations in only three years. My claim to fame was opening my gyms up at full capacity on the first day. So, I opened as many as I could as fast as I could.

My fast pace started getting attention. I got asked to speak at a conference about my advertising method. To me though, I didn't think my process was special. I figured everyone was doing it. So, I walked through my presentation hoping I wasn't boring the audience. They were silent.

The moment I stepped off stage, a mob formed around me. They hurled questions at me left and right. I could barely keep up. They even followed me into the bathroom. I felt like a celebrity. It was wild. To this day, I've never been more bombarded in my life. Everyone wanted me to teach them how to do what I had just presented. They wanted my help. Me. But I had nothing to sell them. Although, over one hundred people left me their phone numbers and business cards in case I did. Then a wild idea came to me.

I could make some money doing this...

3 months later—an idea turns into a business

Since I used advertising to launch my gyms at full capacity I thought, maybe, I could "launch" other people's gyms to full capacity, too. I called the company Gym Launch. Original, I know.

My offer was simple. *I'll fill your gym in 30 days for free. You pay nothing. I pay for everything. I sell new members and keep the first 6 weeks of membership fees as payment. You get everything else. If I don't fill your gym, I don't make money. You spend nothing either way.*

It was an easy offer to sell. I'd fly out. Turn on my lead machine. Work the leads. Then sell the leads. Except, instead of selling them into my gym, I'd sell them into whatever gym I was camped at for the month. Every month I'd go to a new gym. Rinse and repeat. *It worked.*

Word of this kid who'd fill your gym for free got around fast. Unless I hired help, referrals would've booked me out for more than two years straight. I couldn't keep running my gyms *and* doing this, so I sold my gyms and went all in on Gym Launch.

I saw a problem though. I filled their gyms, and *they* got to keep all the long-term profits. I left so much money on the table. But, if I were part owner of some of the gyms, I could stack revenue month over month. *Bingo.* Not much later, one of the gym owners made such an offer. We'd be fifty-fifty. I would fill the gym with members, and he would fill it with staff. With this new model, I could open up 1 to 2 gyms per month and own them all. This would work much better than only collecting the upfront cash. A win-win partnership.

A slight hitch in the plan, though. My new partner had "poor financials." So nice guy Alex offered to pay all the expenses and take on all the liability for the first launch. I personally guaranteed the lease and would spend *my* time and money to fill it with members. Once filled, I would hand the gym over to him. I put all the money from selling my gyms, including my life savings, into this "launch and go" model. It took everything I had.

A few weeks later, halfway through the launch, I woke up to find all the money in the account gone. All of it. The partner accused me of stealing and took the money as "his share" of the profits. But, *we hadn't made any profit.* Then, he sent the money to a foreign contact and filed for bankruptcy. That's what he told me anyway. When I offered to walk through the financials and account for every dollar, he refused. That's when I knew I had made a terrible mistake.

It turns out he had been indicted for fraud a few years earlier. And to make matters worse, *I already knew.* He told me it was "just a big misunderstanding." I believed him. As the saying goes, *when money meets experience... the money gets the experience, and the experience gets the money*. Lesson learned.

In three months, I went from a successful multi-location gym owner. To selling all my gyms. To a cool new launching gyms thing. To completely broke. Everything I made from selling my gyms was gone. My life savings was gone. Wiped out. All of it. Four years of work, saving, sleeping on the floor– erased in a…oh no… *Leila*.

Leila quit her life as she knew it to do this with me. She weathered my constant changes. She supported me in the half-baked partnership even though she opposed it. Even with this huge failure, she never once even hinted, *I told you so*. Instead, she told me, "The Gym Launch model is still good. Let's do more of those." So we did.

I put $3,300 *per day* on a credit card to pay for ads, airfare, hotels, rental cars, etc. for six sales reps. Leila's friends. I say this lightly, but I covered what a nightmare it was in the first book. So I won't repeat it here.

In the first month, we launched six gyms and collected $100,117. We made enough to cover the $100,000 credit card bill. And for the record, that meant I was still broke. The next month we made $177,399 with $30,000-$40,000 in profit. It gave me some room to breathe. *Finally*.

And that's when Leila tapped me on the shoulder to share $150,000 worth of bad news.

Now you're caught up.

The morning after Leila told me we had $150,000 in refunds and lost all our money. Again.

A honking horn startled me at 3 AM. My problems flooded back. *Welp. I'm awake now.* I pulled myself out of bed and slinked to my work corner. I walked over out of habit more than desire. I slid the chair out and plopped down - notebook and pen at the ready. I had to make $150,000 in profit, not revenue, in thirty days. And I had to do it with no money to my name, and no experience making that much profit in a month. Ever. So I started scribbling ideas:

…Charge an upfront fee for new gyms

…Ask for a percentage of revenue from old gyms

...Get gyms I already launched to pre-pay for a future launch

...Call every old customer and sell them supplements over the phone

I kept penciling the math. None of these would make enough money. Not in thirty days anyway. I felt glued to the chair. *I have to figure this out.* I stared at the notebook, hoping it knew something. It didn't. *God I suck.*

A few hours later, Leila woke up. Like clockwork, she walked into the kitchen and poured a cup of coffee. She got straight to work at the kitchen table behind me.

"Whatcha doin'?" I asked, trying to distract myself.

"Check-ins with online fitness clients." she said.

"What does that bring in again?"

"$3600 last month."

"What do you charge?"

"300 bucks a month. Why?"

"How long does it take you?"

"A few hours a week"

"And there's no overhead? just time?"

"Yea...why?"

I plowed on "I know these are old personal training clients, but do you think you could do it with strangers?"

"I don't know...probably...what're you thinking?".

"I think I have something." I said.

"Wait, for what?"

"To come up with the hundred and fifty grand."

"What, my online training? How?" She looked skeptical.

"We just cut the middleman and sell direct. I think I can just run ads to a sales page that books phone appointments. Then we can sell the fitness programs we've been selling at the gyms, but sell it as an online program. We already have the materials. We already know the ads work. And there won't be any cost to fulfill. Plus, no more flights. No rentals. No motels. And no gym owner telling them to refund..."

She hesitated. "You think it could work?"

"Honestly…no idea. But every day we don't do something is one less day to come up with the money."

She thought hard. "Alright, let's do it."

That was all I needed.

I worked thirty-eight hours straight to make the offer go live. A few hours later, leads started flowing. She took her first call the next day. I walked in as the call finished:

"$499...yea…and what card did you want to use?" *she had the candor of a pro.*

A few minutes later, I asked with anticipation, "Was that a sale??"

"Yep." *Dang, she is a pro.*

I even snapped a picture of Leila closing our first sale because it felt so momentous.

Within days, we were doing $1000 per day in online fitness sales. We also got the cash up front with almost no risk of refunds. *This was working.* But, we were still *way* short of the $150,000.

At lunch, she listened to my master plan between mouthfuls. "Okay, the sales guys can stay home and sell this over the phone. If they do the same $1000 per day as you, with eight guys, we should hit $8,000 per day. In thirty days, we'll make $240,000. After ad spend and commissions, we'll have enough to cover the $150,000."

"What about the gyms we're supposed to launch?"

"I'll call 'em and tell 'em we're going in another direction. They haven't paid us anything, so there's not much they can object to. I'll start calling them after lunch."

The first call was to a gym owner in Boise, Idaho.

"Hello?"

I looked down to read the bullet points on my little script. "Hey man - we're not doing launches anymore. We're selling direct-to-consumer weight loss. So we won't be coming out and—"

He interrupted. "But I *really* need this right now. I just refinanced my house and maxed out all my credit cards to keep my gym afloat. I put my life savings into this place. Is there any way you can help me? You launched my buddy's gym. I know what you can do."

Given my *worse than yours* situation, I didn't care how bad his finances were. So I tried to sound polite. "I get that it's a hard time, but we're not flying out. I'm sorry."

"Okay, okay. I get you can't fly out. But is there any way you can just show me what to do? We really need this."

I was beat up, exhausted, broke, and felt betrayed by the entire industry. I should have said "no" but instead, I said… "Fine. I'll show you how to get leads, but I'm not flying out there to save you if you can't sell."

"Totally get it. It's on me. I can close. I just don't have anyone walking in the door. I need LEADS. How much to show me how to launch?"

I looked down at my script. *This is not how it was supposed to go.* I wanted to say no and hang up. Our weight loss offer was working, and I didn't want distractions. He'd already told me he was broke, so I said the biggest number I could think of to get him off the phone.

"$6000. Consider it my 'selling my secrets' sale."

"6k?"

"Yes. Six thousand." I said, articulating the whole number, hoping to scare him off.

"6k? Okay - done."

What. I stood there slack-jawed, frozen in disbelief. *Six. Thousand. Dollars.* I floated out of myself and watched the conversation happen. I still get choked up thinking about it.

"Oh…uhh…great…what card do you wanna use?" Now, trying *not* to scare away the *Six. Thousand. Dollars.* Panicked, I wrote his card information on the flap of a cardboard box.

"When do I start?" he asked.

"I'll send you everything Monday morning." Giving myself the insane task of packaging my entire gym leads and sales system in forty-eight hours. He agreed.

I hung up and sat in shock. Once I came to my senses, I ran the credit card. *$6000…success. Is this real?*

I desperately wanted to tell Leila, but she was on a sales call. Fifteen minutes later, she walked in.

"Got another one," she said.

"You won't believe this. I just sold our Gym Launch system for $6000 to the gym in Boise."

"What? I thought we were doing weight loss."

"Yea, I know. So did I, but…" She waited. "…I think we're still in the gym business…I think we were just doing it wrong." She needed more details. I didn't have any yet. "I'm gonna call the gyms we planned to launch next month and see if they'll buy it too."

"Uhhh…okay." She said.

The next call went the same except when he said "How much?" I said, "$8,000." He agreed.

Next call, same thing, except I said, "$10,000." He agreed.

All eight gyms we planned to launch said yes to licensing the launch materials instead. *In a single day, I collected $60,000 selling something with zero cost to fulfill.* In a single day, I was a third of the way out of my $150,000 prison. I spent five years developing that advertising system. It finally paid off. Doing the thing that scared me most - *giving away my secrets* - led to the biggest breakthrough in my life.

"I can't believe it," I said. "I think we can get out of this."

"So… are we not doing the weight loss thing?"

"No. I guess not…I think we've had something here all along. We just had to put the pieces together."

"Do you think anyone else will buy it?"

"I'm gonna call the thirty gyms we already launched. They know our system works because we did it in front of them. We also have some gym owner leads from that conference. That should cover the $150,000 and give us a clean slate."

"Ok, then what? Is this what we're gonna do?" She looked for some well-deserved stability.

"I mean - I think so? It makes more money than the other thing, and it's way easier to deliver." She agreed. "So after I call those leads, I'll start running ads. I'll post our success stories in a few gym groups to get leads from there. And I'll also tell the gyms I'll pay $2000 cash for any gym they send that signs up. That gives us ad leads, content leads, *and* referral leads."

***

In the next 30 days, we made $215,000 *in profit*. We covered the $150,000 in refunds with cash to spare. We did so well because the average gym using our advertising system added an extra $30,000 in cash in their first 30 days. *It made them more money than they paid for it.* It delivered - *in spades*. Plus, they got to keep all the cash. They loved it. Referrals poured in.

I found the processing records from May-June 2017, the month it all happened:

	Pending Authorizations		Charges		Refunds		Rtns/Chgbks		Voids		Declines		Totals	
	Count	Amount	Count	Amount	Count	Amount	Count	Amount	Count	Amount	Count	Aprvl Pct	Count	Amount
01/2017	0	$0.00	348	$102,605.64	7	$-2,488.33	0	$0.00	12	$2,002.98	148	70%	515	$100,117.31
02/2017	0	$0.00	847	$190,809.50	56	$-13,243.77	1	$-166.00	5	$1,247.00	232	78%	1141	$177,399.73
03/2017	0	$0.00	782	$177,820.58	61	$-12,701.50	4	$-997.00	21	$3,458.50	285	73%	1153	$164,122.08
04/2017	0	$0.00	704	$204,461.25	49	$-10,725.00	10	$-6,315.00	2	$-50.00	354	67%	1119	$187,421.25
05/2017	0	$0.00	191	$260,754.00	4	$-797.00	11	$-16,984.00	0	$0.00	42	82%	248	$242,973.00
06/2017	0	$0.00	214	$272,835.00	5	$-1,498.00	30	$-55,375.00	0	$0.00	1	100%	250	$215,962.00
07/2017	0	$0.00	282	$316,917.98	0	$0.00	21	$-23,450.00	0	$0.00	7	98%	310	$293,467.98
08/2017	0	$0.00	346	$393,370.62	0	$0.00	28	$-32,998.99	1	$100.00	45	88%	420	$360,371.63
09/2017	0	$0.00	478	$543,376.29	1	$-1,000.00	64	$-65,792.00	0	$0.00	41	92%	584	$476,584.29
10/2017	0	$0.00	799	$828,709.31	7	$-5,798.00	50	$-49,887.00	8	$8,000.00	31	96%	895	$773,024.31
11/2017	0	$0.00	1076	$1,132,319.31	8	$-8,000.00	66	$-64,296.00	1	$1.00	92	92%	1243	$1,060,023.31
12/2017	0	$0.00	1315	$1,363,956.31	13	$-17,296.00	83	$-82,099.00	1	$1,000.00	111	92%	1523	$1,264,561.31
01/2018	0	$0.00	1609	$1,621,972.81	15	$-28,175.00	97	$-88,995.00	8	$9,000.00	102	94%	1831	$1,504,802.81
Totals	0	$0.00	8991	$7,409,908.60	226	$-101,722.60	465	$-487,354.99	59	$24,759.48	1491	86%	11232	$6,820,831.01

We finished that first year at $6,820,000 in revenue. The next calendar year we did $25,900,000 in revenue and $17,000,000 in profit. Yea, *tens of millions.* It was insane. Like, nuts. The company continues to this day with 4500+ gym locations and counting. And no one is more surprised than me. Something I made actually worked... *finally.*

In 2018 we started Prestige Labs to sell supplements through our gym client base. We used Prestige Labs and the gyms as an affiliate network to generate weight loss leads for each other. In 2019, we started ALAN. A new type of software company that worked leads for local businesses. In 2020, we founded Acquisition.com as a holding company for our business interests. In 2021, we sold 75% of ALAN to a bigger company. I'm not allowed to say for how much, but ALAN did $12,000,000 in revenue in the prior twelve months. So you can use your imagination. We sold 66% of our supplement and gym licensing business to American Pacific Group at a $46,200,000 valuation. And that was after taking $42,000,000 in owner pay over the first 4 years.

I share this because I can still hardly believe it. All this was because of a girl who believed in me, a credit card, and *the ability to get leads*.

Important Disclaimer

Knowing how to get leads saved my business, my reputation, and likely my life. It was the only way I stayed afloat. It was the reason I kept getting second, third, fourth, and fifth chances.

Alex Hormozi ✔
@AlexHormozi

•••

During my hardest days, I repeated the same phrase to myself:

I cannot lose if I do not quit.

I advertised a lot of different things, in a lot of different ways. I advertised to get member leads for local gyms. I advertised to get online weight loss leads for Leila. I advertised to get gym owner leads to sell business services. I advertised to get affiliate leads for our supplement company. I advertised to get agency leads for our software. And so on. Getting leads has been my *get out of jail free* card with no expiration date. And at this point, it's faded and worn with use.

I'd like to share this skill with you. I can show you how to get more leads. And here is your first piece of good news: by reading these words, you're already in the top 10 percent. Most people buy stuff and never crack it open. I'll also throw out a spoiler: the further you read, the bigger the nuggets get. Just watch.

Thank you from the bottom of my heart. Thank you for allowing me to do work I find meaningful. Thank you for lending me your most valuable asset—your attention. I promise to do my best to give you the highest possible return on it. This book delivers.

The world needs more entrepreneurs. It needs more fighters. It needs more magic. And that's what I'm sharing with you — magic.

The Problem This Book Solves

"Leads, lots of leads."

You have a problem:

You're not getting as many leads as you want because you're not advertising enough. Period. As a result, your potential customers are ignorant of your existence. How sad! This means less money flows your way.

So now that you know you have a problem, unless you hate helping people and making money, you kinda have to solve it.

How this book solves it:

To make more money, you've gotta grow your business. You can only grow your business in two ways:

1) Get more customers

2) Make them worth more

That's it. I grow our portfolio companies with this exact framework. *$100M Leads* focuses on number one - getting more customers. You get more customers by getting:

1) More Leads

2) Better Leads

3) Cheaper Leads

4) Reliably (think 'from lots of places').

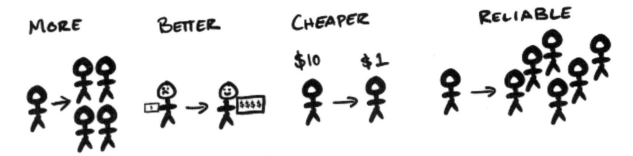

Bottom line: All else being equal…when you double your leads, you double your business.

This book shows you how to transform your business into a lead-getting machine. Once you apply its models, you *instantly* increase lead flow. And, like cash flow, when leads flow, it's hard not to make money. This book will solve your "not getting enough leads" problem for good.

In a nutshell: I will show you how to get strangers to *want* to buy your stuff.

What's In It For Me?

In one word: **_trust_**.

I give this book and the course that comes with it for free (or at cost) in hopes of earning your trust. I want this book to provide more value than any $1000 course, $30,000 coaching program, or $100,000 degree. Although I could sell these materials that way, *I don't want to.* I have a different model. I explain it below.

Who am I looking to help?

I want to provide value to two types of entrepreneurs. The first is *under* $1,000,000 per year in <u>profit</u>. My goal is to help you get to $1,000,000 in profit per year (fo' free) and, in so doing, *earn your trust*. Try a couple of tactics from this book, get some leads, then try a few more, and get more leads. The more leads you get, the better.

Do it enough, and you become the second type of entrepreneur: the type making over $1,000,000 in EBITDA (fancy word for profit) per year. Once you get there, or if that's you now, it would be my honor to invest in your business and help you scale.

I don't sell coaching, masterminds, courses, or anything like that…I invest. <u>I buy equity in growing, profitable, bootstrapped companies</u>. Then, I use the systems, resources, and teams of *all my companies* to fast-track the growth of *your* company.

But don't believe me yet…*we just met.*

Author Note: Our Investment Criteria Have Changed Since Last Book

If you noticed some changes in our investment criteria - you're right. We changed our minimum investment threshold from $3,000,000 in revenue to $1,000,000 in profit.

On top of that, we also used to primarily invest in education and service businesses. But our portfolio has expanded. We've done quite well outside of those industries. So now, as long as a business meets our size requirements and is profitable, cash flowing, and growing, we consider investing in it.

My Business Model

<u>My business model is simple:</u>

1) Provide better free products than the marketplace's paid products.

2) Earn the trust of entrepreneurs who make over $1,000,000 per year in profit.

3) Invest in those entrepreneurs to fast-track their growth.

4) Help everyone else for free, for good.

Our process reverse-engineers success. The winners know my models will work for them because they already have. And I know the winners will use them because they already do. So, we operate on shared trust.

This approach avoids failures *and* increases the likelihood of success. Win-win. Easy to say, but let me show you how much of a difference our process makes...

Within the first 12 months, our average portfolio company **1.8x's revenue and 3.01x's profits**. And we partner for the long haul, that's just the first 12 months. Our average portfolio company who's been with us between 12 and 24 months, **2.3x's revenue and 4.7x's profits**. As a fun exercise, plug your numbers in to see what that would look like for you. This stuff works.

That's how I know the models I'm about to show you work. *They already have.*

Acquisition.com's Mission

To make real business accessible to everyone. Businesses solve problems. Businesses make the world better. There are too many problems for any one person to solve.

And I can't cure cancer, end hunger, or solve the world's energy crisis (for now). But I *can* provide value to the entrepreneurs who build the businesses that will. I want to help create as many businesses as possible so we can solve as many problems as we can. So I share these business-building frameworks rather than hoard them. Fair enough?

Cool. Let's press on.

Basic Outline of This Book

I laid this book out from zero clients, zero leads, zero advertising, zero money, zero skills (Section II) to max clients, max leads, max advertising, max money, and max skills (Section IV). We learn more skills as we progress in the book. And when we have more skills, we can get *more leads in the same amount of time.* So, we finish with the most complex skills that get us the most leads for our time spent. We save them for the end because they take lots of skills *and* money. And, getting good and having money takes time. I want this book to help a person get their first five clients <u>and</u> crack their first ten million-dollar month and beyond.

This order also reminds those *with* skills and money, me included, of the basics we stopped doing. *Our businesses deserve better.* Respecting the tried-and-true methods that got you to your current level will probably get you to the next one. *Masters never don't do the basics.*

So, we go from getting your first lead all the way to building a $100,000,000+ leads machine. Here's the breakdown:

Section I: *You're about to finish reading it right now.*

Section II: I reveal what makes advertising *really* work. Most entrepreneurs think about advertising the wrong way. Since they think about advertising the wrong way, they do the wrong stuff to get leads. You want to do the right stuff to get leads. *This is the way.*

Section III: We learn advertising's "core four." There are only four ways to get leads. So if there is a most important "how to" section, it's this one.

Section IV: We learn how to get other people (customers, employees, agencies, and affiliates) to do it all for you. And this completes the assembly of your fully functioning *$100M Leads* machine.

Section V: We wrap up with a <u>one-page advertising plan you can use to get more leads</u> <u>today</u>.

GOLDEN TICKET:

We invest in companies over $1,000,000+ in profit to help them scale. If you would like us to invest in your business to scale, go to **Acquisition.com**. You can also find **free** books and courses so good they grow your business without your consent. And if you don't like typing, you can scan the QR Code below to grab them.

Section II: Get Understanding

Advertising. Simplified.

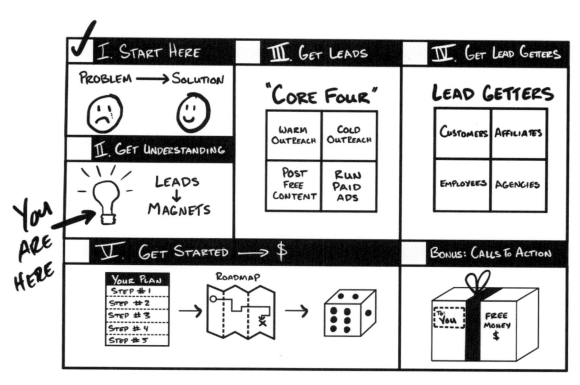

In this section, we cover three things to make sure advertising does exactly what we want it to do.

First, we talk about what a lead actually is. If we want more of them, then we better be darn well sure we're talking about the same thing. Second, we learn how to separate leads that make you money from leads that waste your time. Third, I show you the best ways I know to get the leads that make you money to *show interest in the stuff you sell.*

Let's dive in.

Leads Alone Aren't Enough

"If you cannot explain something in simple terms, then you don't understand it."

- Dr. Richard Feynman, Nobel Prize Winner in Physics

I'll let you in on a little secret. This book started because somebody asked me what a lead was. You'd think it would be simple, but I couldn't give a straight answer. And after six months of trying to figure it out, I was more confused than before. It became clear *I didn't know as much about leads as I thought*. My search for a *clear* definition of "a lead" snowballed into the massive project that became *$100M Leads*. All this to say, we've got to agree on what the heck a lead is before we dive head first into getting them...

So what's a lead anyways?

Someone who clicks an ad?

A phone number?

A person that schedules a call?

A list of names?

A door you knock on?

A walk-in?

An email address?

A subscriber?

A person that sees your content?

Etc...

You see, words matter because they affect how we think. How we think affects what we do. And if words have us thinking the wrong way, then we will probably do the wrong stuff. I hate doing the wrong stuff. So to do the right stuff more and the wrong stuff less, it's best we know what words mean and use them.

To cut the suspense, a **lead** is a _person you can contact_. That's all. If you bought a list of emails, those are leads. If you get contact information from a website or database, those are leads. The numbers in your phone are leads. People on the street are leads. _If you can contact them, they are leads._

But what I came to realize was - _leads alone aren't enough_. We want **engaged** leads: _people who *show* interest in the stuff you sell_. If someone _gives_ their contact information on a website, that is an engaged lead. If someone _follows_ you on social media and you can contact them, that is an engaged lead. If people _reply_ to your email campaign, they are engaged leads. The leads _showing interest_ are the leads that matter.

Engaged leads are the true output of advertising.

Getting more _engaged_ leads is the point of this book. But I couldn't call the book "engaged leads" because no one would get it. But now you do. So the next question is: _How do we get leads to engage?_

Engage Your Leads: Offers and Lead Magnets

"I don't do drugs. I am drugs" - Salvador Dali

April 2016.

I paid $25,000 to be in this group, and *everyone* told me to do a webinar. In fact, my mentor at the time told me, "Do a webinar every week until you make a million dollars. Until then, don't ask me about anything else." *This is my only path to success. I've got to figure this out.*

A webinar, as I understood it, was a magical presentation with a zillion slides. If somebody watched, it would hypnotize them into buying my thing.

There was so much I didn't know. Landing pages. Registration pages. Follow-up emails. Replay emails. Cart close emails. Presentation software. Website integration. Writing ads. Making ad creative. Figuring out where to put the ads. Who to show the ads to. Building a payment page. Processing payments. Never mind *making the actual webinar*. The list overwhelmed me.

So, I started with what I understood most, the landing page. I built a few of those for my gyms. My mentor made millions with webinars, so I modeled his landing page. But I didn't need it to make millions. I just needed it to make *something*.

Okay...now the "thank you" page.

An entire Sunday later, the "thank you" page went live. *Now for the big test.* I put my email into the landing page, clicked "sign me up," and waited. My brand new thank you page loaded. *Success.* I still wasn't a millionaire, sad face. But it was something.

The following Sunday, I sat down for my regular 'work *on* the business, not *in* the business' ritual. I had ten hours to figure out the next piece of this webinar puzzle. After my first cup of coffee, I decided I didn't really want to work, but I still wanted to feel productive. So I went to my advertising group's forum to get some tips.

"Just got off my webinar. $32k in an hour! I ROI'd the entire tuition in my first week! Webinars rock!"

I'm never gonna make this work. He joined the same month as me. He was in the same industry as me. He figured out how to make money with his webinar before me. He was stealing all the clients before I even got a chance. *Everyone is making money except me.*

Desperate, I called other people in the group. "I will do anything for your business: build a sales team… write your sales scripts… fix your sales process… anything… just *help me finish this webinar…*please?" One person agreed to help me. *Thank God.*

Eight Sundays later, and the little circle next to my ad campaign turned green. *It's alive!* I was officially spending $150 per day on ads. All I had to do now was watch the money pour in. I was gonna be rich!

Three days, $450, 80 leads, and 0 sales later…

I shut it all down. *I suck.*

No one even watched my webinar. Meanwhile, that guy posted *again* about how much money he was making off this webinar stuff. *Why do I suck so much?*

I spent most of my money to join this group, and I just set *another* $450 on fire. I didn't have the money to fail again. I *needed* the next thing to work. And if I couldn't even get anyone to watch, what was the point?

The case study:

I scrolled my newsfeed to see what other people were doing. An ad caught my eye. "Free Case Study on How I Spent $1 and Made $123,000 in a Weekend" or something like that. I punched in my email, and the page sent me to a video of walking through a successful advertising campaign. Nothing fancy. No slides. No "presenting." Just a dude explaining how his stuff worked.

This, I can do.

I fired up my screen recorder:

Okay everyone. So here's the ad account of a gym we just launched. Here are the ads we ran. This is how much we spent. We sent them to this page with this offer. You can see how many leads we got here. They got this many people scheduled. This many showed. This is how many they sold. This is how much the gym owner made. This is everything we did. If you want help setting something like this up, we'll do the whole thing for free. And we only get paid off the sales you make. If that sounds fair, book a call.

It took maybe 13 minutes. Simple. I swapped the webinar out for this video and changed the headline:

"FREE Case Study: How we added 213 members and $112,000 in revenue to a small gym in San Diego."

They would book a call on the next page.

I set up a fresh ad campaign and went to bed.

The next morning…

"Alex…what did you do?" Leila asked.

"What do you mean?"

"Strangers have booked my calendar solid for like the next week."

"Really?"

"Yea. Did you start a new campaign or something?"

"Yea… but I didn't think it would go live so fast. Wait. People booked calls!?"

"Yea. Tons."

Seeing Leila's calendar stacked with appointments filled me with joy. *It's working!*

I learned an important lesson. *They didn't want my webinar. But they did want my case study.* This accidental discovery showed me how getting leads actually works…you have to *give people something they want.* The best part is - it's easier than you think.

Lead Magnets Get Leads to Engage

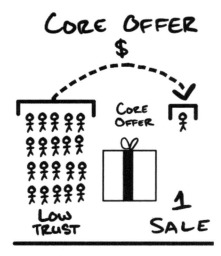

Offers are what you promise to give in exchange for something of value. Often, a business promises to give its product or service in exchange for money. This is a *core offer*. If you advertise your core offer, then you go straight for the sale—the direct path to money. Advertising your core offer might be all you need to get leads to engage. Try this way first.

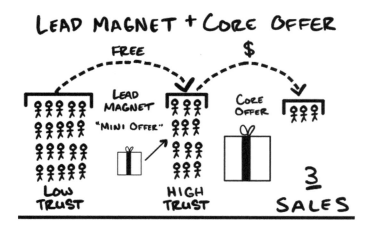

Sometimes, though, people want to know more about your offer before they buy. This is common for businesses that sell more expensive stuff. If that's you, then you'll often get more leads to engage by advertising with a lead magnet first. A **lead magnet** is a <u>complete solution to a narrow problem</u>. It's typically a lower-cost or free offer to see who is interested in your stuff. And, once solved, it reveals another problem *solved by your core offer*. This is important because leads interested in lower-cost or free offers *now* are more likely to buy a related higher-cost offer *later*.

Think of it like salty pretzels at a bar. If somebody eats the pretzels, they'll get thirsty and order a drink. The salty pretzels solve the narrow problem of hunger. They also reveal a thirst problem solved by a drink, which they can get, *in exchange for money*. The pretzels have a cost, but when done right, the drink revenue covers the cost of the pretzels *and* nets a profit.

So your lead magnet should be valuable enough on its own that you *could* charge for it. And, after they get it, they should want *more* of what you offer. This gets them one step closer to buying your stuff. *<u>A person who pays with their time now is more likely to pay with their money later.</u>*

Good lead magnets get more engaged leads and customers than a core offer alone, and do it for less money. So let's make a lead magnet, shall we?

Pro Tip: Even Free Stuff Has A Cost

People will give you time before they'll give you money. But, time is still a cost. If your lead magnet isn't worth their time, *it's overpriced*. And, free or not, they won't buy from you again.

So look at it this way—*if they think your lead magnet is worth their time, they'll think your core offer is worth their money.*

Seven Steps To Creating an Effective Lead Magnet

Step 1: Figure out the problem you want to solve and who to solve it for

Step 2: Figure out how to solve it

Step 3: Figure out how to deliver it

Step 4: Test what to name it

Step 5: Make it easy to consume

Step 6: Make it darn good

Step 7: Make it easy for them to tell you they want more

Something to keep in mind before we start - Grand Slam Offers work for free stuff as much or better than they do for paid stuff. So make your lead magnet so insanely good people will feel stupid saying no. And yes, this means you may have a few insanely valuable offers (even if some are free). But that's a *good* thing. The business that provides the most value wins. Period. So let's get started.

Step 1: Figure out the problem you want to solve and who to solve it for

Here's a simple example we can walk through together…this book is a lead magnet. You are a lead. I want to solve an engaged lead problem. And I want to solve it for businesses making *less than* $1,000,000 in annual profit. With enough engaged leads, they can make *more than* $1,000,000+ in annual profit. Then, they qualify for my core offer: me investing in their company to help them scale.

The first step is picking the problem to solve. I use a simple model to figure this out. I call it the Problem-Solution cycle. You can see it below.

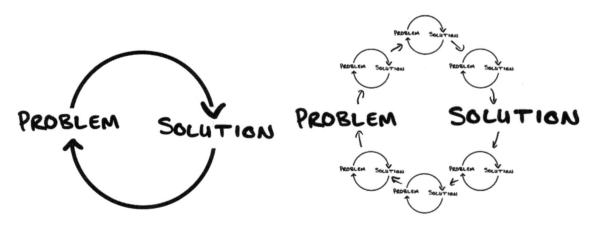

Every problem has a solution. Every solution reveals more problems. This is the never-ending cycle of business (and life). And, smaller problem-solution cycles sit inside larger problem-solution cycles. So how do we pick the right problem to solve?

We start by picking a problem that's narrow *and* meaningful. Then, solve it. And, like we just learned, when we solve one problem, a new problem reveals itself. Here comes the important part- *if we can solve that new problem with our core offer, we've got a winner.* This is because we solve this new problem *in exchange for money.* That's it. Don't overthink it.

Example: Imagine we help homeowners sell their homes. That is a *broad* solution. But what about the steps *before* selling a home? Owners want to know what their house is worth. They want to know how to increase its value. They need pictures. They need it cleaned. They need landscaping. They need minor things fixed. They need moving services. They may need staging. Etc. These are all *narrow* problems–great for lead magnets. We pick one of the narrow problems and solve it for free. And although it helps, it makes their other problem more obvious–*they still have to sell their home.* But now we've earned their trust. So we can charge to solve the remaining problems with our core offer and help them achieve their broader goal.

Action Step: Pick the narrowly defined problem you want to solve. Then, make sure your core offer can solve the next problem that comes up.

Step 2: Figure out how to solve it

There are three types of lead magnets and each offers a different type of solution.

First, if your audience has a problem they don't know about, your lead magnet would make them aware of it. Second, you could solve a recurring problem for a short amount of time with a sample or trial of your core offer. Third, you can give them one step in a multi-step process that solves a bigger problem. All three solve one problem and reveal others. So your three types are: 1) Reveal Problems, 2) Samples and Trials, and 3) One Step Of A Multi-Step Process.

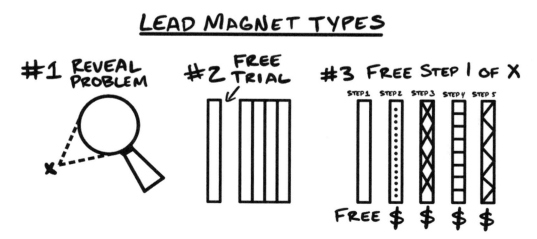

LEAD MAGNET TYPES

1) **Reveal Their Problem**. Think "diagnosis." These lead magnets work great when they reveal problems <u>that get worse the longer you wait</u>.

   o Example: You run a speed test that shows their website loads at 30% below the speed it should. You draw a clear line between where they should be and how much money they lose by being below standards.

   o Example: You do a posture analysis and show them what their posture should look like. You draw a clear line to what their pain-free life would look like if their posture were fixed and how you can help.

   o Example: You do a termite inspection that reveals what happens when the bugs eat their home. If they do have termites, you can get rid of them for cheaper than the cost of… another home. If they don't, they can pay you to prevent the termites from coming to begin with! You can sell 'em either way. Win-win!

2) **Samples And Trials**. You give full but brief access to your core offer. You can limit the number of uses, time they have access, or both. This works great when your core offer is a recurring solution to a recurring problem.

   o Example: You hook them up to your faster server and show their website loading at lightning speed. They get more customers from your faster load times. If they want to keep it, they need to keep paying you.

   o Example: You give a free adjustment for their bad posture and they experience relief. To get permanent benefits, they must buy more.

   o Example: Food, cosmetics, medicine, or any other *consumable*s. Consumables, by nature, have limited uses and solve recurring problems… with recurring use. So single serving, "fun sized," etc. samples are great lead magnets. It's how Costco sells more food than other stores—they give out samples!

Pro Tip: Be A Drug Dealer

Many people make money selling drugs (legally and illegally). A free drug sample is a lead magnet. They can afford to give a 'hit' away because once people try it, they're hooked. It's so good, they come back for more. This is why we don't 'dilute' the value of our lead magnets or give away sucky fluff. If anything, like a drug dealer, you'd wanna give the strongest 'hit' *first*. It keeps them coming back for more. Your lead magnet is your first 'hit.' The next one they have to pay for. Be a (legal) drug dealer, and you'll make money like one.

PS - Whatever you do, make sure it's legal.

3) **One Step Of A Multi-Step Process.** When your core offer has steps, you can give one valuable step for free and the rest when they buy. This works great when your core offer solves a more complex problem.

- ○ Example: This book. I help you get to $1,000,000+ per year in profit. Then you'll have new problems we can help you solve, and scale from there.

- ○ Example: You give away a free wood sealant for a garage door. But the sealing process requires three different coats to protect from all weather conditions. I do the first one free, explain how it only gives partial coverage, and offer the other two in a bundle.

- ○ Example: You give away free finance courses, guides, calculators, templates, etc. They are so valuable people really can do it all themselves. But, they also reveal the time, effort, and sacrifice of doing it all. So you offer financial services to solve all that.

Action Step: Pick how you want to solve your narrowly defined problem.

Author Note: What We Can Learn from Dressing Rooms "Try Before You Buy"

Years ago, you weren't allowed to try things on before you bought them. Then, one savvy business owner created a fitting room. Their sales presumably skyrocketed. So much so, that it's now a standard practice in *all* clothes stores. Here's why the dressing room is so powerful - it is all three types of lead magnet *in one*. You get to try something on - *like a trial*. It also *reveals a problem* as once you try one thing on, you might find that you need something different than you intended. And once you find a shirt you like…a good salesperson would say "do you want pants to go with it?" It becomes step one on a multi-step process of creating *an outfit*. So if you can, try and get a lead magnet that does all three: reveal a problem, give them a taste of the solution, and show it as a small piece of a total package.

Step 3: Figure out how to deliver it

DELIVERY MECHANISMS

#1 SOFTWARE   #2 INFORMATION   #3 SERVICES   #4 PHYSICAL PRODUCTS

There are unlimited ways to solve problems. But my favorite lead magnets solve them with: software, information, services, and physical products. And each of those works great with the three types of lead magnets from step two. I'll show you what I've done to attract gym owners using each lead magnet type.

1) Software: *You give them a tool.* If you have a spreadsheet, calculator, or small software, your technology does a job for them.

>   Ex: I give away a spreadsheet or dashboard that gives a gym owner all their relevant business stats, compares them to industry averages, then gives them a rank.

2) Information: *You teach them something.* Courses, lessons, interviews with experts, keynote presentations, live events, mistakes and pitfalls, hacks/tips, etc. Anything they can <u>learn</u> from.

>   Ex: I give away a mini course for gyms on how to write an ad.

3) <u>Services</u>: *You do work for free.* Adjust their back. Perform a website audit. Apply the first layer of garage sealant. Transform their video into an ebook. Etc.

Ex: I run gym owner's ads for free for thirty days.

4) <u>Physical Products</u>: *You give them something they can hold in their hands.* A posture assessment chart, a supplement, a small bottle of garage door sealant, boxing gloves to get boxing gym leads, etc.

Ex: I sell a book for gym owners called *Gym Launch Secrets*.

With three different types of lead magnets and four ways to deliver them, that's up to twelve lead magnets that solve a single narrow problem. So many magnets, so little time!

I make as many versions of a lead magnet as I can and rotate them. This keeps the advertising fresh *and* low effort. Plus, you see which ones work best. Like my case study story at the beginning of the chapter, the results are often surprising. And you won't know until you try.

<u>Action Step</u>: As a thought exercise, think of a lead magnet and then a version of it for each delivery method. You always can, I promise. Then, pick how to deliver *your* lead magnet.

Step 4: Test What To Name It

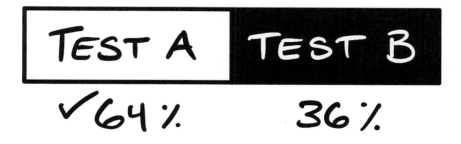

David Ogilvy said, "When you have written your headline, you have spent 80 cents of your (advertising) dollar." What that means is, five times more people read your headline than any other part of your promotion. They read it and make a snap decision to read further… or not. Like Ogilvy hints, leads have to notice your lead magnet *before* they can consume it. Like it or not, this means how we present it matters more than anything. For example, improving the headline, name, and display of your lead magnet can 2x, 3x, or 10x your engagement. It's *that* important. Besides, if no one shows interest in your lead magnet, no one will ever know how good it is. You can't leave it to chance. So listen up. Here's what you do next - **you test**.

The three things you'll want to test are the headline, the image(s), and the subheadline, in that order. The headline is the most important. So if you only test one thing, test that. For example, I had no idea what to title this book. So here's what I did to figure out which name would do the best - **I tested**. The results may surprise you as much as they surprised me.

Headline Tests

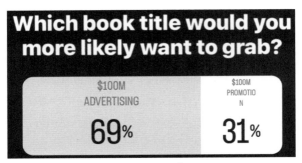

Round I: Advertising ✔ vs Promotion

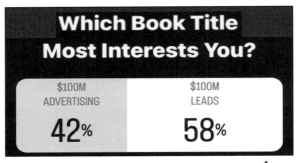

Round II: Advertising vs Leads ✔

Round III: Marketing vs Leads ✔

<u>Image Test</u>

✔ Real vs. Cartoon

<u>Subheadlines</u>

<u>Round I:</u>

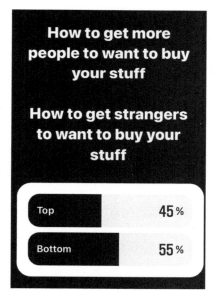

<u>Round II:</u>

'How to get more people to want to buy your stuff'

'How to get strangers to want to buy your stuff' ✔

How to get more strangers to want to buy your stuff

"How to get strangers to want to buy your stuff" ✔

Round III:

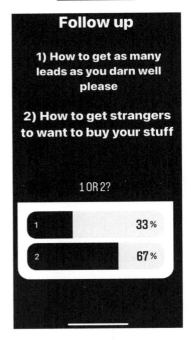

Round IV:

"How to get as many leads as you darn well please"

"How to get strangers to want to buy your stuff"✔

"Get strangers to want to buy your stuff"

"How to get strangers to want to buy your stuff"✔

Note two things with the subheadline tests:

1) "How to get strangers to want to buy your stuff" overwhelmingly beat "Get strangers to want to buy your stuff." The only difference is two little words: "how to." And it also beat "how to get *more* strangers to want to buy your stuff" with a single word removed '*more*.' Small changes can make big differences.

2) Since so many people asked, I figured I'd answer it here. I didn't subtitle the book "How to get strangers to buy your stuff" because that's sales, not getting leads. The point of this book is to get strangers to show interest, not to buy (yet). A raised hand is where this book ends. *'$100M Sales'* or *'Persuasion'* (I haven't decided yet) will be a future book. One problem at a time.

Action Step: Test. If people engage in droves, you've got a winner.

And if you have any following at all, you can run polls like these. You don't need a lot of votes to get a directional idea. If you can't do that, make a post on every platform and ask people to respond with a '1' or a '2', then count 'em up. If you still can't even do that, then just message people and ask. There's always a way, and this is one of the highest leverage things you can do with your time - make sure how you package it gets engagement and you give yourself a big head start.

Bonus Points: If people respond to the poll *and* ask when they can get their hands on it, you have a mega winner.

Step 5: Make it easy for them to consume

People prefer to do things that take less effort. So if we want more people to take us up on our lead magnet, and consume it, we gotta make it easy. You can see 2x, 3x, and even 4x+ increases in take rates *and* consumption simply by making it easier to consume.

1) Software: You want to make it accessible on their phones, on a computer and in multiple different formats. This way, they'll pick the one easiest for them.

2) Information: People like to consume things in different ways. Some people like watching, other people like reading, others like listening, etc. Make your solution in as many different formats as you can: images, video, text, audio, etc. Offer them all. That's why this book comes in every format people consume.

3) Services: Be available at more times in more ways. More times of day. More days of the week. Via video call, phone call, in person, etc. The easier you are to get a hold of, the more likely people will become engaged leads to claim the free value.

4) <u>Physical products</u>: Make it super simple to order and fast to get to them. Make the product itself fast and easy to open. Give simple directions on how to use the product. <u>Example</u>: Apple made its products so well they didn't even need directions. And the packaging is so good, most people keep the boxes.

<u>Action Step</u>: Package your lead magnet in every way you can. It dramatically increases how many engaged leads come your way. And more leads engaging with your lead magnet means more leads getting value from it. This is huge.

Fun fact: My book *$100M Offers* has a near perfect ¼, ¼, ¼, ¼ split between ebooks, physical books, audiobooks, and videos (free on Acquisition.com). Making the book available in multiple formats is the easiest way I know to get 2-3-4x the amount of leads for the same work. If I only made it available in one format, I'd miss out on the 3-4x the people who wouldn't have read the book otherwise. What a shame that would've been and what a waste.

Step 6: Make it darn good:

Give Away The Secrets, Sell The Implementation

The marketplace judges everything you have to offer - *free or not*. And you can never provide too much value. But, you *can* provide too little. So you want your lead magnet to provide so much value people feel obligated to pay you. The goal is to provide more value than the <u>cost of your core offer</u> *before they've bought it.*

Think about it this way. If you're scared of giving away your secrets, imagine the alternative: You give away sucky fluff. Then, people who might've become customers think *this person sucks! They only have sucky fluff!* Then, they buy from someone else. So sad. Not only that, they tell other folks who might've bought from you, not to. It's a vicious cycle you don't want to ride.

But remember, people buy stuff based on how much value they think they'll get *after* they buy it. And the easiest way to get them to think they'll get tons of value after they buy is… drum roll please… to provide them with value *before* they buy.

Imagine a company scaled from $1M to $10M just by consuming my free content. The chance they'll partner with Acquisition.com is huge because *I paid for my share before we even started.*

<u>Action Step</u>: 99% of people aren't gonna buy, but they will create (or destroy) your reputation based on the value of your free stuff. So, make your lead magnets as good as your paid stuff. Your reputation depends on it. Provide value. Stack the deck. Reap the rewards.

Step 7: Make it easy for them to tell you they want more

Once the leads consume the lead magnet, some of them will be ready to buy or learn more about your offer. This is the time to give a Call To Action. A **Call To Action (CTA)** *tells the audience what to do next.* But, there's a little more to it than that. At least, if you want your advertising to work. Good CTAs have two things: 1) what to do and 2) reasons to do it *right now.*

<u>What to do</u>: CTAs tell the audience to call the number, click the button, give information, book the call, etc. There are way too many to list. Just know CTAs tell the audience how to become engaged leads. Good CTAs have clear, simple, and direct language. Not *"don't delay"* but instead *"call now."* Read the next paragraph to learn more (see what I did there?).

<u>Reasons to do it right now</u> - If you give people a reason to take action, more people will do it. But a couple things to keep in mind: first, good reasons work better than bad reasons. And second, any reason (even bad ones) tends to work better than no reason at all. So to get more people to take action, I include as many effective reasons as I can. Here are my favorite reasons to act now:

a) Scarcity- Scarcity *is when there is a limited amount of something.* Especially when there is a small supply compared to demand. When something is scarce, like your lead magnet or offer, people also tend to want it more. And this is why they're more likely to act *right now.* The fewer you have, the more valuable people think it is. But there's a catch- the fewer you have, the fewer engaged leads you can get before running out. So the best strategy I know for scarcity is - *reality.* Let me explain. If you sold 1000x the customers tomorrow, could you handle it? If not, you have *some* limit to how much you can sell. Maybe you're limited by customer service, onboarding, inventory, time slots per week, etc. Don't keep it a secret - advertise it. This gives you *ethical* scarcity. If you can't handle more than five new customers per week, <u>say so</u>. Draw attention to the natural scarcity in your business. If you have limitations you may as well use them to make money.

> Ex: *"The most convenient class times fill up fast. Call now to get the one you want."*
>
> *"I can only handle five people per week, so if you want it solved soon, do xyz…"*
>
> *"We only printed one batch of shirts and will never reprint this design, get one so you don't regret missing out forever…"*

b) Urgency. You can have unlimited units to sell, but let's say you stop selling them in an hour… *on purpose.* I bet more people than normal will buy your thing in that hour. This is urgency in action. **Urgency** *is when people act faster because they have a short amount of time.*

And the less time people have, the faster (more urgent) they tend to act. So if you make the time they can act on your CTA shorter, you can get *more* of them to act on it *faster*. You can also use the same urgency with discounts or bonuses that go away after X minutes or hours. After which, this offer will never be available again.

Ex: *"Our July 4th promotion ends Monday at midnight, so if you want it, take action now."*

"Our Black Friday promotion ends at midnight. There are only four hours left. Get it while the gettin's good."

"Through Friday, I'll also throw in a free hat to anyone who buys more than three books. So if you wanna look slick in an Acquisition.com hat, buy now."

Pro Tip: The Urgency Tactic I Use The Most

<u>I put time limits on bonuses</u>. This way, I don't need to change my pricing or products all the time. I can just change the bonus. I like to make a handful of valuable bonuses and rotate them each week. And if they don't take action by the end of the week, they'll *actually* miss out on the bonus. The best part is that it's an *easy* way to make CTAs more effective *without capping sales*.

---

c) Fraternity Party Planner (my favorite) - Make Up A Reason. Fraternities don't need a reason to party - but they sure make up some doozies. "John got his wisdom teeth removed…kegger!" "Margherita Monday!" "Toga Tuesdays" "Thirsty Thursday!" etc. Your reason doesn't even have to make sense, *and it will still* get more people to act. In fact, Harvard ran an experiment showing that people were more likely to let someone cut in line *if they only gave a reason*. The number of people that let others cut *increased* if the reason made sense (like scarcity and urgency). But *any reason* still works better than *no reason*. So I always try to include one. Think 'the stuff you say' after the word *because*. Examples:

- *Because*…moms know best.
- *Because*…your country needs you.
- *Because*…it's my birthday, and I want you to celebrate with me.

<u>Action Step:</u> Give a clear, simple, action-oriented CTA. Then, give them a 'reason why' using scarcity, urgency, and any other reasons you can think of. And, do it often. Don't be clever, be clear.

Even if your lead magnet costs money to deliver, it should still *lower* your cost to get a new customer. This is because more engaged leads means more chances to get customers. And the extra customers *more than* cover your costs. That's the point.

Let's say you make $10,000 of profit on your core offer. And it costs you $1000 in advertising to get someone on a call for it. If you close one out of three people, it costs you $3000 in advertising to get a customer. Since we have $10,000 in profit to work with, that's fine. But we're savvy, we can do better. So, let's do better.

Imagine you advertise a free lead magnet instead of your core offer. Your lead magnet costs you $25 to deliver, and because it's free to them, more will engage. The extra engagement means it only costs $75 in advertising to get someone on a call. All in, it's $100 per call. By delivering value before they buy, *you get ten times more engaged leads for the same cost.* Note: this happens all the time when you nail the lead magnet.

Now, let's say one out of ten folks who get the lead magnet buys your core offer. This means your new cost to acquire a customer is $1000 ($100 x 10 people). We just cut our cost to get a customer by 3x. So instead of spending $3000 to get a new customer, by using a lead magnet, we spend only $1000. Given we make $10,000, that's a 10:1 return. So if we keep our advertising budget the same, and use a lead magnet, *we triple our business.* Remember: the goal is to print money, not just make our "fair share."

This is where experienced business owners beat newbies. With a $25 budget to deliver your lead magnet, you can provide FAR more value than a $0 budget. Crazy, I know. You attract more customers because your lead magnet is more valuable than other people's. Oftentimes, by a lot. This translates into more strangers becoming engaged leads. It also translates into more sales because you provided value in advance. Win. Win. Win.

Action Steps:

Step 0: If you're struggling to get leads, make an <u>amazing</u> lead magnet.

Step 1: Figure out the problem you want to solve for the right customer

Step 2: Figure out how you want to solve it

Step 3: Figure out how to deliver it

Step 4: Make the name interesting and clear

Step 5: Make it easy to consume

Step 6: Make sure it's darn good

Step 7: Tell them what to do next, why it's a good idea, do it clearly, and do it often

Section II Conclusion

My goal with this book is to demystify the lead-getting process. In the first chapter, we covered why leads alone aren't enough–you need *engaged leads*. In the second chapter, we covered how to get leads to engage - *a valuable lead magnet or offer*. And a good lead magnet does four things:

1) Engages ideal customers when they see it.

2) Gets more people to engage than your core offer alone

3) Is valuable enough that they consume it.

4) Makes the right people more likely to buy

So, more people show interest in our stuff. We make more money from them. And we deliver more value than we ever have–all at the same time.

Next Up:

We've armed ourselves with a powerful lead magnet. Now, I'll show you the four ways we can advertise it. In other words, now that we have "the stuff,"–we gotta tell people about it. Let's get some leads.

FREE GIFT: Bonus Tutorial on Making The Ultimate Lead Magnet

If you want a more in depth look at how we create insanely good lead magnets, go to **Acquisition.com/training/leads**. It's free and publicly available. As promised, my goal is to earn your trust. And trust is built brick by brick. Allow this training to be the first of many bricks. Enjoy. You can also scan the QR code below if you hate typing.

Section III: Get Leads

The Core Four Advertising Methods.

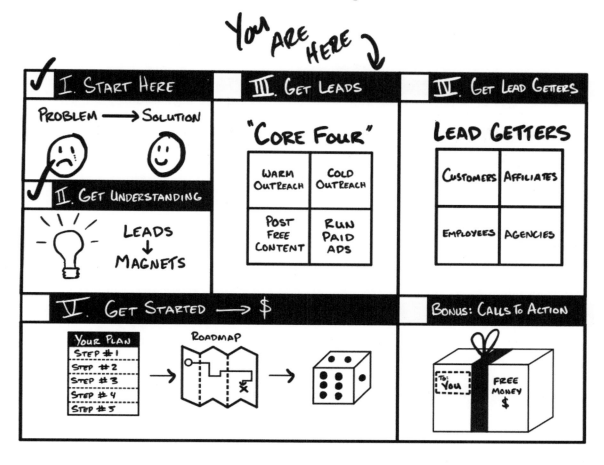

We get engaged leads by letting people know about our stuff. And there are two types of people we let know: people who know us and people who don't. And there are two paths of letting them know about it: one-to-one and one-to-many. Those combine into the four basic ways one person can let other people know about anything. Let's break down how we can use those four ways to get us leads.

Two Types of Audiences: Warm and Cold

Warm audiences are *people who gave you permission to contact them.* Think "people who know you" - aka - friends, family, followers, current customers, previous customers, contacts, etc.

Cold audiences are *people who have not given you permission to contact them.* Think "strangers" - aka - other peoples' audiences: buying contact lists, making contact lists, paying platforms for access, etc.

The difference matters because it changes *how* we advertise to them.

Two Ways To Communicate: One to One (Private), One to Many (Public)

We can contact people 1-to-1 or 1-to-many. Another way of thinking about this is private or public communication. Private communication is when only one person gets a message at a time. Think "phone call" or "email." If you announce something publicly, many people can get it at the same time. Think "social media posts" or "billboards" or "podcasts."

Now, automation can make this *seem* confusing. Don't let it. Automation just means some of the work is done by machines. The nature of the communication stays the same. Email, for instance, is one-to-one. Emailing a 10,000 person list "once" is more like one-to-one *really fast* by a machine. Automation, which we cover later, is one of the many ways we can get leads on steroids. Like audiences, the difference between public and private communication matters because they change *how* we advertise.

Section III Outline: Get Leads

CORE FOUR

	PEOPLE WHO KNOW YOU	PEOPLE WHO DON'T
1 TO 1 PRIVATE	WARM OUTREACH	COLD OUTREACH
1 TO ∞ PUBLIC	POST FREE CONTENT	RUN PAID ADS

Combining warm and cold audiences with 1-to-1 and 1-to-many leads us to the only four ways we can let anyone know about anything: the core four. I combined them below for you.

- 1-to-1 to a Warm Audience = Warm Outreach

- 1-to-many to a Warm Audience = Posting Content

- 1-to-1 to a Cold Audience = Cold Outreach

- 1-to-many to a Cold Audience = Paid Ads

These are the *only* four things you can <u>do</u> to let other people know about the stuff you sell. And each method takes us one step closer to the land of overflowing leads. I refer to the core four throughout the rest of the book - so get to know them. In fact, make them part of yourself.

Once you do, you will have your own "get out of jail free" card to carry around forever. It will give you as many chances to succeed at business as you could ever want *for the rest of your life*. Or at least, it has for me.

So if you aren't getting as many leads as you want, you're not doing the core four with enough skill or with enough volume. We cover all this stuff in lots of detail. How they work. How to do them. When to do them. And show how to measure your progress along the way. This simplifies the overly confused world of advertising into four core <u>*actions*</u>. Either do them and get as many leads as you darn well please, or get crushed by those who do.

> **FREE GIFT: Bonus Training - The Core Four Framework**
>
> I did a live training where I explained the 50+ iterations that created this simple 2 x 2 box. I explain how to use the core four framework to get the most leads possible and create goals within your company. If you want it, you can get it fo' free here: **Acquisition.com/training/leads**. You can also scan the QR code below if you hate typing.

#1 Warm Outreach

How To Reach Out To People You Know

"The world belongs to those who can keep doing without seeing the result of their doing."

May 2013. Starting out.

For the third time that day, I pulled out my phone and checked my bank account. *$51,128.13*. I let out a small sigh of relief. It's amazing how years of work and saving can fit into such a tiny screen. Feeling good for the moment, I switched over to social media to get more dopamine. Friends from college were applying to business school. Acceptance letters filled my newsfeed. I, too, started the business school application process.

I had a choice: I could either quit my job and go to business school, or I could quit my job and start a business.

The application stared at me - *How will a Harvard MBA help your short and long-term goals?*

That question changed my life. I spent three days trying to answer it. At the end of the third day, I saw the truth - *it wouldn't.* $150,000 in loans and two years without income *wouldn't* help me start a business. At least not as much as starting a business and taking two years to figure it out. *I could make the same amount by the time I graduate and skip the debt.* Or at least, that's what I told myself.

So I quit my job and took the steps to start my business. I set up Impetus Group LLC. Check. I set up a business banking account. Check. I set up a merchant account to process payments. Check. There still wasn't any money coming in, but at least I felt 'legit.'

Impetus Group LLC. (say it out loud...)

The first person I told about my new business said, "Impotence?" *God, I suck. No wonder the name was available.* I immediately changed it to 'The Free Training Project.' Name that doesn't suck? Check. I was in business.

But I had a problem - I didn't know anything about advertising or sales. But I did know I needed clients. So, I just asked around where I could. I called, texted, and sent Facebook messages to a bunch of people I knew.

"Hey, do you know anyone who's trying to get into shape? I'm training people for free for twelve weeks. On top of that, I'll make them a custom nutrition plan and grocery list. All they have to do is donate to a charity of their choice and let me use their testimonial."

Only six people said yes. Six. Two high school friends. One college friend. And three people they referred.

I emailed everyone fitness plans and we got to work. We texted during the week to keep tabs on progress. Thankfully, they were all friends of mine, so they gave it their all. They encouraged me more than anyone in the beginning. A decade later, I still have their before and after pictures.

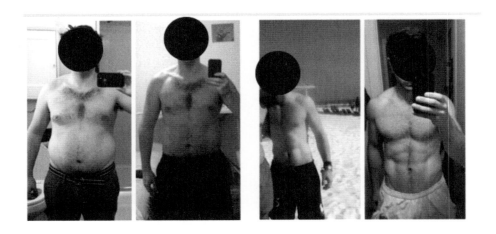

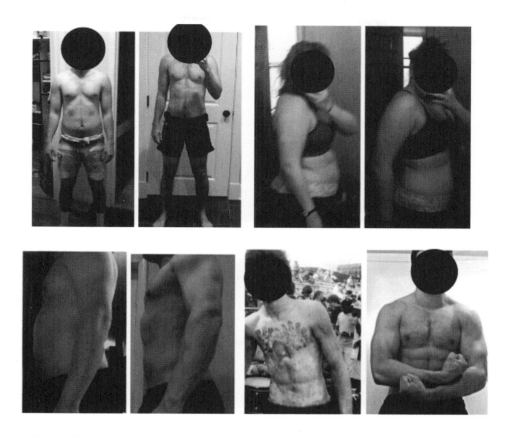

And this is where the decision to skip business school started coming back to haunt me. A few months into this, I was less sure of myself. My 'pile' of money didn't look as big without new money coming in every month. And it started turning into a real problem. So, after twelve weeks of the "pay a charity period," I asked them to pay me instead. I was the charity now. Ha. I worried they'd be upset to pay me instead, but they didn't seem to mind.

Once they got results, I asked them to send their friends over. To my surprise, I got another five or six clients from their referrals. I asked the referrals to pay me directly. Again, none of them minded. That little business made about $4000 per month and replaced the income from my first job. It gave me enough money to live on (and some). My savings started to grow again. Sigh of relief.

_____ iness sounds straightforward, that's because it was. I emailed clients their plans _____ the questions they had along the way. That's about it.

_____, you don't need a lot. All you need is a tax ID, a bank account, a _____ a way to communicate with people.

_____ ay to communicate with people - is the most important part. It's _____ though I had no idea I was doing warm reach outs, one of the *core four,* it's how I got my first leads. I *still* get leads this way (just with bigger numbers). And I'll show you how you can too.

How Warm Reach Outs Work

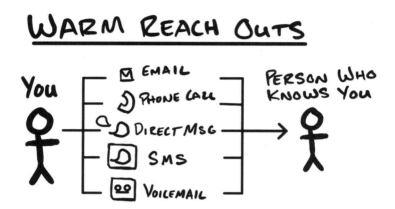

Warm reach outs are when you make one-to-one contact with your warm audience - aka - the people who know you. It's the cheapest and easiest way to find people interested in the stuff you sell. It's super effective–and most businesses don't do it. Don't be like most businesses. Also, you *do* have a warm audience, even if you don't know it. Everybody knows somebody. So your personal contacts are the easiest place to start.

Warm reach outs usually come in the form of calls, texts, emails, direct messages, voicemails, etc. And like we learned in Section II, you advertise one of two things. You let them know about your lead magnet (something free and valuable), or you let them know about your core offer (the main thing you sell).

When you start doing warm reach outs, you don't get many engaged leads for your time. You do everything on your own and make each message personal. But, for that reason, it is *reliable*. As certain as the sun rises and sets, *it works*.

<u>Note</u>: Reaching out to your warm audience works whether you have 100 contacts or 1,000,000. So as your business grows, you will use automation and employees to make it more efficient. The systems start small, with you, but they scale *all the way up*. I detail how to scale these systems to larger audiences in Section IV.

each Outs in 10 Steps

a fantastic way to get your "First Five Clients" *For any new product*
lks: Think re-engagement and new product lines. Here's how to do

rm

our message

up

riends

he easiest offer in the world

op

ng

List Warm

have any leads…" → Everyone Has A List

mans. Let me prove it to you.

phone. Inside you have contacts. *Each contact has subscribed to from you*. They have given you the means *and permission* to contact

- Pull up *all* the email accounts you've used over the years. Pull your contacts and address list from each. Bingo! Look at all them leads.

- Now, go to all your social media profiles. See your followers, subscribers, friends, connections, or whatever kids call 'em these days...eureka - you got more leads!

Add up <u>all</u> your contacts from <u>all</u> the platforms. Seriously, *figure out the number.* Between your phone, email, social media, and other platforms you will have more than enough contacts to get started. For many of you, this will be your first 1000 leads. Would ya look at that! "I don't have any leads." Psh. Just found some.

And if you're terrified you'll have to talk to people. Relax. You'll like what I'm gonna show you next.

(Step 2) "But I don't know where to start…" → Pick A Platform

Pick the platform you have the most contacts on. Phone, email, social media, mail, carrier pigeon, etc. It doesn't matter. Just pick the one with the most contacts. You'll hit 'em all eventually anyways.

(Step 3) "But what do I say?" → Personalize your greeting

Use something you know about the contact as your actual reason to reach out. If you don't have much personal info, you can check their social media profiles etc. to learn a bit about them first.

Don't be a weirdo. Pay your social dues. Remember, you haven't asked for anything. You're just checking in and providing value. *So…relax.*

Ex: *Saw you just had a baby! Congrats! How is the baby doing? How are you?*

(Step 4) "Now what?" → Reach. Out. To. One. Hundred. People. Every. Day.

"To get what you want, you have to deserve what you want." - Charlie Munger

Now, reach out to 100 of them per day with your personalized messages. You'll call, text, email, message, send a postcard, etc. And you will reach out to them up to three times. Once per day for three days* or until they respond. Whichever comes first.

*Once per week with physical mail.

ff The Bandaid

ut is always the hardest and takes the longest. Your second reach
es. Your third, seconds. Be okay with sucking. It's new. This is
en thinking about starting new things, I remember this Chinese
ng must be hard before it can be easy"

say when they respond?" → Act like a human.

ce without sounding icky.

A-C-A framework:

what they said. Restate it in your own words. This shows active

o kids. And you're an accountant…

them on whatever they tell you. Tie it to a positive character trait if

.Wow! Supermom! So hardworking! Managing a full-time career and two

question. Lead the conversation in whatever direction you want. In
topic closer to your offer. Examples:

y/Life Coaching: *…Do you get time for yourself?*

s/Weight Loss: *…Do you have time to get workouts in?*

ng Services: *…Do you have anyone who helps you keep the house tidy?*

k is great because it helps you talk to anyone. It just so happens it's
eople know about your stuff. This means you can learn about the
onversation toward your offer.

bout themselves. So let them. They also love to be complimented,
eople feel good when talking to you, they'll like and trust you more.
and trust you more. Besides, it's solid practice to find the good in
king of practice, this will take practice. And that's OK.

Pro Tip: On Email You'll Be More Up Front

On email you will have a personalized opener to show that you actually took time to research them in some way. Think 2-3 sentences. Then, you will transition directly to your offer or lead magnet which we talk about next. You sort of 'do it all at once' with email or voicemails.

(Step 6) "How do I know if they're interested?" → Make them an offer.

Get through a 'normal' amount of conversation. Think 3-4 exchanges if on the phone or messaging and 3-4 minutes if in person. Then, you'll make them an offer to see if they're interested.

When I make an offer from scratch, I refer to the value equation. If you're wondering 'what's the value equation?' - it was the core concept of my first book *$100M Offers*. Value, as I define it, has four elements:

1) <u>Dream Outcome</u>: what the person wants to happen, the way they want it to happen

- State the best possible results your product can get. Big bonus points if those results come from people like the one you're talking to.

_____ of Achievement_: how likely they think it is for them to achieve

s, reviews, awards, endorsements, certifications, and other forms
idation. Also, guarantees are huge.

ong they believe it'll take to get results after they buy

fast people _start_ getting results, how often they get results when
how long it takes to get the best results possible.

_e_: The bad stuff they'll have to endure and the good stuff they'll
their struggle to get the result.

good stuff they can keep doing, or get to do, and still get results.
m the bad stuff that they can get rid of, or avoid doing, and still

ze the first two and minimize the second two. So all you have to
e:

tly what they want

teed to get it

a finger or giving up anything they love

iously, that's ideal. We gotta get as close to that as we can without

th a real-life offer:

anybody who is (describe their struggles) _looking to_ (dream outcome)
on five case studies for free, because that's all I can handle. I just want to get
ice/product. I help them (dream outcome) _without_ (effort and sacrifice).
ople get (dream outcome) _or I work with them until they do. I just had a_
_h me_ (dream outcome) _even though she_ (describe the same struggle
had another guy who (dream outcome) _and it was his first time. I'd just_
w it works across different scenarios. Does anyone you like come to mind?

(Pause if on the phone) …and if they say no…*Haha, well…does anyone you hate come to mind?* (ha) This helps break any awkwardness.

Pro Tip: Implied Perceived Likelihood of Achievement

You'll notice *besides the guarantee*, there's no slot for "perceived likelihood of achievement." But how we explain the testimonials fulfills that need. After all, we're not gonna say "hey! I can obviously help you because I've helped someone *exactly* like you." But we *imply* that by selecting a testimonial that's as close to their situation as possible. And the longer you are in business, the more 'perfect fit' testimonials you'll have. So the easier it'll be to show testimonials that *perfectly* match the person you're speaking with. Then, once you can show *one* perfect testimonial, the only thing better is *a buttload of them*.

There's an important feature here. *We're not asking them to buy anything. We're asking if they know anyone.* And of the people who say yes, most say *they* are interested. This entire thing is engineered to boost *their* perceived likelihood of achievement. It's why we show struggles *and* results from people like them who have struggles like theirs. But, we let *them* connect the dots. Since you didn't ask them to buy anything, you don't come off as pushy. Some people will show interest in your stuff. Some will refer you to those who might. Some will do both. In all three outcomes, you win. And you win *without pushing anything on anyone.*

If you have even less time or space to deliver it, just use the value elements back to back:

I help (ideal customer) *get* (dream outcome) *in* (time period) *without* (effort and sacrifice) *and* (increase perceived likelihood of achievement–look at the pro tip below).

Note: These work well for emails, texts, direct messages, calls, and in-person. Just fill in the blanks.

To Increase Perceived Likelihood of Achievement

increase their perceived likelihood of achievement so more
on your offer. Include one or more of the following:

f we have done what they want (our own story)

of of people *just like them* getting what they want (think

sheer volume of happy reviews we've received (think lots of 5-

't have reviews yet, even the number of people you've helped

/Degrees/Third party accreditations that we're legit

ts, research that supports the outcome you want them to believe

hing for us

nique characteristic they haven't failed with before (so it might
e)

no have endorsed us ('they trusted them, so should I')

they'll achieve it (so we put some skin in the game too)

describe them or the current pain they're experiencing. The
the better. (think 'he/she really gets me, they must know how

demonstrate the outcome live. Or, show a recording of it

tising agency plays a recording of a call that a gym owner has to
lead on the sales call. "Could you handle making a call like that
f we get them for you?" It demonstrates the outcome of the
services - people don't want "leads" they want customers.
don't know a better way to ask for them.

(Step 7) "How do I get them to say yes?" → **Make it easy for them to say yes. Make it free.**

After people show interest, make your offer easy to say yes to. I like to start with the easiest offer enhancer in the world - FREE:

And don't try to look advanced if you're not. <u>People aren't dumb.</u> Just be honest and keep it simple:

Since I'm only taking on five people, I can give you all the attention you need to get brag-worthy results. And I'll give it all for free so long as you promise to: 1) Use it 2) Give me feedback and 3) Leave a killer review if you think it deserves one. Does that sound fair?

This sets reasonable expectations upfront. And boom. Now, you're just helping people for free. Winning.

Pro Tip: Stack "Yeses" To Build Early Momentum.

Early on, I felt terrified asking for money. So, if you recall from the story above, I told people I would work with them for free as long as they donated to a charity of their choice. I still got them invested in their results, but asking them for a feelgood tax write-off felt like a much safer way to do it. By the way, this was the first thing I ever sold. Looking back, I wanted easy low pressure YESES under my belt. And those early yeses built my first business. And they can build your business too.

My recommendation - whenever you launch a new product or service - <u>make the first five free</u>. The exact number matters less than knowing why you benefit from it. Here's why:

ps in and become comfortable with making offers to people. It'll
res knowing you're just helping…for free…for now (winky face).

suck (for now). People are far more forgiving when you haven't
ng.

robably suck, you need to learn how to suck less. <u>You suck less by</u>
s better to have a few guinea pigs to get the kinks out. You'll learn
people you help for free, I promise. Even though it may not feel
1're getting the better end of the deal.

alue, especially for free, they're far more likely to:

ositive reviews and testimonials.

u feedback.

eir friends and family.

some enough, free customers can make you money in three other

paying customers.

ying customers via referrals.

bring in paying customers.

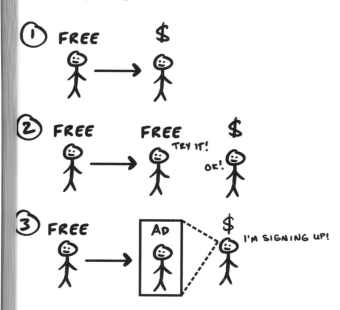

u win.

Pro Tip: Apply the "Hinge Method" to Referrals

If you ask for a referral, get a three-way introduction. My favorite way to do this in person is to grab the customer's phone, take a picture of the two of us, then text that picture to the referral <u>and</u> your own number. If I'm virtual, screenshot a video call and do the same thing. If you can't do that, then at least get a three way conversation going with *them* initiating it.

<u>What if they say no?</u>

Often, the most expensive part of what you sell isn't the price–it's the hidden costs. **Hidden costs** are the time, effort, and sacrifice it takes to get results from the thing you sell. In other words, <u>the bottom part of the value equation</u>. If you struggle to give your stuff away for free, it means either people don't want it (dream outcome), they don't believe you (perceived likelihood of achievement) *or* the hidden costs (time, effort and sacrifice) are too high. In short, your 'free' stuff is *too expensive*. So figure out the hidden costs. Once you do, you unlock even more value–that you'll eventually be able to charge for.

To build your understanding of hidden costs… *ask.* So when someone says "no" ask "why?":

> *"What would I have to do to make it worth it for you to continue?"*

Their answers give you a chance to solve their problem. And if you solve that problem, they'll probably buy from you. And even if they don't buy from you, they'll give you the ammo to get the next person to.

And remember, failure is a requisite for success. It's part of the process. So rack up failures as fast as you can. Get them out of the way to start paying down your "no tax." If you get thousands of nos, you will get your yeses, I promise. I always tell myself: Yeses give me opportunity. Nos give me feedback. Either way, I win.

arren Buffet and Benjamin Graham

ffet became the greatest investor of our time, he offered to work
raham, for free. Wanna know Graham's response? "You're
knew what was up. The most expensive thing about hiring
heck, but the time to train him. Graham would actually be
And in the same way, your early customers are working for you.
- for free! And you want to minimize that cost to them. *Know*

naged to get Graham to take his free offer. The rest is history.

g or Earning

not to "undervalue yourself" by giving your services away for
, tell them to hush. Sure, you're a special snowflake. But the
sn't valuable *yet*. You've barely started. The objective right now
We'll get to the earning once we've learned more. But we must
Don't get the objectives mixed. The earning will come, *I promise.*

Once I've Reached Out To Everyone?" → Start Back At

l the leads on one platform, switch to the platform you have the
er you reach out to those leads, go to the platform you have the
forth.

Let's say you follow this to the tee because being poor sucks more than helping people for free. If between all platforms, you have 1000 leads, that gives you ten solid days of work. A month of work including follow-ups. By this point, I promise, *five or more people will have accepted your free offer*. And some will have converted into paying customers. If you did a good job, they'll send friends, and they'll become paying customers too.

So, let's make our first dollar.

(Step 9) "But I can't work for free forever…" → Start Charging.

This is important. This is your litmus test to know when you're "good enough" to charge. <u>*Once people start referring, start charging*</u>. When that happens, swap out '*…free…*' in the script above to '*80% off* for the next five'. Then '*60% off* for the next five.' Then '*40% off* for the next five,' and so forth. The "I increase my prices every five" rule also adds urgency because prices *actually* go up. And if you're curious, you don't have to stop raising your price. Feel free to keep raising it by 20% every five until you find your sweet spot. It's your business. You can do what you want. Charge more as you get more experienced - a nice reward.

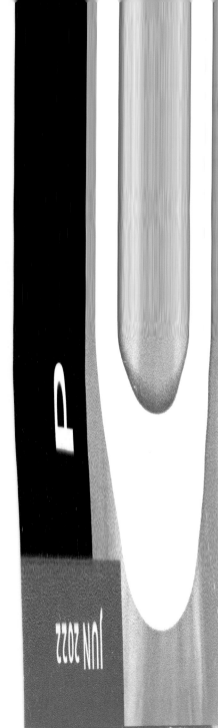

: Cash Up Front & More Yeses → Prepay + Guarantee

...e gets more people to buy because it reverses risk. Here's a
...ee that'll get you more yeses *and* more cash.

...rantee *only* to people who pay up front. Reason why: *People who*
...*mmitted. And as a result, we're able to guarantee their outcomes. So if*
...*ou can prepay our service.*

...wording I got my good friend Dr. Kashey: After the person
..."*would you rather pay less today or get all your money back?*" Paying
...plan, so less money down. Get all your money back = prepay
...at you get the result you want.

...2000/mo for 3 months = $6000 (no guarantee)

..."ey Back" = $6000 up front *with* a guarantee.

...he majority of the people take the up front cash option with
...planned on offering one anyways, you may as well weaponize
...eople to pay up front.

...lo from here?" →Keep your list warm.

...r list through email, social media, etc. to keep it warm. A warm
...rm reach outs in the future. We cover exactly how to give that
...Once you've given value for a while, or see who wants value,
...ckson's timeless "9-word email" template":

Are you still looking to [4 word desire]?

No images. No frills. No links. Just a question. Nothing else. This message is money for
getting leads to engage. And it's among the first things I do when I invest in a new business.
Here are a few examples:

Are you still looking to

   …buy your dream home?

…get more sales leads?

...tone up your arms?

...open an online store?

...start a YouTube channel?

You get the idea. Swipe and deploy. You make the ask to see who replies - aka - engaged leads. And *these replies should be your top priority for warm reach outs.*

I'll end step 10 here because I break down this "give-ask" process in the next chapter. The main point is that a warm list is a huge asset because it's a consistent and *growing* source of engaged leads. If you treat them well, your audience will feed you forever.

Advertising Checklist Summary

Now let's look at this in ten lines because it took ten pages to get here.

Warm Reach Outs Daily Checklist	
Who:	Yourself
What:	First five free
Where:	Phone/Email/Physical Mail/SMS/Etc
To Whom:	Your Contacts
When:	First four hours of your day
Why:	You want to get customers or intros
How:	Personalized Message using ACA
How Much:	100 Attempts Per Day
How Many:	Follow up two more times after first.
How Long:	Until you get customers

Benchmarks: How well am I doing?

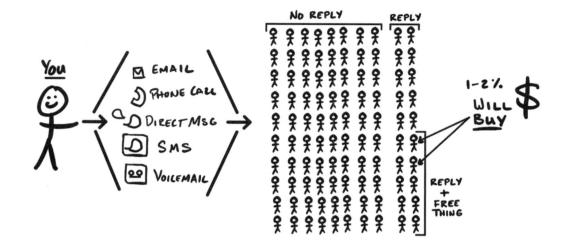

Warm reach outs should get about one in five contacts to engage. So one hundred warm reach outs should get about twenty replies. Of the twenty who reply, another one in five*ish* will take you up on your free offer. So, four people. Of the four who take your free offer now, you should be able to convert *one* into some sort of paid offer later. Hooray - money.

This framework allows you to predict how many customers you get per 100 warm reach outs. In the example, you would get one customer per 100 reach outs. These numbers vary based on the value of your offer and how much they trust you. But, no matter what, with enough volume, *you will get a customer.* And the more you do it, the better your numbers will get. It just takes effort. You'll also learn a lot about what engages your audience: what they value and how to make offers to them. This knowledge can make you millions. You get to learn while you earn - score.

This process *alone* can take you to $100,000+ per year with nothing else. Wild, I know. Here's the money math:

This assumes 1% of your list buys a $400 offer using *only* warm reach outs.

500 reach outs per week = 5 customers per week

$400 product → 5 customers per week x $400 each = $2000/wk

$2000/wk x 52 weeks = $104,000…bingo.

Which, as of this writing, is still two times the median household income in the US. Not bad.

Alex Hormozi ✔
@AlexHormozi

You can get "good enough" at almost anything in 20 hours of focused effort.

The problem is, most people spend years delaying the first hour.

You'll learn more in the first ten days of *doing* 100 reach outs than you did from everything you've ever read or watched. Get that learning done as fast as you can. Remember, *we want to get rich, not just "get by."*

What's Next?

Warm reach outs have two limitations.

The first is time. When you're starting out, getting new customers should take the majority of your time. Think four hours per day, minimum. It should be the first thing you do when you get up. And you shouldn't stop until you achieve your goal. Embrace the work. It will be part of the story you tell one day. It has been for me.

The second limiter is the number of people who know you. You'll eventually "run out." Don't worry though. We can get more. A lot more. Now we *add* the second of the core four advertising activities: posting free content.

FREE GIFT: Bonus Training - Warm Reach Outs

If you like this stuff, I go deeper in a no-holds-barred breakdown of the many different strategies you can use within warm reach outs to get your first or zillionth customer. If that sounds cool, go to **Acquisition.com/training/leads**. And, if you needed another reason, it's free. I hope you use it to get as many leads as you need. You can also scan the QR code below if you hate typing.

#2 Post Free Content Part I

How To Build An Audience To Get Engaged Leads

No one's ever complained about getting too much value.

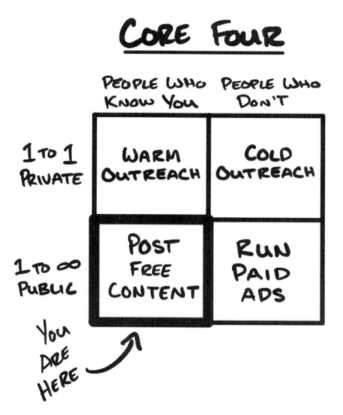

January 2020

"Did you hear about Kylie Jenner?" Leila asked.

"No, why?" I replied.

"She's now the youngest female self-made billionaire."

"Wait, what?"

"Yea, she's twenty. Forbes just put her on the cover."

I was ten years older than her and *not* a billionaire. *Why do I suck so much?* How could she make so much more than me? I thought I was pretty good at business–we took home $13M in personal income the year before. But, I was clearly missing something. And I felt horrible about it.

My ego protected me… *Well, Kris Jenner is her mother and she must have organized all this.* I wrote it off as "rich parents" and moved on.

A few months later…

Leila looked up from her computer.

"Dude - Huda just sold a minority stake in her company at a $600M valuation."

"Huda, the makeup girl?" I replied.

"Yea."

"Holy cow." *Again? How have I been screwing up so bad?* How was someone so young making so much more money than me?

…*She's in beauty, she can do that, I can't.* I told myself, then carried on.

A few months later…

A headline caught my eye:

"Conor McGregor's Proper 12 whiskey hits a $600M valuation within 12 months of launching."

Seriously!? - Another person making gobs of money in what felt like seconds.

A few months later…

I saw another headline. *"With an Insane $3.5 Billion Worth, Dwayne Johnson's 'Teremana' Sweeps the Floor With Conor McGregor's 'Proper 12'."*

Dwayne "The Rock" Johnson was now a multi-billionaire. And he never even talked about business! *What am I doing wrong?*

Alex Hormozi ✓
@AlexHormozi

⋯

If someone makes more money than you, they are better at the game of business in some way.

Quiet the ego, look for the lesson.

A few months later… at a famous friend's house…

Up to this point, I stayed behind the scenes for the most part. I did not want to be famous. I wanted to be rich. And I succeeded at that. But seeing these successes chipped away at my beliefs. Could building a personal brand be *that* powerful? Simple answer - yes. But, I wanted my privacy…

We sat around his kitchen table, and I asked him, "You get all these weird messages from strangers. People threaten your family. Are you still happy you became famous?" He replied with something that changed my life forever:

"If getting weird messages and hate from people I don't know is the price I have to pay to make the impact I want to have, I'd pay that price any day of the week."

I felt exposed. I was being a pansy. I claimed I wanted to make the impact, but wasn't willing to pay the price for it. After that conversation, Leila and I went all in on building personal brands.

***

I have a core belief I'd like to transfer to you. <u>If someone is making more money than you, they are better at the game of business in some way.</u> Take it as good news. It means you can learn from them. Don't think they had it easy. Don't think they had a shortcut. Don't tell yourself they broke some moral code. Even if it's true, none of those beliefs serve you. None of those beliefs *make you better.*

Years ago, I was vocal about "making content." I didn't see the point. Why would I waste my time making something that would disappear in a few days? I thought it was a stupid waste of time and let everyone know. I was wrong. It really wasn't about the content at all - it was about the audience. What I didn't understand was - the content you create isn't the compounding asset - *the audience is*. So even though the content may disappear in time, your audience keeps growing.

This was a lesson my ego prevented me from learning for too long. It took an entire year of getting hit in the face with solid evidence before I changed my ways. *Building an audience is the most valuable thing I've ever done.*

I saw Kylie Jenner, Huda Kattan, Connor McGregor, and The Rock become billionaires "overnight." My famous friend said a massive audience was crucial to his success. The overwhelming evidence broke my beliefs, so I rewrote them. I now saw the power of having an audience. But, I didn't know where to start. So, I did what I always do. *I paid for knowledge.* Buying somebody else's experience saves the time it would take to figure everything out yourself. Leila bought me four calls with a big influencer who had the type of audience I wanted to build. She paid $120,000.

On my first call, he told me to post regularly on every platform. So, that's what I did. Twelve months later, my audience grew by more than 200,000 people. On my second call, he noted the progress. But I wanted more, "Do you have a blueprint for your personal branding? How do you put out all that content?"

He said, "Bro, anyone telling you there's some secret is trying to sell you something. We just put out as much as we possibly can. Pull up your Instagram and pull up my Instagram... Look. You've posted once today. I posted three times. Pull up your LinkedIn… Look. You posted once this week. I posted five times *today*." He went platform by platform. I grew more embarrassed with each comparison.

"You just gotta do more bro."

Simple. Not easy. Over the next six months I put out *ten times* the content. And over the next six months, I added 1.2M people to my audience. Also, when I put out ten times the content, my audience grew ten times as fast. Volume works. Content works. A growing audience is the result. And in this chapter, I'll break down how I did it so you can too.

How Building An Audience Works - You Post Great Free Content

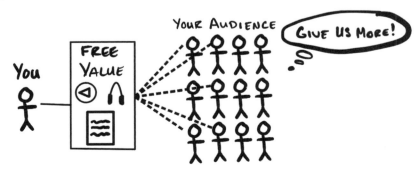

Warm reach outs don't get a lot of engaged leads for the time we invest. If we want to reach ten people, we have to repeat ourselves ten times. Lots of effort. By posting free content, we can say it once and reach all ten. So, posting free content can get a lot more engaged leads for the time we invest. Hooray.

The people who think it's valuable become part of your warm audience. If they think other people will find it valuable, they share it. And if the people they share it with like it, they become part of your warm audience too. Rinse and repeat. The sharing can go on infinitely. The more they share your stuff, the larger your warm audience gets. And once in a while, you'll make them an offer. If your offer has enough value, they'll take it. When they do, you make money. And the bigger the audience, the more money you make. Look at it this way:

- Posting free content grows your warm audience.

- So constantly posting free content means you'll have a constantly growing audience of people more likely to buy your stuff.

- Free content makes all other advertising more effective. If you reach out to someone and they can't find content related to your services, they're less likely to buy. On the other hand, if they find lots of valuable content, they are more likely to buy.

This is what my ego prevented me from learning. Now the headlines with Jenner, Huda, McGregor, and The Rock all made perfect sense.

But, posting free content is not all sunshine and rainbows. It has trade-offs. First, it is more difficult to personalize your message. So fewer people respond. Second, you compete with everyone else posting free content. This makes it harder to stand out. Third, if you do stand out, people will copy you. This means you need to constantly innovate.

That being said - A bigger audience means more engaged leads. More engaged leads means more money. More money means you more happy. Just kidding - it won't do that. But it'll give you the resources to remove stuff you hate. Anyways...

This chapter covers only two topics. First, we demystify audience-growing content by showing it's all made of the same basic units. A content unit has three components - Hook, retain, and reward. Second, how linking basic units together will make audience-growing content for any platform or media type. The next chapter (Post Free Content Part II) shows you how to weaponize this content to make money. But for now, you can't monetize content until you know how to make it.

The Content Unit - Three Components

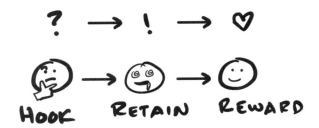

All audience-growing content does one thing - it rewards the people consuming it. And a person can only get rewarded by the content if they:

1) Have a reason to consume it and

2) Pay attention long enough to

3) Get that reason satisfied.

Thankfully, we can reverse those three outcomes into the three things we have to *do* to make audience-growing content. This means we have to:

a) **Hook** attention: get them to notice your content.

b) **Retain** attention: get them to consume it.

c) **Reward** attention: satisfy the reason they consumed it to begin with.

The smallest amount of material it takes to hook, retain and reward attention is a **content unit**. It can be as little as an image, a meme, or a sentence. Meaning, you can hook, retain, and reward *at the same time*. This is how short tweets, meme images, or even a jingle can go viral. They do all three. I separate them so we can discuss them more clearly, but they can all happen at once.

Let's dive into each of the things we do to create a content unit. This way you can create effective content that grows your audience.

1) Hook: They cannot be rewarded unless we first get their attention.

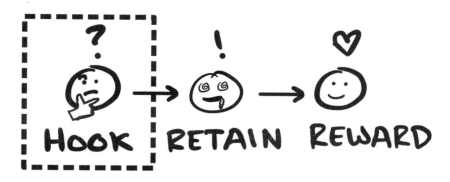

The objective: We give them a reason to redirect their attention from whatever they are doing towards us. If we do that, we've hooked them. The effectiveness of your hook is measured by the percentage of people who start consuming your content. So if you hook attention well, *many* people will have a reason to consume your content. If you do a poor job, *few* people will have a reason to consume your content. Remember, this is a competition for attention. We have to beat every alternative they have to win theirs. Make yourself the best option.

We increase the percentage of people who pick our content by picking *topics* they find interesting, *headlines* that give them a reason, and matching the *format* of other stuff they like. Let's dive into each.

Topics. Topics are the things you make your content about. I prefer to use personal experiences. Here's why: there's only one of you. The easiest way to differentiate is to say something no one else can say. And no one else has lived your life but you. I divide topics into five categories: Far Past, Recent Past, Present, Trending, and Manufactured.

a) <u>Far Past</u>: The important <u>*past*</u> lessons in your life. Connect that wisdom to your product or service to provide huge value to your audience. Give them the story without the scar. *It's why I write these books.*

   i) Example: A personal lesson where I broke my belief that "I don't have enough time":

      1) Hook: I complained to a friend that I didn't have enough time to do something *while glued to my phone.*

      2) Retain: They yanked it out of my hands and looked at its usage. It showed I spent three hours *per day* on social media.

      3) Reward: They looked back at me and said, "Hey, I found you some time."

It's a simple story other people can relate to. This makes it an interesting topic to more people. And it connects what I do, growing businesses, to a struggle many people experience - not having enough time. The epiphany I give away makes this lesson valuable for *my audience* – people starting, growing, and selling their businesses.

b) <u>Recent Past</u>: Do stuff, then talk about what you did (or what happened). Any time you speak with somebody, there's a chance your audience can get value from it. Look at your calendar for the last week. Look at all your meetings. Look at all your social interactions. Look at all your conversations with warm reach outs. *There's gold in these conversations.* Tell stories from them that would serve your audience. For example:

> As a marketing rule of thumb:
>
> If everyone else is doing it, don't do it.

    i) This tweet came from a meeting I had with a portfolio CEO that was just copying the same offer everyone else in his market was making and was getting subpar results.

    ii) This means taking notes, recordings, and other records to make that stuff easy to access. But it also means a free, easy, and valuable stash of content.

    iii) Testimonials and case studies fall in this category. If you can tell a cool client story *in a way that provides value to your audience*, you'll both promote your services and provide value. Win-win.

c) <u>Present</u>: Write down ideas *at the exact time they come to you*. Always have a way to record your ideas in arms reach. I'll even pause meetings to make note of, text, or email ideas to myself. People don't mind when you ask to take notes anyway, so it's not weird. Then, when you make content, you have a bucket of fresh stories to work with.

    i) *I note my ideas publicly:* I used to keep ideas to myself. Now, I tweet them publicly as they happen. If a post does better than normal, I know it's something people find interesting. Then, I make more stuff on that topic.

d) <u>Trending</u>: Go where the attention is. Look at what's trending right now and make stuff about it. Apply your own experiences to it. If you have relevant commentary or it touches your expertise in some way, talk about it. Talking about trendy stuff is very effective for gaining the attention of a broader audience.

e) <u>Manufactured</u>: Turn your ideas into reality. Pick a topic people find interesting. Then, learn about it, make it, or do it. Then, show it to the world. This costs the most time and effort since you have to create the experience versus talking about one you already had. But, it can have the biggest payouts.

    i) Example manufactured experience: *I lived on $100 for a month. Here's how.* Now I don't live that way, but I could manufacture that experience then make content about it.

Author Note: Manufactured vs Documenting

Manufactured content has the most potential to grow and monetize an audience, <u>*by far*</u>. This is because skilled content creators can engineer the maximum reward for every content unit. To give you an idea, as of this writing, the top ten videos on the most popular video platform are all music videos. And they've racked up about 60 *billion* views. Watching or listening- that's *a lot* of attention! But for us mortals, the lower cost of documenting our experiences (versus manufacturing them) lets us keep the volume high. And - I believe it's more sustainable over a lifetime. A quote I heard from a famous content creator "I don't want to be filling my living room with sand when I'm fifty." And, personally, I'd rather see entrepreneurs put out more content, more often, and in more places. Just one man's 2 cents.

Action Step: Life happens–profit by sharing yours.

Headlines. A headline is a short phrase or sentence used to grab the audience's attention. It communicates the reason they should consume the content. They use it to weigh the likelihood they will get a reward for consuming your content versus another.

Rather than give you a bunch of templates, I'd rather give you the timeless principles that make great headlines. And, there's no greater headline creator than "the news." So let's study them.

A meta-analysis of news revealed headline components that drove the most interest in stories. They are as follows. Try and include at least two in your headline.

a. Recency - As recent as possible, quite literally the 'new's

   i. Example: People pay attention to something that happened an hour ago more than a year ago.

b. Relevancy - Personally meaningful

   i. Example: Nurses pay more attention to stuff that affects nurses compared to stuff that affects accountants.

c. Celebrity - Including prominent people (celebrities, authorities, etc.).

   i. Example: Normally, we wouldn't care what another human has for breakfast every day. But if it's Jeff Bezos, we do. Since he's a celebrity, many people care.

d. Proximity - Close to home - geographically

   i. Example: A house on fire across the country doesn't get your attention. If it's your neighbor, it sure does. Make it as close to home as possible.

e. Conflict - of opposing ideas, opposing people, nature, etc.

   i. Example: Pineapple vs no Pineapple on pizza? Conflict!

   ii. Example: Good vs Evil. Hero vs Villain. Left vs Right.

   iii. Example: Freedom vs Security. Justice vs Mercy. You get the idea.

f. Unusual - odd, unique, rare, bizarre

   i. Example: Think of a six-fingered man at the old-time circuses. If it's outside of the norm, people pay more attention.

g. Ongoing - Stories still in progress are dynamic, evolving, and have plot twists.

   i. Example: If someone goes into labor, people want updates every ten minutes because *anything could happen.*

Action Step: Include one or more of these components to give yourself meatier, attention-grabbing headlines.

82

Format. Once we have a good topic and communicate it with a headline using one or more components, we need to match our format to the best content on the platform. People consume content because it's similar to stuff they've liked in the past. And matching the popular format of the platform gets the most people to interact with it. So, we want to make our content look like the stuff they've liked before.

Format example:

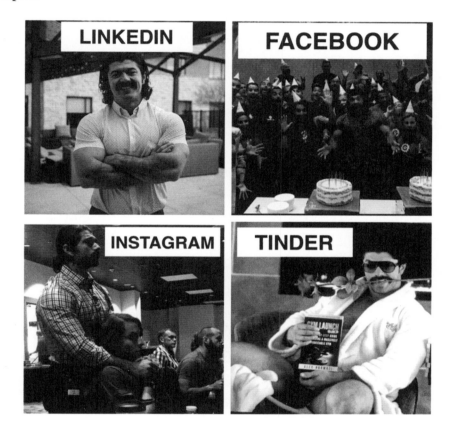

This meme communicates the point better than I can with words. All four images above are…well…images. But, they have a different look and feel. This is because formatting depends on the audience you want to hook *and* the platform your audience is on.

Bottom Line: You've gotta make your content look like *what they expect will reward them.* Otherwise, no matter how good it is, better-looking content will hook them before yours even has a chance.

Action Step: Format your content for the platform first. Then, tweak it so it hooks your ideal audience. Use the best content on the platform that targets your market as your guide.

This concludes the "hook" step of our content unit. *Always* following these basics will already put you in the top 1%. At least, it has for me.

2) Retain

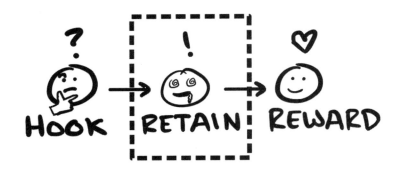

My favorite driver of retention is *curiosity*. It's my favorite because, if done correctly, people will wait *years*. People want to know what happens…*next*. For example, I get messages daily, for years now, about when I will release a book on sales.

My favorite way to get the audience curious is to embed questions in their minds. Unresolved questions can be explicit or implicit. You can directly ask the question. Or, the question can be implied. My three favorite ways to embed questions are: lists, steps, and stories.

a) Lists: Lists are things, facts, tips, opinions, ideas, etc. presented one after the other. Good lists in free content also follow a theme. Think "Top 10 Mistakes" or "5 Biggest Money Makers" and so on. Giving the number of listed items in your headline, or in the first few seconds of your content, tells people what to expect. And in my experience, this retains more of the audience's attention for longer.

    i)   Example: "7 Ways I invested $1000 in my 20s That Paid Off Big"

    ii)   Example: "28 Ways To Stay Poor"

    iii)   Example: "A content unit has three pieces…",

b) <u>Steps</u>: Steps are actions that occur in order and accomplish a goal when completed. Provided the early steps were clear and valuable, the person will want to know how to do them all to accomplish the overall goal.

    i)   Example: "3 Steps to Creating a Great Hook"

    ii)   Example: "How I Create a Headline in 7 Steps"

    iii)   Example: "The Morning Routine That Boosts My Productivity"

Note: Here's the difference between steps and lists. Steps are *actions* that must be done in a *specific order* to get a result. So steps are less flexible but have a more explicit reward. Lists can have just about anything on them in any order you want. So lists are more flexible but have a less explicit reward.

c) <u>Stories</u>: Stories describe events, real or imaginary. And stories worth telling often have some lesson or takeaway for the listener. You can tell stories about things that *have happened*, *might happen*, or *will never happen*. All three drive curiosity because people want to know what happens next.

    i)   Ex: Almost every chapter in this book has a story.

    ii)   Ex: "My editor made me do 19 drafts of this book - here's what I did to him."

    iii)   Ex: "My journey from sleeping on the bottom floor of a gym to the top floor of a 5-star hotel."

You can use lists, steps, and stories on their own or interweave them. For example, you can have lists within steps, and a story about each list item. You can have stories to reinforce the value of a step. You can have a list of stories or many ongoing storylines. Etc. Your creativity is the only limit here. That's why people who make a lot of content call themselves content *creators*. This chapter, for example, has lists within steps and stories interweaving them.

Action Step: Use lists, steps, and stories to keep your audience curious. Embed questions in their minds to make them want to know what happens *next*.

3) Reward

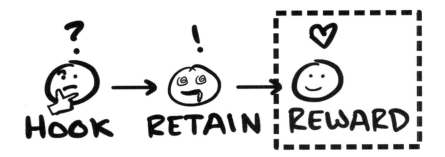

Anyone can think of cool hooks and organize their content using lists, steps, or stories. But the real question is - is it good? Does it satisfy the reason they watched to begin with? Does it make people want to share it? <u>How good your content is depends on how often it rewards your audience in the time it takes them to consume it.</u> Think *value per second*. For example, the same person who gets bored three seconds into a ten-second video may also binge a 900-page book. And that same person may binge a television series for eight hours straight. So there is no such thing as too long, only *too boring*.

Now, we can't guarantee a specific reward. But, we can increase the chance reward happens by:

- Hooking the *right* audience with proper topics, headlines, and formatting

- Retaining them with lists, steps, and stories to get them curious and wanting more

- Clearly satisfying the reason the content hooked them to begin with.

Example: If your hook promises "7 Ways to Make Up with Your Spouse" and you give:

(A) four ways (B) seven ways that stunk (or they've heard them all before). (C) you're talking to a room of single guys who don't have spouses, *you did a bad job of rewarding*. People will not want to watch again, and certainly won't share it.

Example: If your hook promises "4 Marketing Strategies Dentists Can Use" and they can't use them, they will not share it or watch your content in the future. *You did a bad job of rewarding.*

<u>Bottom line:</u> I've had tons of content I thought would smash records but the audience smashed the next button instead. So no matter how good you think your content is, the audience decides. Rewarding your audience means *matching or exceeding their expectations when*

they decide to consume your content. Here's how you know if you succeeded: *your audience grows.* If it's not growing, your stuff isn't that good. Practice and you'll get better.

Action Step: Provide more value than anyone else. Make good on your promises. Clearly satisfy the hook you used to get their attention. In other words, completely answer the unresolved questions you embedded in their minds.

So what's the difference between short and long form content? Answer: not much.

If you recall from earlier, the smallest amount of material it takes to hook, retain and reward attention is a **content unit**. So to create a longer piece of content, we simply link content units together.

For example, a single step in a five-step list might be a content unit. When we link all five together, we have a longer piece of content. Here's a visual to drive it home.

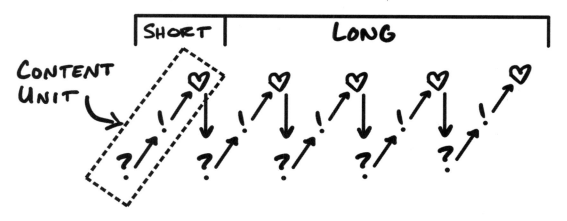

Shorter content hooks, retains, rewards fewer times. Longer content does it more times. And doing it more times takes more skill because you have to string more "good" content units in a row. For example, a new comedian typically will only get a few minutes on stage to perform their "bit." Only a master comic gets an hour. It takes practice to reward attention just often enough to keep it for that long. So, start small, then build from there. Even if you start with longer content, which is fine, I suggest starting with shorter versions. You'll have an easier go of it. Many successful authors with epic-length novels started by writing…you guessed it…short stories.

> **Pro Tip: Make All Your Content For Strangers:**
>
> This is important. Pay attention. If you want to *grow* your warm audience, then you need to make content assuming the people consuming it have never heard of you before. If you make it for strangers then strangers will like it because... *you made it for them*. And they'll share it. And your audience will grow that much faster. And consider the alternative, you litter your content with "inside jokes" that no one gets besides your audience. Cool for you guys, but no one else will feel welcome. And your audience growth will slow down. This is one of the most common mistakes I see content creators make - so don't make it. So make every piece of content assuming the person has never heard of you before. And everyone who already knows you won't mind. They'll appreciate the reminders.

Once you understand how to make a content unit, all you have to do is *more*. Then, your audience will grow. And once your audience grows big enough, you may want to monetize it. I had too much to say to fit into one chapter, so we'll talk about how to monetize the audience in the next one.

See you there.

#2 Post Free Content Part II

Monetize Your Audience

"Give-give-give, give-give-give, until they ask"

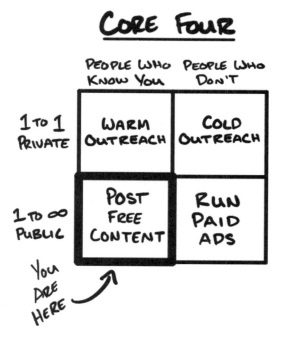

The point of this chapter is to show you how to monetize your warm audience. First, we talk about how we can make offers and not be a spam monster - mastering the give : ask ratio. Then we'll talk about the two offer strategies to monetize the audience. After that, I'll talk about how to scale your output so you can grow a bigger audience faster and make even more money. Then, I'll share a bunch of lessons I've learned in building my own audience that I wish I had known sooner. Finally, I'll wrap this up with how you can take action on everything *today*.

Mastering the Give : Ask ratio

Gary Vaynerchuk popularized "jab, jab, jab, right hook." It simplifies the idea of giving to your audience many times before making an ask. You deposit goodwill with rewarding content, then withdraw from it by making offers. When you deposit goodwill, your audience pays more attention. When you deposit goodwill, your audience is more likely to do what you ask. So I try to "under-ask" my audience and build as much goodwill as possible.

Thankfully, the give : ask ratio has been well-studied. Television averages 13 minutes of advertising per 60 minutes of air time. That means 47 min are dedicated to 'giving,' and 13 min are dedicated to 'asking'. That's roughly a 3.5:1 ratio of giving to asking. On Facebook, it's roughly 4 content posts for every 1 ad on the newsfeed. This gives us an idea of the minimum give : ask ratio we can sustain. After all, television and Facebook are mature platforms. They care less about growing their audiences and care more about making money from them. So they give less and ask more. Which means "give, give, give, ask" is the ratio that gets us closer to *maximally monetizing* an audience without shrinking it. But, most of us want to grow, so we shouldn't model them. We should model growing platforms.

So what do growing platforms do? They display lots of content without many advertisements at all. In short, they give give give…give give give…give give give…give give give…maybe ask. They dramatically over give and under ask. Why? Because the more you reward your audience, the bigger it gets. So if you want to grow an audience, give far far more than you ask.

And now that I have some experience with it, I've got a slight tweak on the traditional give-ask strategy that puts it on steroids: *Give until they ask.*

People are always waiting for you to ask for money. And when you don't, they trust you more. They share your stuff more. You grow faster, etc. But I'm not some altruistic saint. I'm here to make money. After all, I wouldn't be a good businessman if I weren't making any.

So, it's simple. If you give enough, *people start asking you*. It makes people uncomfortable to continue to receive without giving back. It is core to our culture and DNA. They'll go to your website, DM you, email you, etc., to ask for more. Not only that, when you use this strategy, you get the *best* customers. They are the ones who are the biggest 'givers.' They are the ones who, even as paying customers, still feel they get the better end of the deal. And best of all, if you advertise this way, *your growth never slows*. When you use this strategy, you *give in public, ask in private*. You let the audience self-select when they're ready to give you money. That's why, in my opinion, *give until they ask* is the best strategy. But, if you feel like asking, I get it. So, let's talk about how to ask. If you're gonna do it, you might as well do it well.

Bottom Line: The moment you start asking for money is the moment you decide to slow down your growth. So the more patient you are, the more you will get when you finally make your ask.

Action Step: Give give give give give give *until they ask*

Pro Tip: Give in public, ask in private.

If you continue to give in public, people will ask you privately to sell them stuff. Bank on it. The best of both worlds is to never stop giving in public and get an increasing number of people asking you privately to buy your stuff. Give give give, and you will get - without losing goodwill or slowing your audience growth.

How To Make Money From Content: Ask

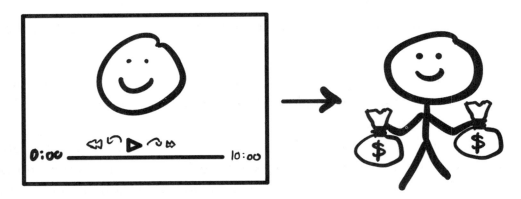

To be clear, I think you should use the *give until they ask* strategy. But, if you need to pay rent, feed your family, etc., I get it. Sometimes you gotta ask. So let's talk about how to do that without sounding like a nincompoop.

Think of 'asks' as commercials. You *interrupt this program with a very important message*. Since you are the one providing the value, you interrupt your own content with commercials about the stuff you sell. But, since it's your audience, you pay the cost of potential loss of trust, slowing growth, and of course, the time it took you to gather the audience in the first place. But money-wise, it's free. Now, I use two strategies to weave promotions into content: integrated offers and intermittent offers. Let's cover both.

INTEGRATED

SINGLE PIECE OF CONTENT

Integrated: You can advertise in every piece of content so long as you keep your give : ask ratio high. You will continue to grow your warm audience *and* get engaged leads. Win-win.

For example, if I make an hour-long podcast, having 3 x 30-second ads means I'd have 58.5 min of giving to 1.5 min of asking. Well above the 3:1 ratio.

On the flip side, I had a friend who had a podcast that blew up quickly. Eager to monetize his new audience, he started making offers (asking) too frequently -*in*- the content. His podcast not only stopped growing, it actually shrank! Don't be like that. Don't kill your golden goose. It's a balancing act. Over-give to protect your most valuable asset - the goodwill of your audience.

Action step: I most commonly integrate the 'asks' - aka - CTAs after a valuable moment or the end of the content piece. Consider trying one of those places first - and make sure your audience growth doesn't slow. Then add in the second and so forth.

Pro Tip: PS Statement Asks

The "PS" statement is one of the most read parts of any content. Often, because it summarizes the main thing the author wants the audience to do. So, I try to include them in everything I write. It's also one of my favorite places to put make asks.

PS - see, everyone reads these.

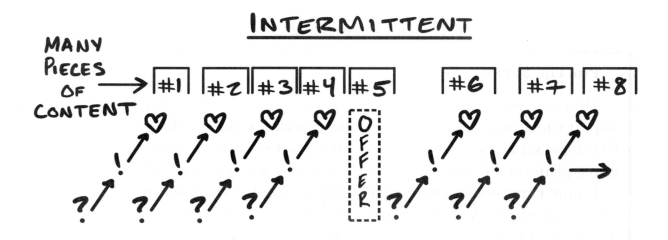

Intermittent: The second way you can monetize is through intermittent asks. Here's how it works. You make many pieces of content of pure 'gives' then occasionally make an 'ask' piece. Example: You make 10 'give' posts, and on the 11th, you promote your stuff.

The difference between the first way and the second way depends on the platform. On short platforms, the intermittent way will dominate. On long-form platforms, integrations are often your best bet.

When you make your ask, you either advertise *your core offer,* or *you advertise your lead magnet.* That's it. Don't overcomplicate this.

<u>Lead Magnet Example:</u> If I just talked about a way to get more leads on a post/video/podcast/etc., I would then say, "I have 11 more tips that have helped me do this. Go to my site to grab a pretty visual of them." And as long as I have an audience that wants to get more leads, this will get some of them to engage. Then, the thank you page after the opt-in page for my lead magnet would display my paid offer with some video explaining how it works. Bonus points if your lead magnet is relevant to your content advertising it.

<u>Offer Example:</u> You can also 'go for the jugular' with your core offer and go straight for the sale. The direct path to money. We model our offer from the last chapter.

"I'm looking for 5 (specific avatar) to help achieve (dream outcome) in (time delay). The best part is, you don't have to (effort and sacrifice). And if you don't get (dream outcome), I will do two things (increase perceived likelihood of achievement): 1) I will hand you your money back 2) I will work with you until you do. I do this because I want everyone to have an amazing experience with us and because I'm confident I can deliver on my promise. If that sounds fair, DM me/book a call/comment below/reply to this email/ etc."

After you make your ask, get back to providing value.

Pro Tip: $100M Offers

My first book, $100M Offers, breaks down the offer creation process step by step. If you want to know how to create a valuable offer that the *right* person would feel stupid saying no to…go check out that book (the kindle version is sold as cheap as the platform will allow me to sell it, if you're strapped for cash). If it helps you feel more comfortable, more than 10,000 people left it a 5-star review in the first fifteen months since it was published. And it has sat atop the #1 best seller in marketing, advertising, sales lists for 100+ weeks and counting. If you don't know what to sell, read that book to get it right the first time.

---

*^This box is an example of an integration.

Action Step One: Pick whether you integrate it or make an intermittent ask. Then, pick whether you'll advertise your core offer or lead magnet. If you're not sure, do the lead magnet. It's lower risk.

How to Scale It

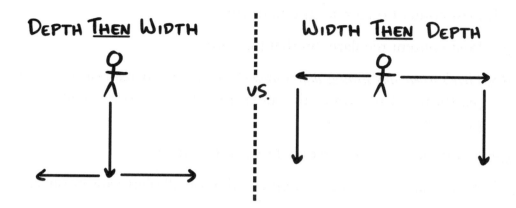

After you start asking, you're gonna start getting leads and making money. But you don't want to stop there, do you? Didn't think so. Cool, so let's talk about scale.

There are two opposing strategies to scale your warm audience. They both follow progressive steps. First, you have the depth-then-width approach. Then, you have the width-then-depth approach. Both are right. Here's how they work:

Depth then width: Maximize a platform, then move onto the next platform.

Step #1: Post content on a relevant platform.

Step #2: Post content regularly on that platform.

Step #3: Maximize quality and quantity of the content on that platform. Short form, you may sometimes be able to get up to ten times per day per platform. Long form, you may have to get up to five days per week (see soap operas).

Step #4: Add another platform while maintaining the quality and quantity on the first platform.

Step #5: Repeat steps 1-4 until all relevant platforms are maximized.

Advantages: Once you figure out one platform, you maximize your return on that effort. Audiences compound faster the more you do. You take advantage of this compounding. Fewer resources are required to make this work.

Disadvantages: You have less low hanging fruit of new platforms and new audiences. You don't accomplish the feeling of 'omnipresence.' In the beginning, you risk your business being reliant on a single channel. This is a risk because platforms change all the time and sometimes ban you for no reason. If you only have one way to get customers, it can kill your business if it gets shut down.

Width then depth: Get on every platform early, then maximize them together.

Step #1: Post content on a relevant platform.

Step #2: Post content regularly on that platform.

Step #3: *Here's where this strategy differs from the one before.* Instead of maximizing your first platform. Move onto the next relevant platform while maintaining the previous.

Step #4: Continue until you are on all relevant platforms.

Step #5: Now, maximize your content creation on all platforms at once.

Advantages: You reach a broader audience faster. And, you can "repurpose" your content. So with a little extra work, you can capture tons of efficiency. With minimal changes to the format, you can make the same content fit multiple platforms. For example, it takes little extra effort to format a single short video across all platforms distributing short video content.

Disadvantages: It costs more labor, attention, and time, to do this well. Oftentimes, people end up with lots of bad content everywhere. Sucky fluff. No bueno.

If you already have a sizable business, scale up faster and reap the rewards of an asset that only gets better with time. I said it before and I'll say it again. The best day to start posting content was the day you were born. The second best day is today. Don't wait like I did.

Pro Tip: How I Get It Done

I am not a full time content creator. I run businesses. But, content creation is a part of my responsibility. Here's my simple process for recording.

1) I find topics using the five ways from the "topics" section in Part I of this chapter. This takes me about an hour.

2) I sit down twice every month and record thirty or so short clips based on Step 1.

3) On the same day, I record 2-4 longer videos unpacking tweets that had more stories or relevant examples. This creates my longer form content.

If this sounds simplistic, it's because it is. Just start. You can add volume over time.

Action Step: Pick an approach. Start posting. Then, go up the scaling steps over time.

> ### Pro Tip: Only One Call-To-Action At A Time
>
> *'A confused mind doesn't buy'* is a common saying in the sales and marketing world. To increase how many people do what you want, only ask them to do one thing per call to action. For example, don't ask people to "share, like subscribe, and comment" at the same time. Because instead of doing them all, they'll do none. Instead, if you want them to share, *only* ask them to share. And if you want them to buy, *only* ask them to buy. Make up your mind, so they don't have to.

Why You Should Make Content (even if it's not your primary advertising strategy)

January 2020.

I called all the major departments to a meeting to answer an important question: *Why isn't our paid advertising working like it used to?* Opinions flooded the room. "The creative…the copy…the offer…our pages…our sales process…our price…" They shot back and forth at each other, every bit as invested as I was in solving the problem.

Leila and I sat quietly as the team debated. After the din died down, Leila, in her wise fashion, asked a different question: *What did we stop doing in the months before the decline?*

A new debate arose and a unanimous answer surfaced: Alex stopped making gym content and started talking about general business. Now, I didn't know how important that was, but I had to find out. So, I sent a survey to our gym owners. I asked if they had consumed any content of mine *before* they booked a call. The results astounded me.

78% of all clients had consumed at least TWO long form pieces of content, prior to booking a call.

I had fallen into my old ways and given paid ads all the credit. But, our free content was nurturing the demand. Don't make the same mistake I did. Your free content gives strangers an opportunity to find, get value from, and share your stuff. And, it warms people on the fence that go to and come from the cold audience methods we dive into next. So even if it's hard to measure, free content gets you better returns on all advertising methods.

Bottom line: Start making content relevant to your audience. It will make you more money.

7 Lessons I've Learned From Making Content

1) **Switch from "How to" to "How I." From "This is the best way" to "These are my favorite ways" etc.** (especially when starting out). Talk about what you've done, not what others should do. What you like, not this is *the* best. When you talk about experience, no one can question you. This makes you bulletproof.

   a) I make my oatmeal this way vs. you should make your oatmeal this way.

   b) How I Built My 7-Figure Agency vs. How To Build a 7-Figure Agency.

   c) My favorite way to generate leads for my business vs. This is the best way to generate leads for your business.

   It's subtle. But when you tell your experience, you are sharing value. When you tell a stranger what to do, it's hard to avoid coming off preachy or arrogant. This helps avoid it.

2) **We Need To Be Reminded More Than We Need To Be Taught:** You're a silly goose if you think 100 percent of your audience listens 100 percent of the time. For example, I post about my book every single day. I surveyed my audience and asked them if they knew I had a book. One in five that saw the post said they didn't know. Keep repeating yourself. You'll get bored of your content before your whole audience even sees it.

3) **Puddles, Ponds, Lakes, Oceans.** Narrow the focus of your content. If you have a small local business, you probably shouldn't make general business content. Not at first, at least. Why? The audience will listen to people with better track records than you. But you can narrow your topics to what you do and the place you do it. Example: plumbing in a certain town. If you do that, you can become king of that puddle. Over time, you can expand your plumbing puddle to the general local business pond. Then the lake of brick & mortar chains and so forth. Then eventually, the ocean of general business.

4) **Content Creates Tools For Salespeople.** Some content will perform well and get more people interested in buying your stuff. That content *helps your sales team.* Create a master list of your "greatest hits." Label each 'hit' with the problem it solves and the benefit it provides. Then, your sales team can send it before or after sales calls and help people decide to buy. They work especially well if the content resolves specific concerns prospects commonly face.

5) **Free Content Retains Paying Customers**. How a customer gets value from you matters less than where they got it. Imagine a person pays for your thing and then consumes your free content. If your free content is valuable, they will like you more and stay loyal to your business longer. On the flip side, if they consume your free content, and it sucks, they will like your paid product less. Here's something you may not know. Somebody who buys your stuff is *more likely* to consume your free content. This is why it's so important to make your free content good - your customers will include it in how they calculate their ROI from your paid thing.

6) **People don't have shorter attention spans, they have higher standards.** Repeated for emphasis: *there's no such thing as too long, only too boring.* Streaming platforms have proven that people will spend hours binging long form content *if they like it.* Our biology hasn't changed, our circumstances have. They have more rewarding stuff to choose from. So make good stuff people like and reap the rewards rather than whining about people's "short attention spans."

7) **Avoid Pre-Scheduling Posts**. The posts I manually post perform better than ones I pre-schedule. Here's my theory. When you manually post, you know that within seconds you will be rewarded or punished for the quality of the content. Because of that close feedback loop, you try *that much harder* to make it better. When I schedule stuff out, I don't feel that same pressure. So whenever I post, or my team does, we strongly believe in someone pressing the 'submit' button because it gives that last bit of pressure to get it right. Try it.

Benchmarks - How Well Am I Doing?

If our audience grows, we did good. But if our audience grows fast, we did *gooder*. So I like to measure my audience size and speed of growth monthly.

Here's what I measure:

1) Total followers and reach - *How big*

   a) Follower Example: If I go from 1000 followers across all platforms to 1500, I grew my audience by 500.

   b) Reach Example: If I go from 10,000 people seeing my stuff to 15,000 people seeing my stuff, I grew my *reach* by 5,000 people.

2) Rate of getting followers and reach - *How fast*

   You compare the growth between months:

a) Example: If I gained those 500 followers in a month, that would make it a 50% growth month. (500 New / 1000 Started = 50% growth rate).

b) Example: If I reached those 5000 extra people in a month, that would make it a 50% growth month. (5000 New / 10,000 Started = 50% growth rate)

Remember, we can only control inputs. Measuring outputs is only useful if we are consistent with inputs. So, pick the posting cadence you want to stick with on a particular platform. Then pick your 'ask' cadence on that platform (how you will direct people to become engaged leads). Then, start, and…Do. Not. Stop.

Alex Hormozi ✔
@AlexHormozi

It's amazing what you can accomplish if you don't stop once you start.

For reference, I posted a new podcast twice a week for four years before even getting picked up on the Top 100 list. Because I did the same thing every week for years, I knew I could trust the feedback. In the beginning, it didn't grow much. It took time for me to get better. And I knew I had to make more, over a long time, for that to happen.

So if your listeners go from ten to fifteen in a month, that's progress baby! Even with small absolute numbers, that's fifty percent monthly growth! It's why I like to measure both the absolute and relative growth and pick the one that makes me feel better (ha!). As my friend Dr. Kashey says, "The more ways you measure, the more ways you can win." Be consistent. Measure a lot. Adapt to feedback. Be a winner.

To close the loop, in its <u>fifth year</u>, my podcast- *The* Game, became a Top 10 podcast in the US for business and top 500 in the world. This was only possible *after 5 years* of *multiple podcasts per week every week*. Remember, everyone starts at zero. <u>You just gotta give time, time</u>.

Your First Post

You've probably been providing value to other humans knowingly or unknowingly for a while. So the first post you make, *you can make an ask*. My hope is that it gets you your first engaged lead. If it doesn't, you need to give for a while, then make an ask once you've earned the right to. To show you that I'm not making this up, below you can find my first business post ever. Is it ideal? No. I had no idea what I was doing. Should you copy it, probably not. Main point: don't be afraid of what other people think. If someone won't speak at your funeral, you shouldn't care about their opinion while you're alive. Honor the few who believe in you by having courage.

 Alex Hormozi ✓
April 9, 2013 · Baltimore, MD · 🌐   ...

Everyone,

For those of you who know me, you know two things:

1) I am terrible with all things technological. For example, I just heard about spotify a few weeks ago, seriously.
2) I love training/nutrition and "fitness" more than, well, a whole lot.

So, today is sort of special because it marks a day when my love of training vanquished my fear of technology.

What do I mean?

For the better part of a year I have been taking part in a free personal training project with the idea that I would give away free personal training to anyone who was willing to give some of their $500-$1000 to a cause of their choice. This way, they wouldn't have to be motivated by the same thing as me, but be motivated to give to their cause and benefit themselves. When I first introduced the idea, I was happily surprised with the amount of positive support I received.

So, almost a year from my first client, I NOW HAVE A WEBSITE!! to formally show some of the transformations that have gone underway using my programming and as a formal means of contacting me about signing up.
I CURRENTLY HAVE A FEW SLOTS OPEN IN MY ROSTER, SO DROP ME A NOTE QUICKLY IF YOU ARE INTERESTED! THANKS SO MUCH!

Take a second to check out some of the ridiculous transformations in record. time. CHECK IT OUT

Whenever I read this, I just think "you goon." But hey, I was trying. And for that, I'm proud.

Recap

We covered eight things:

1) The Content Unit - done

2) Short vs. Long Form Content - done

3) Mastering the Give:Ask Ratio - done

4) How to Ask - done

5) How to Scale It - done

6) Lessons From Content - done

7) Benchmarks - done

8) Your First Post - done

Now, you know. Nothing's stopping you.

So What Do I Do Right Now?

Posting free content is less predictable than, but complementary to, warm reach outs. So *keep doing warm reach outs*. Also, posting free content grows your warm audience. And a bigger warm audience means more people for warm reach outs. So free content gets engaged leads on its own and *keeps getting* engaged leads through warm reach outs. Instead of ditching one for the other, I recommend you post free content *in addition to* warm reach outs.

Let's fill out our daily action commitment for our first platform.

Post Content Daily Checklist	
Who:	Yourself
What:	Value: Give give give until they ask
Where:	Any media platform
To Whom:	People who already follow you
When:	Every morning, 7 days a week
Why:	Build goodwill. Get engaged leads.
How:	Written, image, videos, audio posts
How Much:	100 min per day
How Many:	As many times as the platform shows it
How Long:	As long as it takes.

Next Up

First, we start with warm outreach. We reach out to every person we have permission to contact. Second, we post publicly about the successes and lessons we have from our first clients. We post testimonials. We provide value. Then occasionally ask. We commit to doing both of these activities every day.

With these two methods alone can eventually build a six- or seven-figure business. But you may want to go faster. So we venture from warm audiences who know us, to cold audiences who don't. We begin *reaching out to strangers*. This begins the third step in our advertising journey: cold outreach.

> **FREE GIFT: Everything I've Learned From Posting Content**
>
> I had to cut a lot of material to make this book manageable. If you want to know the fast and easy way to make content that builds trust in an audience - go to **Acquisition.com/training/leads**. And, if you needed another reason besides 'it'll make you money'....it won't cost you any. It's free. Enjoy. And as always, you can also scan the QR code below if you hate typing.

Free Goodwill

"He who said money can't buy happiness hasn't given enough away." - Unknown

People who give without expectation live longer, happier lives *and* make more money. So if we've got a shot at that during our time together, darn it, I'm gonna try.

To do that, I have a question for you…

Would you help someone you've never met if it cost you nothing, but you didn't get credit?

Who is this person you ask? They are like you. Or, at least, like you used to be. Less experienced, wanting to make a difference, and needing help, but not sure where to look.

Acquisition.com's mission is *to make business accessible to everyone*. Everything we do stems from that mission. And, the only way for us to accomplish that mission is by reaching…well…*everyone*.

This is where you come in. Most people do, in fact, judge a book by its cover (and its reviews). So here's my ask on behalf of a struggling entrepreneur you've never met:

Please help that entrepreneur by leaving this book a review.

Your gift costs no money and less than 60 seconds to make real, but can change a fellow entrepreneur's life *forever*. Your review could help…

….one more small businesses provide for their community.

….one more entrepreneur support their family.

….one more employee get meaningful work.

…one more client transform their life.

…one more dream come true.

To get that 'feel good' feeling and help this person for real, all you have to do is….and it takes less than 60 seconds…leave a review.

If you are on audible - hit the three dots in the top right of your device, click rate & review, then leave a few sentences about the book with a star rating.

If you are reading on kindle or an e-reader - scroll to the bottom of the book, then swipe up and it will prompt a review for you.

If for some reason these changed- you can go to Amazon (or wherever you purchased this) and leave a review right on the book's page.

If you feel good about helping a faceless entrepreneur, you are my kind of people. Welcome to #mozination. You're one of us.

I'm that much more excited to help you get more leads than you can possibly imagine. You'll love the tactics I'm about to share in the coming chapters. Thank you from the bottom of my heart. Now, back to our regularly scheduled programming.

- Your biggest fan, Alex

PS - Fun fact: If you provide something of value to another person, it makes you more valuable to them. If you'd like goodwill straight from another entrepreneur - and you believe this book will help them - send this book their way.

#3 Cold Outreach

How To Reach Out To Strangers To Get Engaged Leads

"Quantity has a quality all of its own" - Napoleon Bonaparte

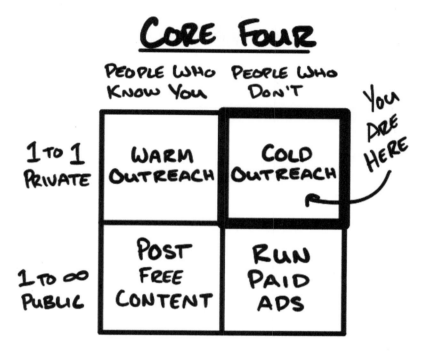

July 2020.

COVID-19 raged. In a matter of months, thirty percent of my customers went out of business. Protestors filled every platform with hate and anger. Politicians made promises. Small businesses suffered in silence. Unemployment skyrocketed. The most tumultuous election ever was upon us. And here we were, trying to generate leads to pay our bills. Employees everywhere, and their families, depended on it.

All three of my companies at the time (Gym Launch, Prestige Labs, and ALAN) relied on brick-and-mortar businesses staying open. And, they were closed. *Brilliant strategy Alex.* To make matters worse, Apple did a software update that crippled our ads. The market was crap. Our paid ads were crap. And I carried the bucket.

I ran through worst-case scenarios. *How much cash would it take to keep us afloat? How long do I keep paying people when there's no end in sight? Should I dip into personal accounts? Give up a third of my life savings? Half? All of it? What does that say about me?* I had no idea what to do.

Early that Saturday morning…

I tried to sleep long enough for my alarm to wake me, but it was no use. I went to my office and checked Instagram. I had a new message waiting for me:

"Hey Alex - Cale told me you guys don't need salesmen anymore, so my offer got pulled. I quit my job to accept it. Super honored you considered me. I hope you'll consider me again the next time you have openings."

Looking for context, I scrolled up. Reading our earlier messages rewarded me with a pang of guilt. *I was the one who told him to apply.* He took the rejection well. *A sign of a good salesman.* I felt obligated to reply.

"You on?" I messaged.

"Yes," he replied.

"Got 5?"

"Yes"

We hopped on a call. He sounded a little nervous, but I could tell he knew his stuff. *It sucks we don't have enough leads for this guy…*

"I've wanted to work for you a while now. I read your book and used the scripts to become the top producer at my company," he said.

"That's awesome. I'm so glad to hear it. What kind of company?" I asked.

"A gym software company."

I hadn't heard of them. "Oh interesting. How do you guys get leads?"

"We're 100% cold outreach."

"You cold call and cold email gyms, then sell them software?"

"Yea, pretty much."

"How big is the team?"

"We've got about thirty guys."

A team of 30!? "What's your revenue like if you can share that with me."

"We're doing about $10,000,000 per month now."

Insane. "Just from cold outreach?"

"Yea, we run some ads, but we haven't cracked that yet."

"And you do this with a retention offer? You're not even really making gyms more money?"

"Yea, it's definitely not as easy to sell as the stuff you do for gyms."

"Do you think you could use the same cold outreach system here?"

"I've never started a team, but I bet I could figure it out."

"Alright. What was the offer Cale pulled?"

"I was gonna be a closer, but he said you guys didn't need one anymore."

I thought for a moment. "Well, given our current lead volume, he's probably right. But, *if you can get your own leads*, I'll give you the runway to get cold outreach going. What do you think?"

"It takes a while to get going. I'll have to figure out the scripts for your offer."

"Yeah, that makes sense. How long, you think?"

"I'm confident I could make it profitable in twelve weeks."

"Alright, deal. I'll let Cale know the plan. To be clear, you'll be expected to figure all this out. The software. The lists. Everything. I'll front you the time, but we can't support you much beyond that."

"Understood."

Here's what happened during the months that followed:

September: 0 Sales. Zippola. Nothin'. Zilch. Nada.

October: 2 Sales ($32,000 in revenue) Team asks me to pull the plug on cold outreach.

December: 4 Sales ($64,000 in revenue) Team asks me to pull the plug, again.

January: 6 Sales ($96,000 in revenue)

February: 10 Sales ($160,000 in revenue)

March: 14 Sales ($224,000 in revenue)

April: 20 Sales ($320,000 in revenue)

May: 30 Sales ($480,000 in revenue)

Today: Cold outreach generates millions per month for our businesses

Making this work took every (legal) cold outreach method we knew. Cold calls….Cold emails….Cold Direct Messages….Voicemails. Everything. But, piece by piece, we built a reliable customer-getting machine. I wanted something that would *endure*.

And that's what I'm gonna show you how to build.

I learned five important lessons from this experience:

1) There was another company in my space making *a lot* more money than mine. It broke my belief about how big the market really was.

2) They made all their money through *private* advertising. I had no way of knowing they existed unless they contacted me first. So, they kind of operated in secret.

3) They built a very profitable cold outreach machine in *my* space. If they could do it, so could I.

4) It's good to have proper expectations. Cold outreach veterans told me it would take a year to scale. I figured we could do it in twelve weeks. I was wrong. It took almost a year. Cold outreach takes a long time. At least, it did for me.

5) We tried cold outreach two times before and failed. Working with a person that had done it all before was immensely helpful in getting this going. I hope to be that person for you now.

How Cold Outreach Works

At some point, you'll want one of two things. Either, you'll want to grow faster than you currently are. Or, you'll want to increase the predictability of your lead flow…

Here's how we can do that. We advertise to people who don't know us. Cold audiences. And like before, we can contact them publicly or privately. In this chapter, we focus on private one-to-one communication with cold outreach. For added context, cold outreach sits atop the foundation of warm outreach. So think of this as the more advanced cousin of warm outreach, no longer limited by your warm audience.

If you can figure out a way to contact somebody one-to-one, you can use it for cold outreach. You knock on 100 doors. You make 100 phone calls. You send 100 direct messages. You send 100 voicemails. All these are examples of cold outreach that have made companies zillions. It worked 100 years ago. It works today. And when the platforms change, it'll work tomorrow.

Cold outreach has one key difference from warm outreach: trust. Strangers don't trust you.

And compared to people who know us, strangers present <u>three</u> new problems.

1) First, you don't have a way to contact them. Duh.

2) Second, even if you can contact them, they ignore you.

3) Third, even if they give you their attention, they're not interested.

Let me describe what these problems look like in the real world.

<u>If you're knocking on doors</u>, you don't have the addresses. Then, even if you do, they don't open the door when you knock. If they open, they still tell you to pound sand.

<u>If you're making cold calls</u>, you don't have their phone numbers. Even if you do, they don't pick up. If they pick up, they hang up on you.

<u>If you're sending cold emails</u>, you don't have their email addresses. Even if you do, they don't open the email. Even if they do, they don't respond.

<u>If you're sending direct messages</u>, you don't have a place to send it. Even if you do, they don't read it. Even if they read it, they don't reply.

<u>If you're sending voice memos or text messages</u>, you don't have their numbers. Even if you do, they don't read or listen to it. Even if they read or listen to it, they don't reply.

Now that we got that out of the way, the order we solve these problems is:

1) Get a way to contact them

2) Figure out what to say

3) Contact them until they're ready and able to listen

The Result. We find lots of ways to contact the most qualified strangers. We reach out to a lot of them in a lot of ways a lot of times. Then, we overwhelm them with value upfront to get them to show enough interest to move forward.

Author Note: It'll Take A Few More Steps Than Normal

As a personal rule of thumb, I sell expensive stuff. I sell expensive stuff better when I do it in multiple steps (rather than on the first contact). So my first priority is to get the prospect to show interest in the stuff I sell. When they show interest, I schedule a time to sell them. If my lead magnet requires a second exchange to deliver it, I do that then. If my lead magnet provides value on its own, then the next call is to talk about the value they received. Either way works.

Cold outreach is a numbers game. The more people you reach out to the more engaged leads you get. Once we figure out how much outreach it takes to engage a lead, then we only have one thing to do...*more*. Let's go hunting!

As there are three new problems strangers introduce, I've divided this chapter into three steps. One step per problem. First, we get a targeted list of leads. Next, we need to know what to say to get them to reply. Third, we make up for a lower response rate by increasing the volume and type of our reach out attempts.

Problem #1: "But how do I contact them?" →Build a List

Up until this point, from warm reach outs and posting free content, you've had to accept the leads that came to you from your warm audience. No more. With cold outreach, unlike any other way of advertising, we get to be as specific as we want. Only want to talk to hedge fund managers managing over $1B? Done. You can do that. Only want to speak with golf apparel retail store owners over $3M in sales? Done. Only want to talk to influencers who get over 50,000 unique page views per month? Done. Now *we* get to pick our targets rather than them picking us.

Now, you probably don't have a way to reach out to 1000 perfect fit strangers. And if we're gonna get them to buy from us, we've gotta first find a way to contact them–*duh*. So let's solve that problem first.

There are three different ways I get my targeted lead lists. First, I use software to scrape a list of names. Second, I pay brokers to assemble me a list of targeted leads. And if neither of those work, I manually scrape a list of names myself. Here's the process.

- o <u>Step #1 Softwares</u>: I subscribe to as many softwares as I can that scrape leads from different sources. I search them all based on my criteria. The software then spits out names, job titles, contact information, etc. I try out a representative sample, say a few hundred from each software I use. Then, if the contact information is up to date, the leads are responsive, and they are the type of person the software claims them to be, bingo! Then I get as many leads as the software will give me. But if I can't seem to find the right audience, I move onto step two.

- o <u>Step #2 Brokers</u>: I go to multiple list brokers and ask them to make me a list based on my audience criteria. They then send me a sample. I test out sample lists from each of the brokers. If I get good results from one or more brokers, I stick with their lists. And if I still can't find who I'm looking for, I move to step three.

- Step #3 Elbow Grease: I join groups and communities that I think have my audience. When I find people that meet my qualifications, I check to see if they have ways to contact them in the group's directory–like links to their social media profiles, etc. If they do, I add them to my list. If they don't, I can reach out to them within the platform hosting the group. I prefer to find contact information outside the group so I don't come off as someone solely trying to milk the group for business *but I will if I have to.*

So I work my way from the most accessible leads to the least accessible leads. Here's an important point. If you can search the database, so can everyone else. But if you assemble a list of names yourself, it's less likely that person has already received many cold reach outs from other companies. So they're the freshest. Downside: it takes the most time. Of course, you can pay someone else to do this for you once you figure it out for yourself, but we're only talking about getting started in this chapter. We'll talk about scaling in Section IV.

Action Step: Find your scraping tool by searching "outbound leads scraping tool" or "database lead scraping." Find brokers the same way. With a few clicks, you'll find what you're looking for. Put your first 1000 names together. If you have more time than money, you might want to start at step three since it only costs time.

Pro Tip: Interest Groups Are The Warmest Cold Audience You Can Get

Interest groups contain the <u>highest quality leads</u> because they are concentrated pools of people looking for a solution. Give them one. Nowadays, there's software that can scrape information from these groups. Use it. They're one of my favorite places to fish.

Problem #2: "I have my list, but what do I say to them?" →**Personalize, Then Give Big Fast Value**

Now that you have your list of leads, you gotta figure out what to say. I went over a lot of scripting in the Warm Reach Outs section–this section builds on that one. At the end of this chapter, I also include three sample scripts you can model for cold calls, cold emails, and cold chat messaging. That being said, there are two important factors I emphasize to get strangers to engage: *personalization* and *big fast value*. This is important because they don't know us and they don't trust us. We've gotta overcome both issues in a matter of seconds.

a) They Don't Know Us→Personalize (Act Like You Know Them). To get more leads to engage, we want the message to *look* like it's from someone they know. The best way to do that is to actually know something about the person you are contacting. In essence, we want our *cold* reach out to look like a *warm* reach out.

...Imagine your phone rings from an unknown number and area code. Are you likely to pick it up? Probably not. What about if the number is from your area code? A little more likely. Why is that? Because *it might be someone you know*. So to take this concept further, imagine you pick up the phone...

...The person says "<Your name?>" then pausing (like a normal person). You'd say, "yea...who's this?" Now, if that person then went on to say, "it's Alex...*then pauses*...I watched a few of your videos and read that recent blog post you wrote on dog training. It was killer! Really helped me out with my doberman. She's a beast! That peanut butter trick really helped. Thanks for that."

You'd still be wondering what's going on. But you know what you wouldn't be doing?...*hanging up.* Then you hear, "Oh yea, sorry, I got ahead of myself. I work for a company that helps dog trainers fill up their books. We like to partner with the best in the area. So I'm always on the lookout. We worked with someone about an hour north from you...John's Doggy Daycare...heard of them?"

You'd respond yes or no (it doesn't matter), and they'd say, "Yea, we ended up getting them 100 appointments in 30 days using a combination of text email and some ads. Do you offer similar services to them?" To which you'd probably say yes. Then they'd say, "Oh that's perfect. Then we'd be able to use that same campaign in your market and drive leads over to you. If you got a boatload of high paying new dog training customers you wouldn't be upset with me would you?" You'd laugh lightly. "Okay great. Well...tell ya what...I can walk you through the entire thing soup to nuts later today. Will you be around at 4?" And you'd say - sure - or whatever. The point is, if that person had started the call with "hey man, wanna buy some marketing services?" you'd probably have hung up.

Personalization is what gets your foot in the door to get the sale. Basically one to three pieces of information we can find that a friend might know about the prospect. Then we want to complement them on it, and ideally, show them how it benefited us. People like people who like them. Even if someone doesn't know you, they'll give you more time if you know something about them.

This comes in handy for personal subject lines on emails, the first few messages in chat, or the first few sentences someone hears. Even if someone doesn't know you, they will appreciate the time you took to research them before contacting them. This tiny effort goes a long way.

Action step: Do a little research on each lead before you send them a message. We can do this ourselves, pay people to do it for us, or use software. Batch this work. Then, use your notes to figure out the first thing you'll open with to *feel more familiar*.

Pro Tip: 50% Email Response Rate Bump

I took our cold outreach template and re-wrote it below a third grade reading level. The results: *50% more leads responded*. I recommend running all scripts and messages through a free reading level app online. I won't recommend one because they go out of business all the time, but I promise you can find one. Make your messages easier to understand and more people will respond.

---

b) They Don't Trust Us→Big Fast Value. The key difference between people who know you and strangers is…strangers give you far less time to prove your worth. And, they need a lot more incentive to move towards you. So make your life easier by "giving away the farm." We're not trying to tickle their interest, <u>we're trying to blow their minds in under thirty seconds</u>.

Like warm reach outs, you can directly make your offer, or offer a lead magnet, or both. It gives the person a strong reason to respond.

I specifically call out 'big fast value' rather than "your lead magnet" as a reminder that it needs to be BIG FAST VALUE. If it's not, or it's mediocre, you'll blend in with the ocean of people trying to get their attention. And they'll treat you the same–they'll ignore you. Here's how much it matters:

The first four months of cold outreach felt like torture. We offered a game planning session as our lead magnet. Some gyms took us up on it, but most didn't. We needed something better. I tested many parts of our process but swapping the lead magnet blew everything else out of the water. We swapped from "game planning" - code for "sales call" - to actually giving them as much free service as we could possibly afford. Our take rates 3x'd and cold outreach became a monster channel for us.

If your offer/lead magnet isn't working for you, up the ante. Keep offering more until you *make it so good they feel stupid saying no*. They either buy from you or have nice things to say about you. Win-win.

If you forget everything about this chapter, remember one thing: *the goal is to demonstrate big value as fast as possible.* Give yourself a downhill battle by giving away something crazy. Give away something for free people would normally pay for and they will want it. Note: I didn't say, "so good they should pay for it," I said, "stuff they actually pay for." Big difference. Take this to heart and your results will show it.

Action Step: Provide the biggest fastest value you can afford to with your lead magnet or offer. Then, write your scripts. And don't worry, I got your back there. To give you a headstart, I provide sample phone, email, and direct message scripts at the end of the chapter. Note: Phone and chat scripts are never more than a page or two, and cold emails rarely more than half a page. So don't overthink it. There are no awards for prettiest script. Get your first 100 conversations or 10,000 emails out of the way before tweaking it. Get testing. Then tweak as you learn.

Problem #3: "I'm not getting enough chances to tell people about my amazing stuff, what do I do?" → Volume

Once we have our list of names, personal info, and our big sexy lead magnet, we need to get more strangers to see it. We do this in three ways. First, we automate delivery to the greatest extent possible. Next, we automate distribution to the greatest extent possible. Finally, we follow up more times in more ways.

a) Automated Delivery. To the extent that we can, automating delivery unlocks huge scale as someone doesn't need to literally communicate the message to the prospect. This means you get more engaged leads per unit of time (even if fewer engage by overall percentage). Remember, you have far more people who don't know you than people who do. So you don't have to worry *as much* about 'burning through an audience.' Here's what the difference between manual and automated delivery looks like.

Manual Examples: A live person can say a script to someone over the phone. You can send a personal voice memo to each lead. A person can write a handwritten letter to every person on the list. If it takes a person time to convey the message each time, it's manual.

RECORDED

<u>Automated Examples</u>: We can send a pre-recorded voice memo to someone's direct messages. We can send a pre-recorded voicemail to someone's voicemail box. We can send templated emails to an inbox or a templated text to someone's phone. We can send a pre-recorded video. Etc. You record your message one time and then send the same message to everyone.

> **Pro Tip: Use Technology That Gets You More Engaged Leads For Your Time**
>
> Everyday, artificial intelligence, deep fakes and other technology advance. They become more indistinguishable from human communication. This means we will be able to automate elements of what we currently are forced to spend time on. Embrace technology as it comes out to reap the rewards. Ultimately, technology serves a single purpose - to get us more output per unit time. Use it.

b) Automate Distribution. Once we have our messages prepared, we gotta distribute them. And there's no award for who works the hardest, only for who gets the best results. Although one leads to the other. And as you build your skills, you will find ways to automate portions of the work. I encourage you to automate when ethical and available.

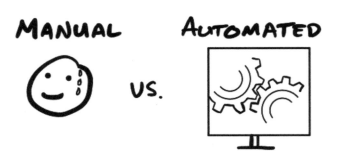

MANUAL vs. AUTOMATED

<u>Manual examples</u>: Dial each phone number. Click send on each email, direct message, text, etc.

<u>Automated examples</u>: Use a robot to dial multiple numbers at a time. Send a blast of 1000 emails, texts, voicemails at one time. Etc.

Generally speaking, you sacrifice personalization for scale. You get a higher response rate with personalized messages. *The fewer leads you have, the less automation you should use.*

For example, if there are only 1000 hedge fund managers who meet your criteria, you're gonna wanna personalize every one of them. On the other hand, if you're targeting women 25-45 trying to lose weight, there are tens of millions of them. So you can get away with less personalization. But…if you personalize…you'll get even more (wink).

Pro Tip: Personalization Tech

The perfect combination for maximum leads is max personalization with max volume. And with tech, you don't *always* sacrifice personalization for scale. Everyday, data becomes more accessible to find personal data. If you can set up the tech to accomplish both - personalization and volume - you create a deadly effective lead-getting combo.

Action Step. Embrace new technology. Allocate ten to twenty percent of your effort towards brand new untested technology. For example, if you make phone calls five days per week, try out a new dialer or tech one of the days and see how it does compared to your standard dialer.

c) Follow up. More times. More ways. There are two more ways you can get more from your list of names.

First, you try to contact them more than once. Shocker. But wanna know something crazy, most people don't. Here's a different way to think about it. Imagine you really needed to get a hold of your parents because something important came up. What would you do? You'd probably call them, text them, leave a voicemail, etc. And if they still haven't responded, what would you do? You'd call and text them again (probably shortly thereafter). It's the same way with prospects. They are in danger of living life without your solution. Be a hero. Save them!

The more ways you try to contact someone, the more likely you are to contact them. People respond to different methods. For example, I never respond to phone calls. But, I reply to direct messages far more.

Contacting someone multiple times multiple ways shows them you are serious. And doing so quickly communicates you have something important to discuss. Curiosity increases because they fear they're missing out.

Personally, I like to email first. You know why? Because most people don't respond. If someone doesn't respond to one of your reach out methods, use that as a reason to follow up with another method. *"Hey I'm calling you to follow up about my email."* We either get a response or a real reason to reach out again. We win either way.

And once you do get them booked for an appointment, expect more than one conversation. Remember, we're contacting complete strangers. Outreach takes more touch points with people who don't know you. So expect two to three conversations before a higher ticket sale. Shoot for less, but expect more when you start out.

<u>Bottom line</u>: Act like you're *actually* trying to get ahold of these people, rather than going through the motions, and you probably will.

Action Step: Contact each lead multiple times in multiple ways.

Pro Tip: Don't be an nincompoop

If someone asks you not to contact them, don't contact them again. Not because there isn't a chance it could work. But because for the same effort, you could reach out to someone who isn't already negatively inclined. It's just more efficient to turn neutrals to YES than NO to YES. On top of that, you don't want a bad reputation. That kind of stuff follows you. Try hard because you have a genuine desire to solve their problems, but be respectful.

Second, once you finish contacting your list, start back at the top again. This actually works for three reasons.

One, because they simply may not have seen your first series of messages. Only a fool would think one hundred percent of people see what you put out one hundred percent of the time. So we make up for that discrepancy with follow up.

Two, even if they do see it, it may not have been a good moment to respond. People's schedules change every day. And there are times when people can't respond to you even if they wanted to. So the more opportunities you give them to respond, the greater the chance they will.

Three, their circumstances may have changed. They might not have needed you then, but need you desperately now. Imagine a person you message about losing weight before the holidays. At that time, they fit into their 'skinny' jeans, so they feel no pain. They probably wouldn't respond. But after they gained ten lbs over the holidays, they may all of a sudden be in desperate need of what you offer. And now, they respond to your reach out attempt. The only thing that changed was their circumstance. So try again in three to six months and get an entirely new group of engaged leads *from the same list*.

Everything may be right except the timing. So the more times we contact them, the more likely we will catch them at the time they're ready to engage.

Action Step. After you've attempted to contact them multiple times, multiple ways, wait three to six months. Then, do it again.

Pro Tip: If You Are New To An Outreach Team, Shadow The Best Guy On The Team.

Then, double their inputs. If they make 200 calls, make 400. If that means you work more - duh. You will suck before you are good. You can make up for your lack of skill with volume. Volume negates luck. And when you do twice as many, you'll get good in half the time. Once you beat their numbers, then you can get cute and try new things. Replicate before you iterate.

Three Problems Strangers Create→Solved

I wrote the book in this order to build on itself. Start with warm reach outs. Get some reps. Post some content to grow your warm audience. Get even more reps. Then, you'll be ready for cold reach outs.

And now, we solved the three core problems cold audiences create: finding the right list of people, getting them to pay attention to you, and getting them to engage. Victory!

Author Note: For People With Low Ticket Products.

I had trouble making cold outreach profitable when selling for my direct to consumer business. Cold outreach teams are expensive, and my average ticket wasn't high enough. But, I learned I could make a low ticket product→a high ticket product, if I sold a lot at once. So I switched from using cold outreach to get customers, to using cold outreach to get affiliates who got customers for me. There were two ways that worked. Either I'd sell the affiliates lots of products in bulk up front, then they'd sell my products to their customers. Or, I'd use cold outreach to recruit them, then get them to sell my products to their customers, and receive a commission after the sale. One affiliate sale can be worth thousands of customers. Both ways transformed my 'low ticket' sale into a 'high ticket' sale by selling many at once. So the numbers pencil out. If you have trouble using cold outreach for your direct to consumer business, consider going after affiliates instead. More on this in the affiliates chapter later.

Benchmarks–How well am I doing?

The two times I failed at cold outreach I hired people who never tracked metrics well. The third person did. And cold reach outs succeeded. The person who runs it (maybe you) has to know the metrics of the sales process like the back of their hand. Every single stat.

Let's break down the numbers with a couple platform examples. I cannot give an example for every platform because it would take too long. My hope is that you can generalize the concept to whatever platform you use.

<u>Phone Example</u>

Let's say I make 100 cold calls per day. And, let's say I get a twenty percent pick-up rate. From there, I am able to get twenty-five percent of people to want to take my lead magnet. That means I got four engaged leads. If it took me four hours to make those calls, it means

I got one engaged lead per hour. I can do this at first. Once the amount of engaged leads that convert to customers makes me more than it costs to pay a cold outreach rep–I teach someone else to do it for me (more on this in Section IV). So you know you do well when you make at least *three times* the lifetime profit of a customer compared to what it costs you to get them.

<u>Email Example</u>

Let's say you send 100 personalized emails per day. From there, thirty percent open our email. From there, 10% reply showing interest. That means we'd have three engaged leads (30% x 10% = 3%). The numbers will vary but <u>shoot for 3% of your list turning into engaged leads</u>. Here's a sample from a new campaign for a very niche high ticket service business in our portfolio. It shows a 4% lead engagement rate. And presumably, a third of them convert into sales. That would net us one new customer per one hundred outreach attempts.

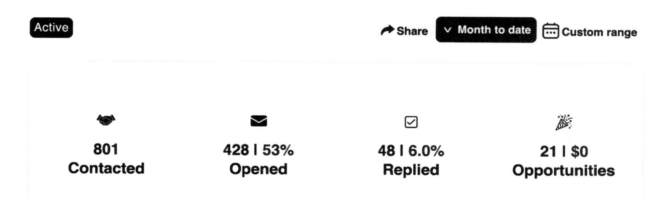

<u>Direct Message Example</u>

Let's say I make a personal video or record a personal voice memo for one hundred people. I say their name and add one personal line before delivering my standard message. From there, twenty percent of people reply. We now have twenty engaged leads. From there we use the same A-C-A format from the warm outreach section to qualify them for a call and so forth. So like the phone example, you know you do well when the cost of doing cold outreach is less than three times what you make in profit from a customer. Note: You can do WAY better than three times, that's the bare minimum. For context, the portfolio company above gets over 30:1 returns from its outreach efforts.

Costs

This method is labor intensive. Nearly all costs are in the form of labor. In order to calculate our return on advertising, we add up all labor and software costs associated with steps one through three in the section before last.

Let's imagine we have a team doing cold calls:

- We pay them $15 per hour and $50 per shown appointment or "shows."

- We have $3600 in profit per sale.

- Leads cost us ten cents.

- They call 200 leads per day.

- We would likely get about two shows per day from one rep.

- If they worked eight hours per day, we would pay $120 in labor and $100 in show commissions per rep and $20 for the leads.

- This means we would pay $240 for two shows or $120 per show.

- If we closed 33% of shows, our cost to get a client (excluding commissions) would be $360.

- Since we get $3600 profit per new client, we would make a 10:1 return.

That's how cold outreach works. Then, you just add bodies. It is boring and tedious, but brutally effective.

Pro Tip: Give Each Rep An Explicit Number Of Leads To Work Every Week.

They should care for these leads like they are their children. If you give a rep too many, they will waste them. If someone can work one hundred leads at full capacity, I'll give them seventy-ish. That way, they have time and energy to squeeze everything they can out of the leads they've got. And since all reps get the same amount of leads every week, you can give them absolute quotas for deals. Ex: I give you seventy leads. You give me back seven appointments. I pay you. No leads left behind.

This Sounds Hard, Why Bother?

Most people dramatically underestimate the amount of volume it takes to use cold outreach. They also underestimate how long it takes. But there are seven *enormous* benefits to using cold outreach:

1) <u>You don't need to create lots of content or ads</u>. You focus only on one perfectly crafted message you convey to all your prospects. Your only goal is to make that one message better every day. There is no 'ad fatigue' or 'banner blindness' since your prospects have never seen anything from you. So, you don't need to be a marketing genius to make this work.

2) <u>Your competition won't know what you're doing</u>. Everything is private. By that fact alone, you can continue to operate in secrecy. You are not educating your competitors about how you acquire customers. They don't know what you're doing, or even, that you exist.

3) <u>It's incredibly reliable</u>. All you have to do to get more is do more. A certain amount of input creates a certain number of responses. It becomes like clockwork, bringing a reliable flow of new engaged leads into your world. You can reverse engineer the amount of sales you want to make to the number of inputs at the top of your lead pathway. Eventually you'll have an equation: for every X people contacted, you get Y customers. Then, you simply solve for X.

> Ex: Let's say for every 100 emails, I get one customer. If I want 100 customers, I need to send 10,000 emails. That's 333 per day. One person can send 111 emails a day. Therefore, I need three people sending emails every day to get 100 customers per month.

4) <u>Fewer platform changes</u>. Private communication is rarely subject to platform changes. Whereas public platforms change rules and algorithms every day. You gotta stay on top of rule changes to remain effective. In contrast, rules for cold calling, door knocking, and cold email have hardly changed in thirty years.

5) <u>Compliance is less painful</u>. Many platforms have stringent rules around claims you can make about the stuff you sell. Some also ban certain industries altogether (tobacco, firearms, cannabis, weight loss, etc.). With cold outreach, you don't need to deal with any of this. You still need to be FTC compliant, but you don't *also* need to worry about platform rules on top. This makes life easier. If you have a phone, you can make money. If you have an email account, you can get leads. This makes you very hard to stop.

6) <u>No spokesperson = Sellable business.</u> If an investor can buy it from you without worrying your business will stop getting customers if you leave….your business is *far* more valuable. Having an established outreach team is how we were able to sell Gym Launch. The business could grow without me dancing in front of the camera or relying on me being super ridiculously good looking (ha!). I don't think they would have wanted to buy us without it, or at least, not for as much.

7) <u>Hard to copy.</u> Even if someone wants to copy your entire cold outreach system, they'll often need to learn how to do each step. And, many steps are invisible. They don't know how you scrape your lists. They don't know how you personalize your messages. They don't know what softwares you use to distribute the messages etc. On top of that, they'd still need to learn how to hire, train, and operate a team of people who can do each step. Once you have a head start, it compounds with time. It becomes very hard to catch you.

Author Note: Belief Breaking Volume - Scaling To 60,000 Emails Per Month

To break your beliefs around what is possible, here's an example. To break past $1,000,000 per month, we automated the entire process of scraping, crafting, and sending emails for one of our portfolio companies. One virtual assistant sends 2000 emails per day using multiple pieces of software. This generates the business 40 engaged leads per day. Note, the response rate dropped because we took out so much personalization. From there, they are able to get 10 percent of engaged leads sold. Meaning, they get four new customers per day. This got them past that 100 customers per month barrier. <u>Fun Facts</u>: They started with us at $250,000 per month (our minimum size requirement for investment at the time). The business makes $20,000 per customer. With four new customers per day, do the math at how big they are now. :)

Your Turn

If you recall our advertising checklist this kicks off your journey to get more engaged leads with cold outreach. You start this as you run out of people to advertise to, or, because you just want more. Here's a sample.

Cold Reach Outs Daily Checklist	
Who:	Yourself
What:	Hook + Lead Magnet/Core Offer
Where:	Any private communication platform
To Whom:	List: Scraped, bought, or software used.
When:	Everyday, 7 days per week
Why:	Get leads to engage to sell stuff
How:	Live calls, voicemail drops, email blasts, text blasts, direct message texts, video messages, voice messages, direct mail pieces, hand written cards, etc.
How Much:	100 Per Day
How Many:	Day 1 - 2x, Day 2 - 2x, Day 7 - 1x
How Long:	As long as it takes.

Pro Tip: Count in 100s

This is a volume game. You will need to do a lot of volume, efficiently, to get the results you want. Don't set a daily goal below 100. And don't stop for 100 days minimum. If you do 100 reach outs for 100 days straight, I promise you will start getting new engaged leads.

Next Up

Now that you have set your commitment for this cold outreach method, we move onto the last thing a single person can do to advertise: run paid ads.

> **FREE GIFT: Cold Outreach Script Samples**
>
> I had to cut scripts to make this book a manageable length. If you want to model your scripts off them, go to: **Acquisition.com/training/leads**. And, if you needed another reason besides 'it'll make you money'....it won't cost you any. It's free. Enjoy. And as always, you can also scan the QR code below if you hate typing.

#4 Run Paid Ads Part I: Making An Ad

How To Publicly Advertise to Strangers

Advertising is the only casino where, with enough skill, you become the house.

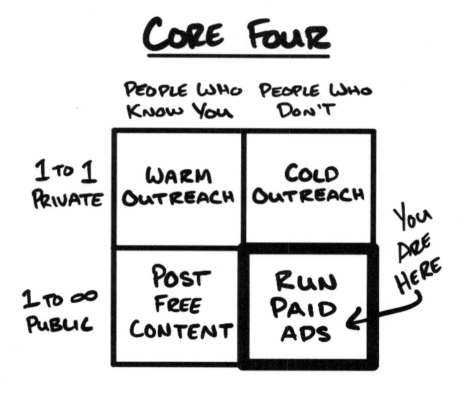

June 2013.

"Let's try some Facebook ads for the gym." I spouted.

Sam's eyebrow went up. "They don't work. I already tried."

Now this was the brief time between quitting my "real job" and starting my first gym. I wanted some experience. So I cold-emailed more than 40 gym owners for a chance to shadow them. Sam was the only one who responded to my pleas for mentorship. He let me work at his gym, *with him*, for minimum wage. I'm forever grateful for that opportunity.

"I promise, I really think they'll work." I said. "Let me give it a shot with the stuff I learned from that workshop last weekend. I'll do everything." *That workshop took most of my puny savings.*

Sam leaned back in his chair, crossing his arms. "I'll tell you what. I'll give you a thousand bucks to play with. If you lose it, then you have to shut up about this Facebook stuff. If you make more, I'll split the profit with you."

"Deal."

I worked with a freelancer to get everything set up. We went back and forth until it was "perfect." A few days later, I marched into Sam's office to show him what I'd made.

"It's ready." I said.

He spun his laptop to face me. "Alright, Hormozi. Show me what you've got."

I placed the ugliest ad you've ever seen:

I'M LOOKING FOR 5 CHINO HILLS RESIDENTS TO TAKE PLACE IN A FREE 6 WEEK CHALLENGE. YOU MUST LET US USE YOUR BEFORE AND AFTER PICTURES IN OUR MARKETING IN EXCHANGE FOR THE PROGRAM. CLICK LINK TO SIGN UP:
[LINK]

No images. No videos. No frills. →Just words. ALL CAPS.

The ad went live.

We got leads within hours. I called them all and booked appointments as fast as I could. I also texted them about an hour before to remind them of our appointment. And as soon as they walked in, I started yapping about our six week challenge. I had zero sales skills. My *conviction made up for my lack of skill.* They bought.

I sold 19 people at $299 each. We made just under $5700 from the $1000 investment. True to his word, Sam cut me a check and handed it over. He made it out for $2500. More than my share.

"Sam, this is—"
He cut me off. "Nice work, Hormozi. *Do it again.*"

***

The "6 week challenge" became the biggest promotion in the gym industry. *For seven years.* It drove at least $1.5B in revenue, more by now. I taught it to over 4,500 gyms. And I bet more than 10,000+ gyms used versions of the promotion without licensing it. Maybe you saw ads for it in your local market. And yes, if you're curious, it got more sophisticated as time went on.

How Paid Ads Work

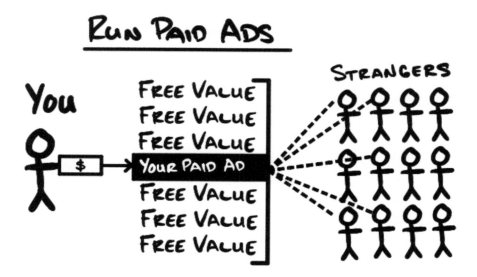

Paid ads are a way to advertise one-to-many to cold audiences. People who don't know you. Paid ads work by paying another person or business to put your offer in front of *their* audience. Think of it like renting eyeballs or earballs. And because you don't need to spend time building an audience, paid ads are the fastest way to get the most people to see your stuff— You trade money for reach. *A considerable advantage when you know what you're doing.* Ads are riskier. But, when done right, they can get you more leads than any other method.

With warm and cold outreach we have to do more stuff to reach more people. To reach more people with free content, we depend on the platform or audience sharing it if they feel like it. Paid ads are different. The reach is *guaranteed*. But getting your money back isn't. So it's a game of efficiency rather than reach. Let me explain:

In principle, if you paid enough money, you could get every person in the world to see your ad. And, if every person in the world saw your ad, someone would buy. Even if only by accident (ha). So the question isn't "do ads work?" it's "*how well* can you make them work?" In other words, it's a push and pull between how much you spend and how much they buy.

And like cold outreach, paid ads go to colder lower trust audiences. So even with good offers, a smaller percentage of people will respond. And like cold outreach, paid ads get over this hurdle by putting your offer in front of more people. And if an ad isn't profitable, most of the time, it's because the right people *never saw it*. So to make an ad profitable, the right people *have to* see it. This keeps our ads efficient.

This chapter reveals how I create more efficient paid ads by finding needles in the haystack. I start with the entire world as my audience (haystack) then narrow down to get a higher percentage of engaged leads (needles). First, I pick a platform that contains my ideal audience. Second, I use whatever targeting methods that exist within the platform to find them. Third, I craft my ad in a way that <u>repels</u> anyone else. Finally, I tell whoever's left standing to take the next step. People overcomplicate it. But that's it. That's all we're doing - narrowing down who sees our ad so we have the highest chance of getting the right type of people to respond.

Once we advertise profitably in a small puddle of an audience, we expand to a pond, then a lake, then an ocean. And as the audience gets bigger it does have more of the wrong people, but it has more of the right ones too. So ads decrease in efficiency, but at that point you can afford it. In other words, the ratio between what you spend and how much they buy goes down but the total amount of money you make goes up. So instead of spending $1000 to make $10,000 with $9000 in profit, you spend $100,000 to make $300,000 with $200,000 in profit. Your ratio goes down, but you make more money. So the risk is higher because you spend more. But so is the reward. This means we want to make the audience as big as possible while still turning a profit.

Paid ads give us four new problems to solve. Let's break them down together:

1) Knowing where to advertise

2) Getting the right audience to see it

3) Making the best ad for them to see

4) Getting permission to contact them

Step 1: "But where do I advertise?" → Find a platform where these four things are true

Platforms distribute content to an audience. If you're not familiar with any available platforms, I invite you to come join me on planet earth. If you've ever consumed content, which you have, you've directly or indirectly used a platform and been a member of its audience. And wherever there's an audience, you can usually advertise. So if you want to become a great entrepreneur, you have to learn about them. Here's what I look for in a platform I want to advertise on:

- I've used it and gotten value from it as a consumer. So I have some idea how it works.

- I can target people on the platform interested in my stuff.

- I know how to format ads specific to the platform (which I'll dive into in step three).

- I have the minimum amount of money to spend to place an ad.

...And yes, platforms change all the time, but these principles stay the same.

Pro Tip: Place Ads Where Your Competitors Place Ads (To Start)

Platforms often have different ad types. For example, on LinkedIn, you can send message ads or you can run newsfeed ads. On Instagram, you can run ads to the newsfeed or stories. On YouTube, you can run ads on the side bar, mid stream, or as pre-roll. So how do you know where to start? Look at the ad placement of other people in your space, and start there. If they can make it work so can you. *Replicate before you iterate.*

Action Steps: Start with one platform that meets the four requirements. And start watching, listening, or reading ads on the platform as a first step to learning how to make one.

Step #2: "But how do I get the right people to see it?" → Target them

So if we start with the entire world, which we kinda do, we need to be a bit more specific. For example, if you choose a platform that has 100,000,000 users, you've already cut out 99% of the world– right off the bat. And, if everyone who buys from you speaks English, you also want to *exclude* the audiences within the platform who don't. If that's half the platform's users, you're already at 99.5% of the world excluded. Specific is good.

The right message to the wrong audience will fall on deaf ears. It doesn't matter how good your ads are. If you're marketing to Florida residents about a local business in Iowa, it's probably not gonna work. So you have only one goal when targeting–get the highest number of people you think will buy your stuff to see your ad.

We did our first round of targeting by selecting our platform. We do the second round *within* the platform itself. Modern advertising platforms have two ways to target. You can use them separately or combine them:

1) <u>Target a lookalike audience</u>. Modern platforms can show your ad to an audience that is similar to, and much bigger than, a list you provide. Advertisers call this a **lookalike audience.** Modern platforms will make lookalike audiences for you so long as you upload their minimum list size. The bigger the list and the higher quality the contacts, the more responsive the lookalike audience will be. Start with your list of current and previous customers. If your customer list is big enough to meet the platform minimum, use it. If it's not big enough, add your warm reach out list. If it's still not big enough, add your cold reach out leads to hit the minimum. This is exactly what I do. Forcing the list to the right size sometimes makes the lookalike audience too broad. And that's OK because you can…

2) <u>Target with factors of your choosing.</u> Targeting options include: age, income, gender, interests, time, location, etc. For example, if you know no one over forty-five or below twenty-five has ever bought your thing, then exclude anyone outside that range. If you sell car parts then show your ad *during* car shows and *on* car channels. If only people with pets buy your thing, then include pets as an interest. Basic filters on top of the platform-generated lookalike audience are a simple way to get more of the right people to see your ads. End result: more efficient ads.

Pro Tip: Local Targeting

Since local markets are already *tiny* in comparison to national markets, you won't want to add many more filters. Be as specific as possible, but no further. The local market on its own is already .1% of a nation, so you're already pretty narrow.

The more filters you use, the more specific the list. The more specific the list, the more efficient your ads but the faster you will "burn" through it. However, this specificity sets you up to get more wins early on. The wins from smaller specific audiences now give you the money to advertise to larger and broader audiences later. *This is how you scale.*

Action Steps: Bring all your lead lists together into one place. Separate them by past and previous customers, warm outreach, and cold outreach. Eventually, you'll have a list of people that engaged with your paid ads by giving you contact information but didn't buy. That'll come in handy. Then, if the platform allows, use these lists in order of quality to create your lookalike audience. Then, if the platform also allows, add filters on top of your lookalike audience to target an even higher percentage of people to engage with your ad. If you are incapable of making a lookalike audience, then simply start by targeting interests.

Step #3 "But what should my ad say?" → Call Out + Value + Call to Action (CTA)

To this day, I don't change the channel when I see an ad. I rarely mute ads or skip ads. In fact, I have no premium subscriptions that remove ads on any media platforms either. Main reason: I *want* to consume the ads. I *want* to see how businesses do three things. 1) How they <u>call out</u> their ideal customers. 2) How they present the <u>value elements</u>. 3) How they give their audience a <u>call to action</u>. When I look at ads this way, it turns what was once an everyday nuisance (ads) into a continuous learning experience. Consuming ads on purpose, with the core elements in mind, makes me a better advertiser. And it will make you a better one too.

Let's use the three chunks to make an ad.

1) Call Outs - I need to get them to notice my ad

2) Value - I need to get them interested in what I have to offer

3) Calls to Action - I need to tell them what to do next

1) Call Out: ***People noticing your ad is the most important part of the ad...by a lot.*** The purpose of each second of the ad is to sell the next second of the ad. And the headline is the first sale. As David Ogilvy says "After you've written your headline, you've spent eighty cents of your advertising dollar." Focus your effort front to back. As crazy as this sounds (and all the pros are nodding their heads), my advertising became 20x more effective when I focused the majority of my effort on the first five seconds. We need the audience's eyes and ears just long enough for them to realize "this is for me, I'll keep paying attention." This "first impression" is the part of the ad I test the most.

Imagine you're at a cocktail party in a big ballroom. Lots of people talking in groups. Loud music playing in the background. In all that noise, a single sound pierces through it all and you turn around. Wanna know the sound? Your name. You hear it, and *instantly* look for the source.

Scientists call it the 'cocktail party effect'. In simple terms, even when there's tons of stuff going on, a single thing can still catch and hold our attention. So our goal with callouts is to harness the cocktail party effect and cut through *all* the noise. After all, if they never notice your ad, nothing else matters.

A **callout** *is whatever you do to get the attention of your audience.* Call outs go from hyperspecific - to get one person's attention - to not at all specific - to get everyone's attention. Let me explain. If someone drops a tray of dishes, *everyone* looks. If a child yells "MOM!", then the *moms* look. If someone says your name, only *you* look. But again, they all get attention. And I try to make my call outs specific enough to get the right people *and* broad enough to get as many of them as I can. So pay close attention to how advertisers use call outs, especially the ones targeting your audience.

Here's what I look for with verbal callouts- *using words to get attention:*

1) Labels: A word or set of words putting people into a *group*. These include features, traits, titles, places, and other descriptors. Ex: *Clark County Moms* *Gym Owners* *Remote Workers* *I'm looking for XYZ* etc. To be most effective, *your ideal customers need to identify with the label.*

    a) People automatically identify with their local area. So with local ads, the more local, the better. A local ad with "LOCAL AREA + TYPE OF PERSON" callout is *still* one of my all-time favorite ways to get someone's attention. It worked two hundred years ago, it works today, and it'll work tomorrow. So think: Americans < Texans < Dallas Residents < Irving Residents. If you live in Irving, you'll immediately think this ad could affect you. So, it catches your attention.

2) <u>Yes-Questions</u>: Questions where if people answer "yes, that's me" they qualify themselves for the offer. Ex: *Do you wake up to pee more than once a night?* *Do you have trouble tying your shoes?* *Do you have a home worth over $400,000?*

3) <u>If-Then Statements</u>: *If* they meet your conditions *then* you help them make a decision. *If you run over $100,000 per month in ads, we can save you 20% or more... *If you were born between 1978 and 1986 in Muskogee Oklahoma, you may qualify for a class action lawsuit…*If you want to XYZ, then pay attention…*

4) <u>Ridiculous Results</u>: Bizarre, rare, or out of the ordinary stuff someone would want. *Massage studio books out two years in advance. Clients furious.* *This woman lost 50 pounds eating pizza and fired her trainer* *The government is handing out thousand dollar checks to anyone who can answer three questions* Etc.

Callouts don't have to be just words. They can also be noises or visuals in the environment. Let's go back to the cocktail party. Sure, a dropped tray of dishes would get everyone's attention, but so would the cling*cling*cling* of a knife against a champagne flute. They both get everyone's attention for different reasons—one signals an embarrassing disaster and the other signals important news… *but, in either case, everyone still wants to know what happens next.* So if the platform allows, good advertisers use verbal and nonverbal callouts *together*.

Here's what I look for with nonverbal callouts- *using the setting and spokesperson to get attention:*

1) <u>Contrast</u>: Any stuff that "sticks out" in the first few seconds. The colors. The sounds. The movements etc. Note what catches your attention. Ex:

   a) A bright shirt almost always gets more attention than a black or dull shirt.

   b) Attractive people almost always get more attention than plain looking people.

   c) Moving stuff almost always gets more attention than still stuff.

2) <u>Likeness:</u> Think visually *showing* labels–features, traits, titles, places, and other descriptors that people identify with.

   a) People want to work with people who look, talk, and act in ways familiar to them (and you may not look, talk, or act in ways familiar to them). So if you serve a broad customer base use more ethnicities, ages, genders, personalities etc. in your ads. If you serve a narrow customer base (ex: medical devices for seniors), then use people who look like them.

      i) Quack like a duck. If you want to attract ducks, look like a duck, walk like a duck, and quack like a duck. If you want to attract plumbers, dress like a plumber, talk like a plumber, be in a plumbing environment. Even with the same message, your ad will do far better if you look the part (or find people who do).

      ii) If you see an ad for doctors, notice the spokesperson. What age are they? Gender? Ethnicity? Are they wearing a lab coat? A stethoscope? Are they in a medical facility? All these things get a specific type of person interested in health related products and services to pay more attention than they would have otherwise.

      iii) Mascots also work well because they don't age, never ask for more money, and never take days off. Think Micky Mouse for Disney. The Geico Gecko. Tony the Tiger for Kellogg's. The Michelin Man. etc. A mascot is a great way to create an enduring spokesperson for your business.

      iv) <u>Advanced:</u> Whichever likenesses you choose to use, if it's not you, the business becomes less dependent on you and therefore more sellable. You also may just be an ugly son of a gun. Plus, pretty people convert better anyways. Good news is, it doesn't cost much to get a pretty person to say stuff to a camera.

3) <u>The Scene:</u> Think *showing* the Yes-Questions and If-Then statements.

   Ex: An ad with…

   a) A person tossing and turning in bed calls out people with sleep troubles.

b) A pear next to an hourglass can call out people with a pear shaped body.

c) A room full of stuff stacked to the ceiling calls out people with too much junk.

d) A rock hitting a window calls out people with broken windows.

e) A local landmark. Locals think - *"Hey, I know that place!"* and pay attention.

Now, this isn't an exhaustive list. *Far* from it. I show you these to pull back the curtain. This way, you can see the infinite ways advertisers cut through the noise, so you can too.

Pro Tip: Infinite Ads

Here's one of the highest ROI tips I can give you about making ads. Record ten or so new ads every week. But, record thirty or more first sentences or questions to begin the ad. Think five second clips. These are the call outs people consume before deciding to watch more. With thirty callouts and ten main ads you can make three hundred variations in a matter of hours. Once you know the best callout, you apply it to all ads.

Action Step: I'm always impressed with the clever and innovative ways advertisers call out their prospects. So instead of muting or hitting "skip ad" *look for the call outs*. Become a student of the game. My goal is that for the rest of your life when you see an ad *you turn up the volume.*

Now, once they've noticed our ad, it leads us to the second chunk of the ad—we need to get them interested…

2) Get Them Interested. If people think an offer or lead magnet has big benefits and tiny costs, they value it. And they'll exchange money or contact information to get it. But if the cost outweighs the benefits, they don't value it, and they won't. *So the best ads make the benefits look as big as possible and the costs look as small as possible.* This makes an offer or lead magnet as valuable as it can be and gets the most engaged leads because of it.

A good advertisement, paid or not, uses clear and simple ways to answer the question: *why should I be interested in your thing?* It tells people why they should want your lead magnet or offer. Now, there are a million ways to do this, but I'll share with you my What-Who-

When Framework. This mental framework hinges on knowing the value equation forwards *and backwards*. So all you have to do is know eight key things about your own product or service: how it fulfills each element of value for your prospect, and how it helps them avoid their hidden costs (remember those?). Think of them like carrots vs sticks. How your offer delivers more good stuff *and* less bad stuff. Then think of the perspectives of the people who would experience them (Who). And finally, what time period (When) they'd have these experiences (positive or negative).

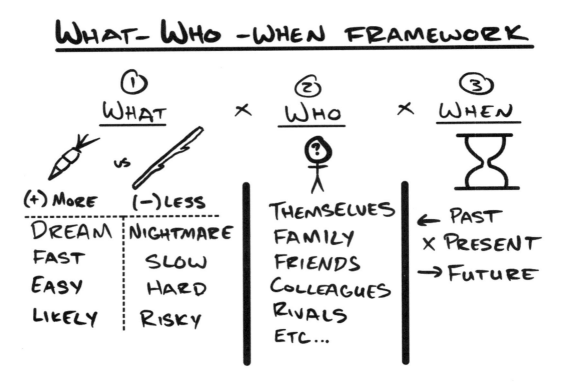

In the words of David Ogilvy "The customer isn't a moron. She's your wife." So you know what that means? *Write to her.* Ads cause the prospect to think questions to themselves. And a good ad answers those questions at precisely the time they think it. So if you can answer what they're thinking with your ad, using the words they'd use, you've won.

So let's start with <u>The What:</u> Eight Key Elements

- **Dream Outcome**: A good ad will show and tell the maximum benefit the prospect can achieve using the thing you sell. It should align with the ideal prospect's dream outcome for that sort of product or service. These are the results they experience after buying the thing.

- **Opposite - Nightmare**: A good ad will also show them the worst possible hassles, pain, etc. of going without your solution. In short - the bad stuff they'll experience if they don't buy.

- **Perceived Likelihood of Achievement**: Because of past failures, we assume that even when we buy, there's a *risk* we don't get what we want. Lower perceived risk by minimizing or explaining away past failures, emphasizing the success of people like them, giving assurances by authority, guarantees, and how what you have to offer will at least give them a better chance of success than what they currently do, etc.

  - **Opposite - Risk**: A good ad will also show them how risky it is to *not* act. What will their life be like if they carried on as they always have? Show how they will repeat their past failures and how their problems will get bigger *and* worse…

- **Time Delay**: A good ad will also show them how slow their current trajectory is or that they'll *never* get what they want at their current rate…

  - **Opposite - Speed**: To get things we want - we know we have to spend time getting them. A good ad will *show* and *tell* how much faster they will get the thing they want.

- **Effort and Sacrifice**: A good ad will also show them the amount of work and skill they'll need to get the result *without* your solution. And, how they'll be forced to keep giving up the things they love and continue suffering from the things they hate. Or worse, that they work hard and sacrifice a ton right now… and have gotten…*nowhere*. In other words, they waste more time and money doing what they currently do than if they just bought our darn solution!

  - **Opposite - Ease**: To get things we want - we know we have to change *something*. But we then <u>assume</u> we have to do stuff we hate and give up stuff we love. And ease comes from a lack of needed *work* or *skill*. A good ad disproves the assumption. It tells and shows how you can avoid the stuff you hate doing, do more of the stuff you love doing, <u>without working hard, or having a lot of skill and *still* get the dream outcome</u>.

Those are the 8 key elements. Now we fully understand <u>The What</u> – how we deliver the four value elements, and how we avoid their four opposites. We now go to the next W - <u>The Who</u>.

Who: Humans are primarily status driven. And the status of one human comes from how the other humans treat them. So if your product or service changes how other people treat your customer, which it does in some way, it *pays* to show how. And talking about the value elements from someone else's perspective shows all the ways it'll improve the status of your customer. So we want to outline two groups of people. The first group is the people gaining status, your customers. The second group is the people giving it to them: Spouse, Kids, Parents, Extended Family, Colleagues, Bosses, Friends, Rivals, Competitors, etc.

All of these perspectives give us different opportunities to show how the prospect's status may improve. And - they give us a *ton* of bonus benefits. As in, if you lose weight, do your kids have a new role model? Does your spouse now decide to get healthy too? Are you more likely to get promoted at work? Science says - yes. Does your frenemy no longer make those little jabs at dinner?

Let's do business examples. If I said something was risk free, I want to spell out how *their spouse* won't nag them about the purchase since there's no risk. I'd talk about how their kids would notice they weren't as stressed or distracted anymore about work. How their competitors notice their phones don't ring as much because all their customers are flowing to your new customer. How their business owner buddies say "business must be good" when they pull up in their new car at the golf range. You get the idea. These are all added benefits to the prospect we'd miss out on if we *only* looked at it from their own perspective.

And, we can apply each new <u>who</u> perspective to each value driver. This is how you get so many different stories, examples, angles, etc., to describe the benefits (more carrot and less stick).

That leads me to the third lens of the What-Who-When framework - <u>The When</u>.

When: People often only think of how their decisions affect the here and now. But if we want to be extra compelling (and we do), we should also explain what their decisions led to in the past *and* what their decisions *could* lead to in the future. We do this by getting them to visualize through their own timeline (past–present–future). This way, we help them to see the consequences of their decision (or indecision) *right now*.

Let's use the weight loss example from earlier *from their perspective*. We'd show them getting teased as a kid (past) struggling to button their favorite pair of jeans (present) or moving up *yet another* belt loop (future). What does that nightmare look like to their spouse? To their rivals? How embarrassing!

Remember, we can also run the same timeline through *someone else's* perspective. Their kid asking why other kids make fun of them (because they passed on bad food habits) (past), or how their kids complain now that the other kids' dads participate at practice when they don't (present), or how their doctor said they might not walk their daughter down the aisle at her wedding (future). Note: this is all the *bad stuff* they want to avoid. Our next copy elements would contrast those with the good stuff that could happen (present and future) *if they buy our thing*.

We use both towards good stuff and away from bad stuff then combine it with the past, present, and future of the prospect's life to create *powerful* motivators in our copy.

Putting the What, the Who, and the When together, we answer *WHY they should be interested.*

If I continued on with the weight loss thing, I might talk about how:

Their spouse (WHO) *will perceive how fast* (WHAT) *they fit into 'that suit your wife loves that didn't fit but does now' in the future* (WHEN). *Or, how their kids* (WHO) *month after month* (WHEN) *got more interested in eating healthy and tagging along during workouts* (WHAT). *Or, how they* (WHO)

143

catch a look at themselves in a reflection in the mall in a few months (WHEN) *and realize 'stuff actually fits me in this store'* (WHAT).

Pro Tip: Make Your Ads As Specific As You Can But No Specific-er

The more specific your copy the more efficient it can get, but also the longer it tends to get. And if it gets too long for the platform it lowers efficiency. So make the *ad in its entirety* as specific as you can in the most efficient space you've got. If you've got audio and visuals at your disposal then use *contrast, likeness,* and the scene itself to <u>match your copy</u> – It becomes more specific without getting any longer. And this makes your ad even more efficient and profitable.

When we combine:

- everything we can to get the prospect going *toward* the four value drivers, while also getting them *away from* their opposites

- the many perspectives we can show them gaining status, *and*

- different timelines for each…

…This adds up to *why* they should be interested. And now we have a lot of ways to get them interested! And - the more angles we cover, the more interested they'll become.

Also - since you asked - the only difference between long ads and short ads is how many angles we have time to cover from the copywriting framework. Longer ads use more. Shorter ads use fewer. So add or take away based on the platform, but keep the callouts (the first few seconds) and CTAs (what to do next) the same.

Pro Tip: Get Unlimited Inspiration.

Many platforms have a database of ads past and present. As of this moment, if you search "[PLATFORM] ad library" in a search engine, in a few clicks you will find them. If you see an ad that runs for a long time (a month or more), assume it's profitable. Then, take notes on the callouts they use, how they illustrate the value elements, and their CTAs. Look for <u>the words they use</u> *and* <u>how they demonstrate them</u>. Break down fifty or so ads and you will have a massive head start to creating winners of your own.

Action Steps: Get as many advertising angles with your offer as you can with the What-Who-When framework.

What: Know the eight key things about your own product or service. How it fulfills each element of value, and how it helps avoid their opposites.

Who: Show how the eight key things about your product or service can change *your prospect's* status. Then, show how *the people they know* give status to the prospect when they buy your thing or take status away if they don't.

When: Get the prospect to see the consequences of buying and not buying through their past, present, and future. Especially through their change in status with people they know. This way, we help them to see the value of their decision (or indecision) at this very moment.

Author Note: You Don't Need to Become a Copywriting Expert.

I'm certainly not. And if I thought copy was the limiter for most, I'd have spent more time on it. Sure, world class entrepreneurs have copywriting skills. But, world class copywriters don't necessarily have entrepreneurial skills. *Don't sacrifice one for the other.* If you explain your offer clearly using the What-Who-When framework, you'll have enough skill to remove copywriting as a limiter on your growth. And that's all you have to do–get good enough to grow. After all, if you call out the right people and have an amazing offer, you barely need any copy to begin with. *You just gotta explain your offer.* Get good enough to make your ads profitable, then scale and see what breaks next.

I also include a few more ad tips and tricks that have served me well in the lessons at the end of the chapter. But even if you never use them, there's only one more thing you'll need to turn these interested folks into engaged leads…

3) CTA - Tell Them What To Do Next

If your ad got them interested, then your audience will have huge motivation… for a tiny time. Take advantage. <u>Tell them *exactly* what to do next</u>. S-P-E-L-L it out: Click this button. Call this number. Reply with "YES." Go to this website. Scan this QR Code (wink). So many ads *still* don't do this. Your audience can only know what to do if you tell them.

<u>Make CTAs quick and easy</u>. Easy phone numbers, obvious buttons, simple websites. For example, a common CTA is to direct the audience to a website. So make your web address short and memorable:

Instead of… <u>alexsprivateequityfirm.com/free-book-and-course2782</u>

Use.. <u>acquisition.com/training</u>

Note: This comes from a guy who spent $370,000 on a single word domain <u>Acquisition.com</u>. So, I may overvalue easy domains, but I don't think I do. I think everyone else *under*values them. Just my two cents.

Assume the audience has no idea who you are, what you do, how it works, they're in a rush, and they have a 3rd grade education.

Beyond these basics which most still forget, you can also use all the tactics like urgency, scarcity, and bonuses from "Step 7" from the "engage your leads" chapter to make even stronger CTAs. They apply here, and everywhere else you tell your audience to do something.

So we can now pick a platform to advertise on, target who we show our ads to, make the ads they see, and tell them what to do next. All we have to do now is get their contact information.

Step #4 "How do I get their info?" → Get Permission To Contact Them

After they take the action–Get. Their. Contact. Information. My favorite way to get contact information is a simple landing page. Don't overthink it. The simpler your landing page, the easier it is to test. Focus on the words and the image. Here are my three favorite templates. Pick one and start testing.

LANDING PAGES

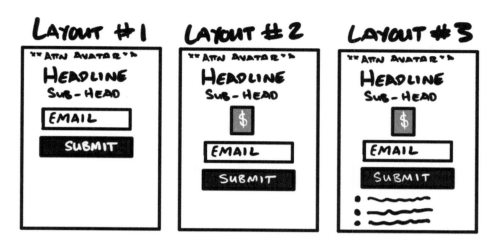

And make your landing pages match your ads. People click an ad because you promised them some benefit. So carry that same look and language over to your landing page. Make sure what you promised in your ad is what you deliver. This sounds simple, but a lot of people forget, and waste money until they remember it. You don't want to end up with some Frankenstein experience where everything looks different. You want a continuous experience from "click to close."

Get more people through more steps. In Robert Cialdini's seminal work, *Influence*, he shows that people like to think of themselves as consistent. So, if you remind them of the action they just took (CTA), and show how taking the next action aligns with it, you'll get more people to take the second action (Contact Info). For example, "Now that you just did A, you need to do B to get the most of A." *Or* "Doing A makes you a 'doing A' kind of person. Doing A kind of people, do B."

To be clear, we aren't selling anything. We are asking if they're interested in the stuff we sell. And if they're interested, they'll give us a way to tell them more about it. And when they do, they become engaged leads. Woo!

Action Step: Build your first landing page. I wasted four years feeling too scared to make a landing page. When I finally tried, I finished before lunch. Nowadays there are tons of "drag and drop" tools to build websites in minutes. And if you're still worried about it, freelancers will build a site, probably using those same drag and drop tools, on the cheap. So just get it done.

→**Now, you have engaged leads from paid ads!** Hooray! We did it!

Run Paid Ads Part I Conclusion

What *has to* happen for advertising to work? Well, we have to show our ad to the right people. So, we pick the right platform and target the people within that platform that have the highest percentage of our audience. Once we do that, we have to get them to <u>notice</u> our ad. Once they notice it, they have to consume it to get a <u>reason</u> to take action now rather than later. We do that using the value equation. And demonstrate it in the past, present and future, from their perspective and the perspectives of the people they know. And once they have a reason to take action, they have to have a <u>way to give us permission to contact them.</u> *That action turns them into an engaged lead.* And since those things gotta happen, they slowly but surely became the three core elements of every ad I create:

1) Callouts (for them to notice it)

2) Value Elements (to give them reason to do something)

3) Calls to action (to give them a way to do it)

Now… only one question remains…how efficient are we? Let's talk about money stuff.

#4 Run Paid Ads Part II: Money Stuff

"I'm just trying to buy a dolla' and sell it for two" - Proposition Joe, The Wire

We focus on efficiency with paid ads throughout this chapter and the last one because *efficiency matters more than creativity.* All advertising works. The only thing that differs between advertisements is how *well* they work. Maybe people get crazy about making paid ads because they have words like "copy" and "creative" and "media" then get hyper-focused on getting all that stuff "perfect" (as if you can). You can tweak all day and night… until the cows come home! The reality is that paid ads, any advertising really, is all about *the return on your investment.* And with paid ads it gets clear as day because you put X dollars in for people to see the ad and get Y dollars out if they buy your stuff. So if you want a *$100M leads* machine, you just need to get it "good enough" to scale. Why? Because good enough is good enough.

Since efficiency matters most, we want to be as efficient as possible so we can scale as much as possible. That way, we get as many leads as our little heart's desire.

That being said, there's enough nuance to scaling paid ads that it felt better to break it into its own chapter. This chapter answers four big questions about ads as I understand them:

- How much do I spend? →Three Phases of Scaling Ads

- How do I know how well I'm doing? →Cost & Benchmarks

- If my ads aren't profitable, how do I fix it? →Client Financed Acquisition.

- What do I wish I had known before I ran my first paid ad? →Lessons

"But how much do I spend on paid ads?"→ The Three Phases of Scaling Paid Ads

There are three stages to spending money on ads as I see it.

Phase One: Track Money

Phase Two: Lose Money

Phase Three: Print Money

Let's break them down together.

Phase One: *Track Money.* Before spending a dollar on ads, set everything up so you can accurately track your returns. If you don't track, you're gonna get cleaned out. It would be like going to a casino and playing your favorite game for as long as you felt like it rather than for as long as you could afford it. But, once you have tracking, you can do more of the stuff that makes you money and less of the stuff that doesn't. It rigs the game in your favor. So get a consultant, watch tutorials, and get it set up. End of story. Once you have the tracking, you can start losing money like a pro (wink).

Phase Two: *Lose money* (half-joking). I prefer to call it 'investing in a money printing machine.' After all, when running paid ads, you pay first. So your bank account has to go down before it comes up.

I emphasize this because I'd rather prepare you: *you're gonna lose money*. In fact, I've lost money more *times* than I've made money running paid ads. But every time I make money with paid ads, I make back everything I lost, *and then a bunch more.* So the number of times I lose is high but the amount I lose is low because I know when to shut it down. And my number of wins is low but the amount I win is very high because I know when to hit the gas. So, think of it like this.

Imagine I spend $100 on ten ads - $1,000 in total. Nine of them lose all $100. Then, one of them makes $500 back for the $100 I spent. I'm still down $500. Many people stop here because they see a $500 dollar loss. But not us. We see a winner. So now we buckle up and 100x down. We spend $10,000 on the winning ad and make $50,000 back.

Note: I still lost *nine times*, but the *one time* I won, I won big. And this is important, because you might lose, nine or ninety-nine times in a row before you win big. But, to win big, you have to see the winners and *double, triple, quadruple, 10x down on them.* This is why paid advertising is a lot like a casino. You'll often lose in the beginning to learn the game. But - with enough skill - you eventually become the house. That being said, during this "lose money" phase, you can still be smart about it. Here's how I do it.

I budget two times the cash I collect from a customer in thirty days (<u>not</u> LTGP) when testing new ads. I wasted tons of money letting ads run too long before I realized they sucked. But on the flipside, I've lost even more money by giving up on ads before I gave them a chance. Eventually, I hit a sweet spot by budgeting <u>two times</u> the cash I collected from a new customer in the first thirty days to test a new ad. For example, if I know I make $100 in profit from a customer in the first thirty days, I'll let an ad go up to $200 in spend before shutting it off (as long as I'm getting leads). If I'm not getting any leads from an ad at all, before I spend 1x thirty-day cash I shut it off ($100 in the example).

It costs money to build an advertising machine. I worked with a business that took a year to get paid ads profitable. It was tough. But other businesses in their space ran profitable ads which meant *we could too*. Once they were profitable, they made their year's worth of 'wasted' money back in the *next month*. It costs money to build an advertising machine…and that's *normal*. Just make sure you measure the returns over a long time horizon, not next week. Can you think of anything more valuable than a machine that prints money? It would be unreasonable for it be cheap (or easy). Once you start making more money than it costs you to make it, you're in phase three.

Phase Three: *Print Money.* If you're making back more money than you spend - the answer is simple - *spend as much as you can*. After all, if you had a magic machine that gave you $10 for every $1 you put into it, what would your budget be? Right. All the money. But realistically, you probably have some other constraint on your business that prevents you from unlimited customers coming in. So here's how I scale my budget.

Instead of asking "How much money should I spend on an ad?" I ask "How many customers do I want?" or "How many customers can I handle?" So once ads break even or better, I reverse my budget from my sales goals. If I can only handle 100 customers next month, and customers cost me $100 to get, I'd need to spend $10,000 to get them (100 x $100). But since ads get less efficient as they scale, I usually pad the budget by twenty percent. So that means $12,000 over thirty days, or $400 per day in ad spend. I reverse my daily ad budget from my lead-getting goal. Then, *I commit to it.* If the number terrifies you, then you're doing it right. Trust the data. This is how you scale. And that's why most people never do.

"How well am I doing?" - Cost & Returns - Efficiency Benchmarks

Efficient paid ads make more money than they cost. If that sounds painfully obvious, good. You've already got most people beat. I measure paid ad efficiency by comparing the lifetime gross profit of a customer (LTGP) with the cost to acquire a customer (CAC). I express this ratio as LTGP to CAC.

I Measure LTGP Instead of "Lifetime Value" or "LTV"

Lifetime gross profit is all the money a customer ever spends on your stuff minus all the money it takes to deliver it. For example, if a customer buys something for $15 and it costs $5 to deliver it, your gross profit is $10. So if that customer buys ten things over their lifetime, then they bought a total of $150 in stuff. But it cost you a total of $50 to deliver that stuff. That makes the lifetime gross profit $100.

Gross profit is important in general because it's the actual money you use to acquire customers, pay rent, cover payroll, and... everything else to run your business.

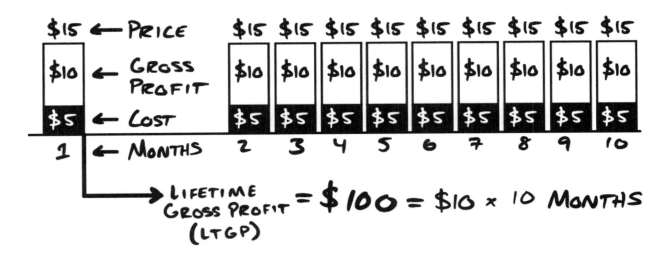

So if you've ever heard me say "I'm getting 3 to 1 on this" I refer to my LTGP-to-CAC ratio. I compare how much I made against how much I spent. So if LTGP is greater than CAC, you have profitable advertising. If it's lower than CAC, you're losing money.

What's a good LTGP to CAC ratio? Every business I invest in that struggles to scale has at least one thing in common - their LTGP to CAC ratio was *less than* 3 to 1. As soon as I get it above 3 to 1 (either through decreasing CAC or increasing LTGP), they take off. *This is a pattern I personally observed, not a rule.*

$$LTGP > CAC = \$+ \quad ☺$$

$$LTGP < CAC = \$- \quad ☹$$

$$\frac{LTGP}{CAC} > 3 \quad ☺$$

You have two big levers to improving LTGP:CAC:

- Make CAC lower - Get cheaper customers. We do this with more efficient ads following the steps we just outlined.

- Make LTGP higher - Increase how much you make per customer. We do this with a better business model.

For maximum money… *I prefer to do both.*

For example, if you made a billion dollars per customer, then you could spend nine hundred and ninety-nine million dollars to get a customer and *still* have a million dollars leftover. You could spend pretty much whatever it takes to get a customer. No matter how crappy your ads - you'd still probably win. On the flip side, if you made one cent per customer, you'd have to get each customer for *less than a penny* to make it work. Even with the best ads, you'd fail.

I bring this up because we speak with hundreds of entrepreneurs every month. They often think they have crappy ads (high CAC) when, in reality, they have a crappy business model (Low LTGP). Here's a finding that will probably surprise you as much as it surprised me. The cost to acquire customers, between competitors in the same industry, is <u>much closer than you'd think</u>. The difference between the winners and the losers is *how much they make off each customer.*

So how do you know if it's your ads or your business model that needs work? I use the industry average CAC as my guide. Research your industry averages for the cost to acquire customers. If your CAC is below 3x your industry average (good), *focus on your business model* (LTGP). If your CAC is above 3x the average (bad), *focus on your advertising* (CAC).

Things can only get so cheap. Eventually you just gotta make more. Think about it like this– lowering the cost of getting a customer by $100 will eventually take more work than making an extra $100 from them. So once your cost is low enough, focus on your business model. Costs can only approach zero but how much you make can go up to infinity. Increasing advertising efficiency beyond a certain point is like trying to "save your way" to a billion dollars. You feel like you're making progress, but you're never gonna get there.

"My ads aren't profitable, how do I fix it?" → Client Financed Acquisition

For many businesses, LTGP is bigger than CAC. Yay. But *not after the first purchase.* Boo. The profit from the customer's *first purchase* is often less than the cost to get them. It can take many months to collect the full LTGP. So you get your money later instead of now. This cash flow problem cripples your ability to scale ads and get more customers. Boo again.

But... if your customer spends more than it costs you to get *and* fulfill them—in the first 30 days—then you have the funds to scale *now* and *forever*. I call this **client financed acquisition.**

I pick thirty days because any business can get interest free money for thirty days in the form of a credit card. And if we make more than the cost to get and fulfill the customer in the first thirty days, we square our balance. Now, we have zero debt and a new customer which we can keep profiting from forever. Then, we repeat the process. Money is no longer your bottleneck. This is the key to limitless scale. *I repeat the same image above so you can reference it.*

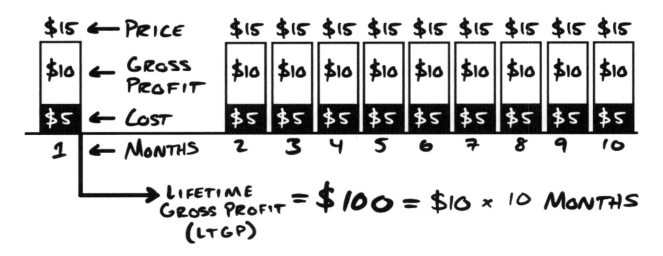

Let's see client financed acquisition in action:

- Say we have a $15 per month membership that costs us $5 to deliver. That leaves us $10 gross profit left over.

  ($15 membership) - ($5 cost) = $10 gross profit per month

- And let's say our average member stays for ten months. That makes our lifetime gross profit $100.

  ($10 gross profit per month) x (10 months) = $100 LTGP.

- If the cost to get a customer is $30 (CAC = $30), we have a 3.3:1 LTGP : CAC ratio.

  ($100 LTGP) / ($30 CAC) = 3.3 LTGP / 1 CAC → 3.3:1 Our ads make money. Hooray.

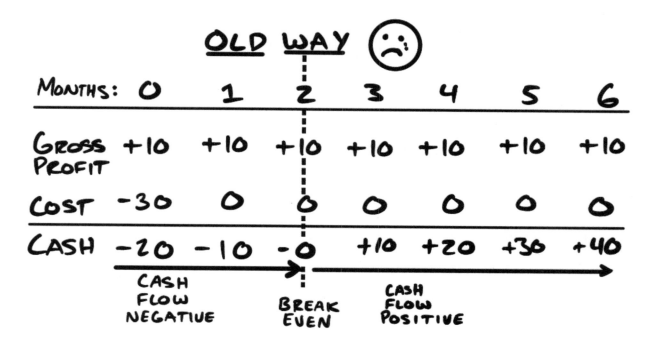

But wait…there's a problem. You spent $30 in ads and only got $10 back. Ten bucks trickles in, one month at a time, until you finally break even…two. months. later. That's tough! Make no mistake, you should 100% make that trade. But, now we have a *cash flow* problem.

Here's the way I fix it- *I immediately sell them more stuff*

- If I offer a $100 upsell (with 100% margins) that one in five new customers take. That adds $20 of gross profit per customer.

  ($100 upsell) / (5 customers) = $20 average upsell dollars per customer.

- This takes us from $10 to $30 in the first thirty days (our break-even window). The first purchase is $10. But now *the average upsell adds $20.*

  $10 + $20 = $30 gross profit per customer in less than 30 days.

- And since it costs $30 to acquire them, we break even. Great!

  $30 CAC - $30 cash collected within thirty days = free customers!

Every $10 a month that comes in thereafter is "gravy." Now, I can go get another customer while I keep collecting that $10 profit per month for the next nine months. This is how you print money. The things you can sell or upsell are unlimited.

If I cover the cost to get and fulfill a customer in the first thirty days I can pay off my card, then do it again. It's how I've scaled every company I've started for the past seven years past $1M/mo in the first twelve months - without outside funding. With efficiency out of the way, creativity is your only limit.

Bottom Line: Figure out a way to get your customers to pay you back in the first thirty days so you can recycle your cash to get more customers.

Personal Lessons from Paid Ads

1. **Don't Confuse Sales Problems With Advertising Problems.** The cost to get customers doesn't only come from advertising (it just mostly does)... For example, a company I invested in spent twelve weeks and $150,000 to run paid ads. They were getting the right leads on the phone, but they weren't buying. The owner said advertising didn't work. But the ads worked fine, great even, *their sales sucked.* The owner threw up his hands and gave up...six inches from gold. Frustrating. Confusing an advertising problem with a sales problem cost them an estimated ~$30M in enterprise value. If your engaged leads have the problem you solve and the money to spend, and they're not buying, then your ads work fine—you have a sales problem.

2. **Your Best Free Content Can Make The Best Paid Ads.** Some of the best paid ads I've ever run came from free content. If you make a free content piece that generates sales, or performs very well, nine times out of ten it'll make a great paid ad.

   a. **User Generated Content (UGC).** If you can get your customers to create testimonials or reviews using your product, post them. If they perform well as free content, they often make killer ads too. Having a system in place to encourage these public posts from customers is my favorite way of getting a steady stream of potential ads. And - the best part is - it's no extra work.

3. **If You Say You Suck At Something, You Will Probably Suck At It.** Never say "I'm not techy" or "I hate tech stuff." It just keeps you poorer than you should be. I said it for…wait for it…FOUR YEARS. Then one day, I snapped because I hated my website designer more than I hated tech itself. "If this idiot can do it, so can I." Four years of wasting time and lost money reversed with four hours of concentrated effort.

Your Turn

I can teach you how to place an ad in twenty minutes. It'll cost ya $100. Worth it? I hope so. It's an important skill. It won't make you money, but you will learn a lesson worth far more than a hundred bucks - *running ads is easier than you think.* In fact, platforms spend zillions to make it as easy as possible (so they can make more money). Here's all you gotta do:

Search "HOW TO PLACE A [PLATFORM] AD." Then place one for $100. Don't go all the way to the end then chicken out. Spend the gosh darn money. Rip off the bandaid. As soon as you do - you're no longer an observer, <u>you're in the game.</u>

Once you have put all these pieces together, it's time to send it. Spend money. Start with an acceptable amount of money you are willing to lose each month. Expect to lose it. You won't be earning, you'll be learning.

If you recall our advertising checklist, you'll need to pick each line to fill out your action card. This kicks off your journey in paid ads to get more engaged leads. <u>Sample Paid Ads Checklist:</u>

Paid Ads Daily Checklist	
Who:	Yourself
What:	Your Offer
Where:	Any platform/audience you can buy access to
To Whom:	Target audience or lookalike audience
When:	Everyday, 7 days per week
Why:	Get engaged leads to sell
How:	Call Out + 3Ws + CTA
How Much:	Learning Budget, Then Reverse to Sales Goal
How Many:	30+ Call Outs x 10 Ads
How Long:	As long as it takes

Paid Ads Part II Conclusion

Paid ads are the fastest way to scale how many leads you get. We spent the lion's share of this chapter talking about efficiency. Because once you understand how ads really make money, it becomes much easier to win. I've been very successful with paid ads, but it wasn't because I was the most creative or had the best copy. It was because I knew the numbers. So follow the steps outlined.

I recommend doing paid ads last for two reasons. First, skills from the other three methods transfer to this one. And second, paid ads cost money. Money you will have if you start with the other three methods first. So learn the skills and make the money from the other three methods, so you have the shortest learning curve on this one.

And once we have all that, we scale it. We expect to lose more times than we win. And once we win, we scale the hell out of it. And that's how we do it.

Paid ads is the last of the core four ways a single person can let other people know about their stuff. But before we transition to the second half of the book, I wanna show you how to put these strategies on steroids.

FREE GIFT: Bonus Training - Paid Ads Fast Track

Running paid ads is the fast track. It's high risk high reward. I recorded a deeper breakdown of paid ads frameworks that have served me across industries and price points. You can find it here for free, as always: **Acquisition.com/training/leads**. My gift to you - money you'll make in the future. And as always, you can also scan the QR code below if you hate typing.

Core Four On Steroids: More Better New

"If at first you don't succeed, use force."

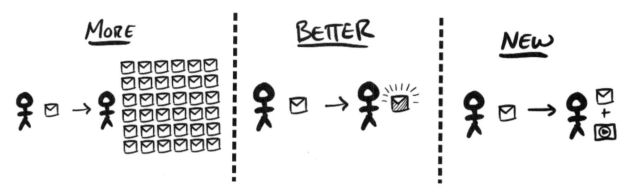

I surveyed the fifty or so faces of the group. All entrepreneurs looking to scale their businesses. Each hungry for the "missing link" that would flood them with engaged leads. After finishing a presentation on lead generation, *I opened up the floor for Q&A:*

The first business owner chimed in, "I just feel like I've saturated the market. I don't think we can get any bigger in the chiropractor niche than we already are."

"What're you doing in revenue?" I asked.

"$2,000,000 a year"

"And how much do you spend on advertising?"

"About $30,000 a month on Facebook"

"What's your conversion rate from click to close?"

"I don't know"

"So you don't track overall throughput?"

"I guess not."

"Okay…What other platforms do you advertise on?"

"None."

"How much content do you make for chiropractors?"

"None."

"How much cold outreach do you do?"

"None."

"And the $30k you spend, on one platform, for a two million dollar business, saturated the $15.1B chiropractor industry? Does that sound reasonable?"

A second business owner chimed in before he could answer "If it helps - I'm in the chiropractor niche too, and I spent $30k in advertising, across *four* platforms, last *week*..."

"Do you still feel like you've saturated your niche?" I asked.

He got the point.

***

I have this conversation daily with entrepreneurs looking to grow. Typically, they have figured out how to get enough customers from <u>one</u> platform to get them to $1M-$3M per year. It's still not completely predictable. And they have their ups and downs. But they have the "gist" of what they need to do and have seen some success. So it's at this point they hit a wall because they think they can't make more money. They assume they've "tapped" their market. I kid you not. I had a conversation with a different entrepreneur making about $3,000,000 per year in the weight loss space. He worried increasing his ad spend past $40,000 per month would saturate his ad platform. For context, that platform has over 1B active daily users. And he was selling weight loss… in America… a $60B industry. Silly.

There are more leads out there than you can possibly imagine. I've used a framework to unlock those leads over and over again and now you can use it too.

How To Get Even More Leads: More Better New

First, you reach out to people who know you. Then, you start making free content. Then you start reaching out to people who don't know you. Then you start running paid ads. This is how you *do* the core four to get engaged leads. And there's really nothing else a single person can do *on their own* to get them.

But what if you are doing the core four and still not getting as many engaged leads as you want? Well, worry not! There are two ways to boost *any* of the core four to get even more engaged leads *on your own*. I use these every time I want to increase the engaged lead flow in a portfolio company. They are easy to remember: **More, Better, New**.

Simply stated:

1) You can do *more* of what you're currently doing.

2) You can do what you're currently doing *better*.

3) You can do it somewhere *new*.

And, just like the story in the beginning with the agency owner, that's *exactly what I was asking him*. Could you advertise more? Could you advertise better? Could you advertise somewhere new?

So let's start with the one I actually do first: *More*.

More

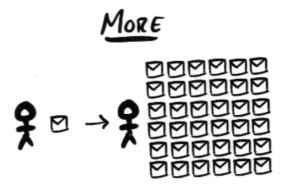

You've done some advertising by now. And you know the advertising that you do works to some degree. So the next obvious thing you can do to get more engaged leads is - *more*. *A lot more*. Crank up the volume to your max capacity.

Even with no improvements at all, if you double your inputs, you'll get more engaged leads. Make twice the reach outs, post twice the content, run twice the ads, double the ad spend, etc. You won't regret it. Unless, of course, you hate money.

So while we'll always focus on testing to make ourselves *better*, which we'll get to in a moment, the <u>biggest</u> increases often come from advertising *more*.

<u>Here's how I do *more*: The Rule of 100</u>

The rule of 100 is simple. You advertise your stuff by doing 100 primary actions every day, for one hundred days in a row. That's it. I don't make many promises, but this is one. If you do 100 primary actions per day, and you do it for 100 days straight, you will get more engaged leads. Commit to the rule of 100 and you will never go hungry again.

Here's what it looks like applied to each of the core four:

<u>Warm Reach Outs:</u>

100 reach outs per day

Example primary actions: email, text, direct message, calls, etc.

<u>Post Content:</u>

100 minutes per day making content.

Release at least one per day on a platform. As you get better, post even more.

Example primary actions: short and long videos or articles, podcasts, infographics, etc

<u>Cold Reach Outs:</u>

100 reach outs per day

Example primary actions: email, text, direct message, cold call, flyers, etc.

As with all cold advertising, expect lower response rates, so use automation.

<u>Paid Ads:</u>

100 minutes per day making paid ads

Example primary actions: direct response media ads, direct mail, seminar, podcast spots, etc.

100 days straight of running those paid ads. Use the daily budget we calculated together in the paid ads chapter. Aim for Client Financed Acquisition.

Here's some inspiration from someone in #Mozination following the rule of 100:

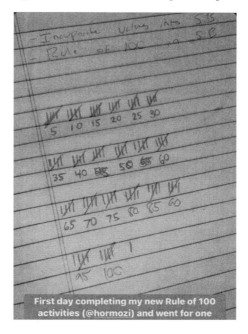

Better

Getting better gets you more leads for the same effort. We want that. And you can only get better by doing one thing–testing. So you do more and more… *until it breaks.* Then, you make it *better.* In other words, if you do *more* for long enough, your CAC will eventually get too high to sustain. So you make a tweak and see if it improves. If it does, keep doing it. If it doesn't, toss it out. Thousands of these tiny tests separate the winners from the beginners.

Every action a lead takes before they become a customer is a potential "drop-off" point. So *I do the most testing at whatever step the most leads drop off.* I call these "constraints." Constraints are the points where the smallest improvements create the biggest boost in results. That's why they're so important. We get the biggest bang for our buck. For example, if you have three steps in your process:

30% Optin (give you their contact information)

5% Apply ← *This is the constraint because it has the biggest drop-off*

50% Schedule

But let's ignore the constraint for a moment. Imagine we improve each step by 5% by itself.

30 + 5%→35% Optin = 16% Increase in leads (1.16x)

5 + 5%→10% Apply = 100% Increase in leads (2x)

50 + 5%→55% Schedule = 10% Increase in leads (1.1x)

We get wildly different results! Improving the constraint also comes out the clear winner. So, *focus on the constraint.* And, again, if you're not sure which step is the biggest constraint, find the step where the most leads drop off. You'll get the biggest reward for the smallest improvement.

Here's how I get better: *I test one thing per week per platform.* And I do it for four big reasons.

1) If you test multiple things at a time on one platform you never really learn what worked.

2) Steps affect each other. A *single* change can affect results at other steps. For example, if you change step one, and more people optin, but *fewer* people apply, no bueno. But you wouldn't know that if you changed both steps. If you make one change *you can see what happened.* If you make a bunch of changes…good luck trying to figure out what worked (or didn't).

3) It forces you to prioritize what will get you the most engaged leads. You can do an infinite amount of tests. But, time is limited. So you must choose your tests wisely. For example, if you only do one "big" test per week per platform, don't waste it on a color change from red to bright red.

4) Maybe the most important, you run the test for long enough to see if you actually get an improvement. Too short and you won't get enough data. Too long and you waste time you could've spent improving the next constraint. With the size of my team and the amount of money I spend on advertising, one week is typically long enough for me.

In every company I own, I set up a testing schedule. Every Monday we run one split test per platform. We give it a week. And the next Monday, we do three things:

1) Look at the results, and pick the winners for each platform test.

2) Then (important), we write down the results of the test in a log of all tests. So the next time we do something, we start a zillion improvements later, not at square one.

3) Come up with our next test to beat our current 'best' version. If we can't beat the version we're currently running in *four tries (or one month)*, we move onto the next constraint.

You continue to allocate effort to make things better. But, at a certain point, the effort you put into making it better brings lower and lower returns. At some point, it makes more sense to invest your effort into something that will bring higher returns. Only at this point, do we try something *new*.

Pro Tip: Front > Back (most times)

In general, the lowest percentage steps usually happen at the front. And, the higher percentage steps happen at the back. As in 1% of people may click an ad then 30% will give you their contact information. This is why (most times) you'll end up focusing on the front more than the back. And that's fine. Those steps are usually the constraint. They have largest returns for the smallest improvements. The call out. The value elements. The offer. The CTA. The landing page headline. Sub headline. Image, etc. Down the pathway you go in order of what the lead will see and then do.

New

So after you've improved your marketing efforts through 'more' and 'better' the only thing you have left is - 'new places in new ways.' In simple terms—*new*. And if you think your business can't possibly get any bigger, let me show you *why* it can. Then, I'll show you *how* it can.

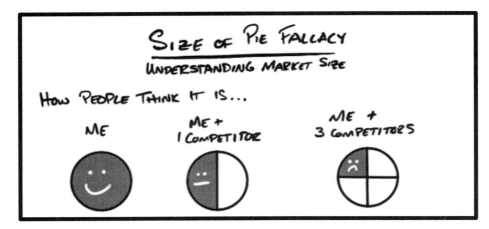

Most business owners look only at the platform and tiny community they market in. And usually, there are only three or four big companies marketing in their niche. So, they assume those companies *must* split the *entire* market between them. This is exactly what the entrepreneur in my intro story did. Think for a moment about how ridiculous this is. I call this problem: **The Size Of The Pie Fallacy**. Here's a drawing to illustrate how the market is, in fact, much bigger than most assume.

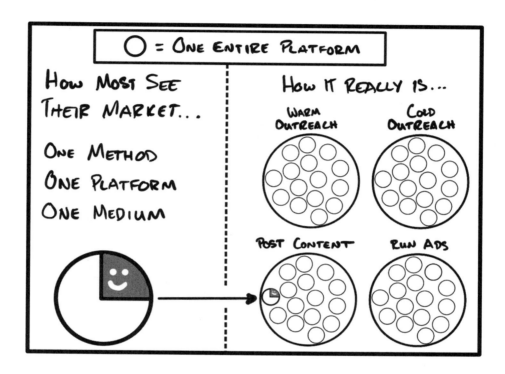

The Size Of The Pie Fallacy. A small business uses one of the core four, on one platform, in one specific way, with a very targeted audience. And in that *same* space, advertising the *same* way, there may only be a handful of other competitors.

They mistakenly assume the <u>tiny</u> slice of the universe they advertise to is the entire available market! This is why most businesses stay small. When they plateau, they think there's no more leads to get. They believe they got as big as they possibly can. Because, for many, saying "I'm as big as I can get" is much easier than saying "I'm not as good at advertising as I thought." This false argument keeps entrepreneurs everywhere poorer than they should be.

<u>When to do *new*</u>: When the returns you get from doing more↔better are lower than what you could get from a new placement or new way of advertising.

There are many other slices of attention (and potential leads) sitting *just inside the tiny universe of "post content."* They could add <u>new placements</u> (since many platforms have multiple places and forms of content). For example, on Instagram you can make stories, messenger ads, and posts. On YouTube you can make shorts, longs, community posts, etc. Or, they could add a <u>new platform</u>. They go from Instagram messenger to Facebook messenger. They go from YouTube shorts videos to Instagram short videos (reels). Etc. And once they've exhausted those, they could add an entirely new <u>core four</u> activity.

And if you're curious, the order I pick my next 'new' comes down to one thing: what will get me the most leads for the amount of work? That is the rule. And nine times out of ten, it goes like this:

New placements→New Platforms→New Core Four.

EASY ⟶ HARD

NEW PLACEMENTS × NEW PLATFORMS × NEW CORE FOUR

<u>Bottom Line</u>: No matter how you advertise, you could do it in new ways (different styles of content) or in new places (think other platforms). Then finally, do a new core four activity altogether. And, you guessed it, each of them gets us what we want - more leads.

Now, this is much harder in practice, which is why I exhaust 'more, better' first. But at a certain point you have to expand to 'new' placements, platforms, and core four activities to let more people know about your stuff.

Action Step: Exhaust more better first. Once you can't do anymore, any better (<u>meaning the returns are lower than putting that same effort into a new platform</u>) try *new*. Use this rough order: new placement, new platform, new core four activity. Get it going. Measure how you do. And scale up from there using more–better. Then, rinse and repeat.

'More Better New' Summary

First, you do *way more* of the advertising that works until it "breaks." Then, *the next drop off point becomes obvious.* Then you keep that level of advertising up while you go back, fix the constraint, and make it *better*. So really, *better* and *more* work with each other more than they work separately. The first question I usually ask myself before we invest in a company that needs to get more customers is "What's stopping them from doing ten times what they're currently doing?" Sometimes, nothing– so we just do *more*. Other times we just need to make something *better* first. So answer that question and you'll know what to do next.

Only once you've exhausted more–better do the real returns come from doing *new*. First, go with new ad placements on a platform you know. Second, go with placements you know on a new platform. Then, once you get the hang of that new platform, use new placements on it. Once you exhaust that, you can add a new core four activity on top of what you currently do. That gives you my simple, *real-world way*, I put the core four on steroids to get even more leads.

Conclusion

Advertising is *the process of making known*. It's what we do to let strangers know about the stuff we sell. Now, we solved 'the stuff' problem with your <u>lead magnet or offer</u>. But to get them to turn into engaged leads, you have to <u>tell them about it</u>. So we spent this section going over the only four ways <u>a single person</u> can advertise–let other people know about their stuff. And to do it, you trade either time, money, or both. And when you do it, you can advertise to people who know you (warm) or you can advertise to strangers (cold). You can advertise publicly (content/ads) or privately (outreach).

As far as what to do when? Whenever I build a business I think about it this way–after I do warm outreach to get my pool of customers going–if I have more time than money, I move to posting content. If I have more money than time, I go with cold outreach or running ads.

But remember, you only need to do <u>one</u> to get engaged leads. So, just pick <u>one</u>. Then, *max it out*. Do more. Do better. Do new. And, all the advertising methods compound together. The money, systems, and experience you earned from the prior method will help you master the next. A business that posts free content and runs paid ads will get more out of their ads *and* their content than a business that does only one or the other. A business that does cold outreach and makes content will get more from their cold outreach *and* work their warm leads better than one that does only one. Every combination of the core four advertising activities boost each other in some way.

And as a personal note, I've done 'em all. I built my first business off posting content and warm outreach. I built my gyms off free content and paid ads. I built Gym Launch off paid ads and cold outreach. I built Prestige Labs off affiliates (which we cover in Section IV). I built ALAN off paid ads and affiliates (also Section IV). I built Acquisition.com off posting content. There are many ways to get engaged leads. If you master one, you will be able to feed yourself for the rest of your life. *They all work if you do.*

Next Up

If you follow the steps in this book, you'll run out of hours in the day. You won't be able to do any more, any better… let alone add anything new! So you'll need help on your journey to the land of endless leads. You'll need allies. Those allies come in four different flavors. And since there are more of them than there are of you, they're the key to getting there. So let's go get them.

> **FREE GIFT: Bonus Training - More, Better, New**
>
> This is one of my favorite topics around scaling businesses. Our portfolio CEOs cite this as one of the most impactful frameworks I've given them. If you want to see a video version of me breaking this down. You can find it here for free, as always: **Acquisition.com/training/leads**. And as always, you can also scan the QR code below if you hate typing.

172

Section IV: Get Lead Getters

Get people who get you more leads

"Give me a lever long enough and a fulcrum on which to place it, and I shall move the world."

- Archimedes

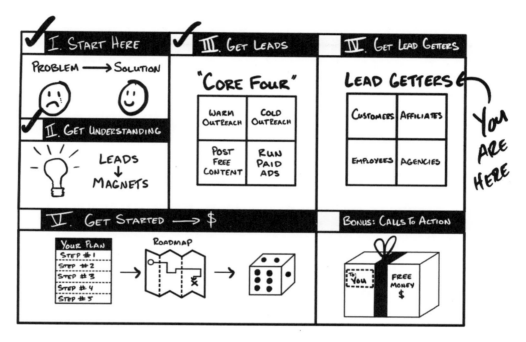

Building A $100M Lead Machine Is All About Leverage

An old lady can lift a semi-truck with a long enough lever. The strongest man in the world, without one, *can't*. The length of the lever determines how much someone can lift. This is leverage. We can use the principle of leverage in advertising. Let me explain:

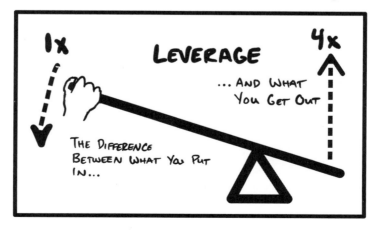

Someone with internet can send a message to millions of people at once. Someone writing postcards by hand *can't*. The internet allows us to reach more people for the same time spent. So, it's higher leverage.

That means leverage boils down to how much we get for the time we spend getting it. So we want to use higher leverage activities to get what we want. More stuff we want. Less time getting it. Good.

And we want *leads. Lots of leads.*

Pro Tip: Don't Mistake Leverage for Speed

One person can only move so fast. A person 1000x ahead of you isn't moving 1000x faster. They *can't*. They're doing different stuff. So the future that feels so far away, with leverage, is closer than you think.

Lead Getters Give You Leverage

Alex Hormozi ✔
@AlexHormozi
...

Only two people can let strangers know about the stuff you sell:
1) You
2) Other people

There are more of them than you.

People can find out about the stuff we sell from two sources. *We* can let them know using the core four. Or, *other people* can let them know using the core four. I call these other people **lead getters**. When other people do it for us, we save time. That means we get more engaged leads for less work. Leverage baby.

Imagine four scenarios:

Scenario #1: You <u>are</u> the lead getter. You do the core four all day everyday by yourself. You get enough leads to pay the bills.

Work: HIGH Leads: LOW Leverage: LOW

Scenario #2: You <u>get</u> a lead getter. You get a lead getter to do the core four on your behalf. Now, the lead getter brings enough leads to pay the bills without you advertising. You work less than scenario #1 and get the same number of leads.

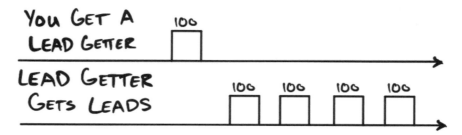

Work: LOW. Leads: LOW. Leverage: HIGH.

Scenario #3: You get lots of lead getters. You spend all your time getting other lead getters. Your leads go up every time you get another one. You work all day everyday, but you get way more leads than you did when it was just you. You work more than scenario #2 but get *way* more leads.

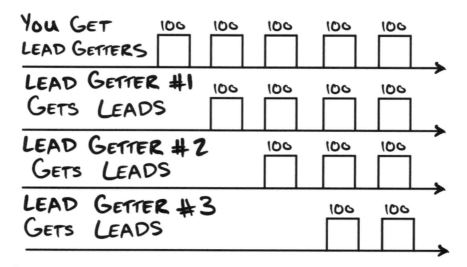

Work: HIGH. Leads: HIGH. Leverage: HIGHER.

Scenario #4: You get a lead getter who gets lead getters. You recruit somebody who recruits other people to advertise on your behalf. They get more lead getters every month. You only had to work to get the first lead getter *once*, but his leads continue climbing without you working. You works less than scenario #3, and you get more leads each and every month.

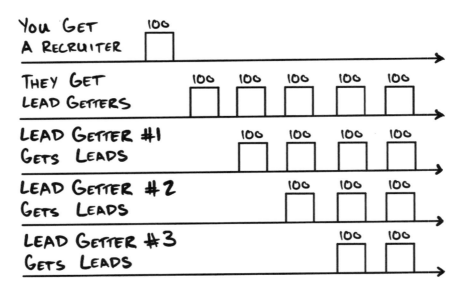

Work: LOW. Leads: HIGH. Leverage: HIGHEST.

Now you've got the makings of a *$100M Leads* machine.

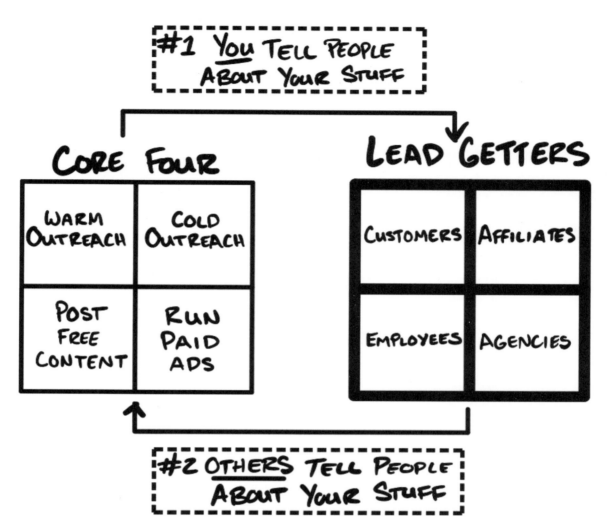

Outline of The "Lead Getters" Section

The lead getters aren't part of the "core four" because they're not things you do. You do not 'do' affiliates or 'do' customer referrals or 'do' agencies or 'do' employees. But, *you have to do the core four to get them.* They come from warm outreach, cold reach outs, posting content, and running paid ads. And once you get them, *they* do it for you.

So the core four stacks. One time to get them, and a second time for when lead getters get engaged leads on your behalf. But it doesn't have to end there. In fact, it shouldn't. The process repeats. Lead getters can go get lead getters! So we do something once then lead getters can do it forever.

But wait, I thought this book was about getting leads? So am I trying to get leads? Or do I want lead getters? Answer: Yes. Lead getters start out as leads, then get interested in the stuff you sell and become engaged leads like anyone else. The difference is they get other people interested in the stuff you sell, too! And ideally, every lead becomes a lead getter.

The following chapters explain, in detail, *how to get other people to advertise for you*. And, if you want to scale to $100M+, you have to understand them:

#1 Customers- they buy your stuff then tell other people about it to get you leads.

#2 Employees- people in your business that get you leads.

#3 Agencies- businesses with services that get you leads.

#4 Affiliates- businesses who tell their audiences about your stuff to get you leads.

*All four lead getters let other people know about *your* stuff. In other words, all four are higher leverage than you doing it on your own.

Once you do understand the four lead getters, you can build a lead getting machine for every company you start for the rest of your life. I'll break down how I use all four lead getters. How each is different. How to work with them. When to use them. Best practices. And how to measure your progress along the way. At the end of this section, you will understand how to get other people to bring you more leads than you can possibly imagine.

And since we already use the core four to get customers, let's start with something we can do right now–get those customers to refer more customers.

FREE GIFT: Advanced Bonus - Get People To Do It For You

That may have been one of my favorite chapters in the book. It took me so so long to figure out how to recombine everything into a simple model. If you want even more training on getting other people to get you leads, and how it applies to scaling go to: **Acquisition.com/training/leads**. And as always, you can also scan the QR code below if you hate typing.

#1 Customer Referrals - Word of Mouth

"The best source of new work, is the work on your desk" - Charlie Munger

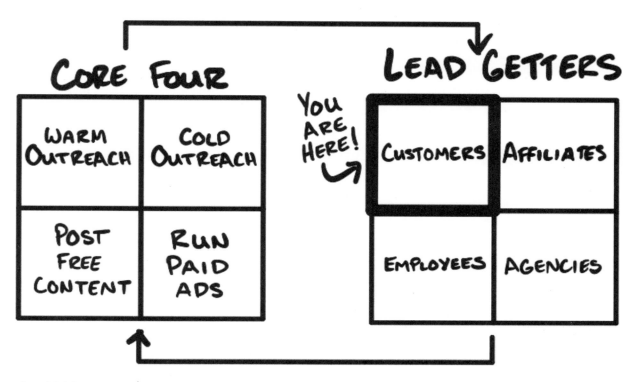

October 2019.

Leila and I sat together on her parents' living room couch. The one she watched movies on as a kid. The faded edges of the coffee table begged us to kick our feet up. We balanced laptops on our thighs. Extension cords snaked around the couch to outlets down the hall. Her stepmother clanged in the kitchen. This was *not* a work environment. But, we made due.

Two years earlier, I lost everything and met her parents *on the same weekend…*

Hey dad, I met this guy on the internet. He lost everything and has no money. But don't worry, I quit my job and moved in with him to help with his next big business idea. By the way, can we crash here for a while?'

…Great first impression, Alex.

But a lot had changed since then. We were multi-millionaires now. We made enough to buy her childhood home in cash. *Every week.*

Leila reviewed reports from our department heads. Oh yeah, we had executives now, too.

"Hey, sales numbers look a little soft this week." she said.

"Really? How many did we close?"

"Fifteen. And sales started dipping last week too. Is there anything different on your end?"

"I don't know. Let me check." I logged into Facebook's advertising portal. Red rejection notifications filled the screen.

"Welp. That'll do it" I said.

"What? What happened?"

"All the ads got shut off."

"Well…that's a problem. When do you think you can get them back up?"

"It'll take a day or two to get a new campaign started."

I squinted at the screen. Something even more alarming jumped at me. *Facebook rejected the ads two weeks ago.* I acted like nothing was wrong.

"So we closed 15 this week, and how many the week before?" I asked.

"21"

"Well, I've got good news and I've got bad news."

"Uhh…Ok…"

"The bad news is…the ads got shut off two weeks ago, so that explains the dip. The good news is…our product is so good that we're still doing $500,000 a week from word of mouth alone.

"You ignored the ads for two weeks!?" She had *oh no you didn't* written all over her face.

I shrugged with a sheepish grin. "You still love me, right?"

We busted out laughing at the absurdity of it all.

Those two years were insane. The amount of money we were making didn't make sense. We didn't comprehend how much until years later. We were just grateful to be doing this together, flaws and all. And this accidental stretch without running paid ads made something very clear: *Our customers were telling their friends.*

A few months later

I stood on stage and looked out over the 700+ gym owner audience. Everyone paid $42,000 to be there. All wore black "Gym Lord" t-shirts and stick-on mustaches. It. Was. Nuts.

I was mid-presentation, explaining how excellent service generates leads through word of mouth. All the while, I obsessed over whether the money we made during two weeks without running paid ads was a fluke. Feeling confident, I paused the presentation. *Time to find out:*

"Alright, just to show you how important this is, who here learned about Gym Launch from another gym owner? Raise your hand." As soon as the words left my lips, I felt instant regret. *What if no one raises their hand? What if our growth was all forced? I'm such an idiot.*

I looked around the room with my arm raised like a monkey. The room stood still. *Oh no.*

Then…a few gym owners raised their hands. *That doesn't look great, but it could be worse.* Then, more. *Thank God.* Then, more. Then, a *wave* of hands. *Holy cow.* People looked to their sides and behind them. *It was almost the entire room.* I let the moment sink in for all of us. I'll never forget it. I knew we had good word of mouth, but not *this* good.

"That" I said, "is the power of word of mouth."

***

I know you weren't there when Leila and I realized we were making $500,000+ per week from word of mouth. I know you weren't there to see $30M in customers say someone referred them. The first time I realized the power of referrals - *it was by accident*. Seeing how much it made me, I studied what had gone right. I wanted to make sure I could recreate it *on purpose*. For me to transfer that ability to you, I have to transfer the beliefs that created it. And these experiences formed those beliefs. *This is why I share them.*

People copied our offers, ads, and lead magnets. They copied our landing pages, emails, and sales scripts. They copied everything they could—but they did it with little success. They think it's about "advertising," and it is. But the *best* advertising is a happy customer. An amazing product turns every customer into a lead getter.

The world loses trust by the second. Every day, more customers do their research. They arm themselves with information to make purchasing decisions. As well they should. So to play at higher levels, we need our product to not only deliver... but *delight*. Customers must get *so much value* it compels them to tell other people about us. The good news is, once you know how, it's easier than you think.

In this chapter, I explain how to get the lowest cost, highest profit, and best quality leads out there: referrals.

How Referrals Work

A referral happens when somebody, a referrer, sends an engaged lead to your business. Anyone can refer, but the best referrals come from your customers. So this chapter focuses on getting more referrals from your customers.

How Referrals Grow Your Business

Referrals are important because they grow your business in two ways:

1. **They're worth more (higher LTGP).** Referrals buy more expensive stuff and buy it more times. They also tend to pay in cash upfront. Lovely.

2. **They cost less (lower CAC).** If one customer sends you another customer because they like your stuff, that new customer costs you nothing. And free customers are cheaper than customers that cost money. So free customers = good.

But what does this stuff really mean? Check this out...imagine you had an LTGP to CAC ratio of 4 to 1. That means it costs twenty-five percent of your lifetime gross profit of one customer to get another. Not bad. But now *imagine if every customer brought you two more customers*. You'd now have an LTGP to CAC ratio of 12 to 1— you'd use just over 8.3% of your lifetime gross profit to get a new customer. So you get three customers for the price of one. Now we're talking. Hooray. What a deal! On top of that, *referrals are exponential*. Let me explain.

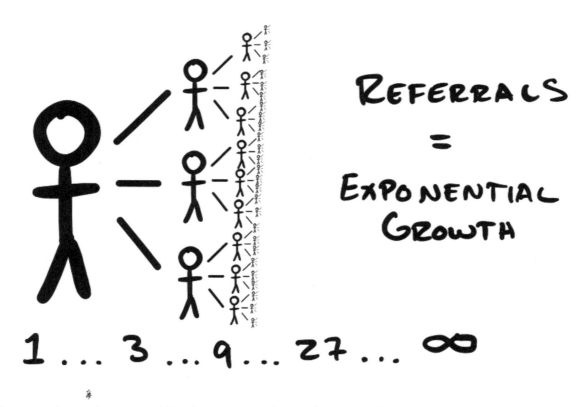

The number of engaged leads you get from the core four depends on *how much* you do them. The inputs to outputs have pretty linear relationships. If you do 100 reach outs you get engaged leads. If you double it, your leads roughly double. If you spend $100 on ads, you get engaged leads. If you double it, your leads roughly double. So no matter how well you advertise, how much you get depends on how much you do. And that's great. But with word of mouth, we can do even better. With word of mouth, one customer brings two. Two bring four. Four bring eight. And so forth. It's not linear, it's *exponential*.

Nothing scales like word of mouth. Want to know why so few people scale by word of mouth? They lose customers faster than they get them. Look at the referral growth equation to see it in action. Referrals (in) minus churned customers (out).

REFERRAL GROWTH EQUATION

$$\%\ \text{Clients Referred Monthly} - \%\ \text{Clients Churned Monthly} = \%\ \text{Monthly Compounding Growth}$$

- If referrals are greater than churn: you grow without any other advertising (yay!)

- If referrals are equal to churn: you need other advertising to grow your business (meh)

- If referrals are less than churn: you've got to advertise to break even (boo - most folks)

This gets nutty when you look at percentages. If the percentage of referrals every month is bigger than the percentage of customers who leave, your business compounds every month. You'd have to spend that much more money on ads, do that many more reach outs, or post that much more content just to maintain that growth. You eventually hit a wall. But with referrals, you can maintain growth *no matter how big you get*. This is how companies like PayPal and Dropbox exploded into multibillion dollar businesses. I'll break down their exact strategies later in the chapter.

On the other hand, small businesses barely scrape by because they have about the same customers exiting as they do entering. A hamster wheel of death. Here's why…

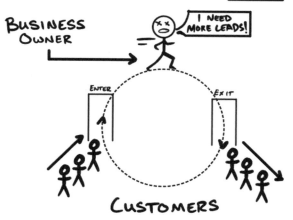

Two Reasons Most Businesses Don't Get Referrals

Most businesses don't get referrals for two reasons. First, their product isn't as good as they think it is. Second, they don't ask for them.

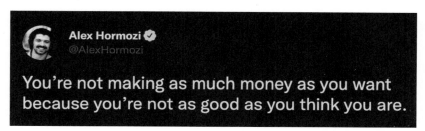

Problem #1: The Product Isn't Good Enough

"Everyone loves our stuff, we just need to get the word out!" - says every small business owner with a product that's not as good as they think it is.

I'm gonna take off my nice guy hat for a second. If your product were exceptional, people would already know about it and you'd have more business than you could handle. So if you sell direct to consumers and they are not bringing you more customers, your product has room to improve.

I like to ask myself: "Why are my customers too embarrassed to tell everyone they know about my product?" It may be okay, but it's *unremarkable*, as in - not worthy of remark.

In fact, most of the stuff I pay for, kind of sucks. My pool guy forgets stuff half the time. My landscapers make tons of noise at the worst hours. My cleaners routinely put my clothes in my wife's closet (I guess that's what I get for extra schmedium t-shirts). The list goes on.

Business owners wonder why they don't get referrals. The answer is right in front of them. *They're just not good enough.* Let me show you how I think about it:

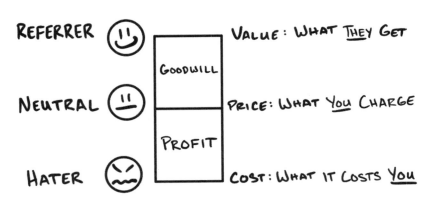

Price is what you charge. Value is what they get. The difference between price and value is **goodwill**.

This means that price not only communicates value, but it's also how we *judge* value. Economics dorks call it 'customer surplus'. But I'm just gonna call it goodwill. You want lots of goodwill. Lots of goodwill creates word of mouth. Word of mouth means referrals.

There are two ways to build goodwill with your customers. You can lower your price or you can give more value. After all, if you lower the price of your product enough, people would line up to get it. But you'd probably lose money. So, lowering the price is, at best, a temporary solution. You can only lower the price so much for so long. And, as marketing legend Rory Sutherland says, *"Any fool can sell something for less."*

So, to build goodwill to get referrals, the question isn't how do we lower our price but, how do we give more value?

Six Ways To Get More Referrals By <u>Giving</u> More Value

There are six ways I get referrals by giving more value. And it just so happens to map to the parts of an ad. Neat-o.

1. Call Outs → Sell Better Customers

2. Dream Outcome → Set Better Expectations

3. Increase Perceived Likelihood of Achievement → Get More People Better Results

4. Decrease Time Delay → Get Faster Results

5. Decrease Effort and Sacrifice → Keep Making Your Stuff Better

6. Call to Action → Tell Them What To Buy Next

1. **Call outs → Sell Better Customers.** We want to sell better customers because they get the most value from our products. Customers that get the most value have the most goodwill. And the customers that have the most goodwill are most likely to refer. Yes, it's that simple. Let me give you a real-life example:

   We have a portfolio company that did public relations for generic small businesses. They had a lot of sales, but they had a lot of churn. So they plateaued. They didn't grow for years.

   To see what we could do, we looked at their lowest churning customers to see if they had anything in common - they did. They were all in a specific niche and looking to raise funding from investors. So the solution looked obvious–get more of them! But the founder had a big worry–these customers were only fifteen percent of his business. If he changed his targeting, and it failed, he would lose eighty-five percent of his business(!). But the business wasn't growing anyway. A tough situation for any entrepreneur. But, after reviewing the data many times, he agreed to *change the advertising call outs to match this narrower, "perfect fit" customer.*

   The results: The company broke through its plateau. They grew for the first time in years - and now on track to adding *millions per month*. Plus, their cost of advertising– a huge expense for their stagnating business–went down. They got *even cheaper leads* since they could be more specific with their messaging. But not only that, the cheaper leads got even more value from the product because *it was meant for them.* And those customers, because they had more goodwill toward the business, started referring like clockwork.

Action Step: *Increase the quality of the prospect, and you'll increase the quality of the product.* Figure out what your most successful customers have in common. Use those similarities to target a new audience that has the greatest chance of getting the most value. Then, sell <u>only</u> people who meet those new criteria. Set yourself up to build more goodwill. More goodwill means more referrals.

SET <u>BETTER</u> EXPECTATIONS

2. **Dream Outcome→Set Better Expectations:** The fastest, easiest, and cheapest way to make your product remarkable - make it better than they expect. And that's easier than you might think because <u>*you*</u> set the expectations.

Pro Tip: Dating Advice

On first dates, I like to set the bar as low as possible by admitting all my flaws. After telling my (now) wife all my flaws, I joked - I can only go up from here!

Have you ever had a stranger tell you a new movie was awesome? Then you go see it and think 'that wasn't as good as I expected.' On the flip side, have you ever had someone tell you a movie was terrible, then you ended up seeing it anyways and thought 'That wasn't as bad as I expected.' Our expectations of an experience can *dramatically* affect the experience itself. We can increase goodwill by lowering expectations. It gives us room to overdeliver.

In the beginning, I promised everything and the kitchen sink to get people to buy.

Fulfilling on that turned into a nightmare. So, I began inching down my promises while maintaining quality. It gave me more room to overdeliver and I netted a major benefit - referrals. Customer expectations are fickle. That's why we set the expectations for them. And if we set those expectations, then we can exceed them.

Action Step: Slowly lower the promises you make when making offers. Keep lowering them until your close rates lower. At that point, stop. This maximizes how many customers you get *and* the goodwill you build with them. Maximized customers and more goodwill means more referrals.

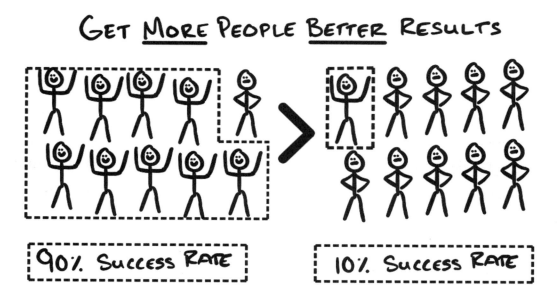

GET MORE PEOPLE BETTER RESULTS

90% SUCCESS RATE   10% SUCCESS RATE

3. Increase Perceived Likelihood of Achievement → Get More People Better Results:

The customers with the best results get the most value from your product. Figure out what they do to get the most value, and you can help your other customers do the same. Two steps ago, to sell better customers, we figured out who the best ones *were*. So now, to get everyone the best results, we figure out what the best ones *did*.

Let me show you what it looked like at Gym Launch. We started by tracking customer activities. Speed to running their first paid ad. Speed to their first sale. Their attendance on calls. Etc. Then, we compared the activities of our *average* customers to the activities of our *best* customers. We found out something huge. If a gym owner ran paid ads and made a sale in the first seven days, their LTGP *tripled*. Once we realized this, we focused on getting *everyone* to launch ads and make sales in the first seven days. The results of our average customers skyrocketed. More customers, more testimonials and more referrals followed.

Here's the process I use to get more people better results:

Step #1: Survey customers to find the ones who got the best results.

Step #2: Interview them to find out what they did differently.

Step #3: Look at the *actions* they had in common.

Step #4: Force new customers to repeat the actions that got the best results.

Step #5: Measure the improvement in average customer results (speed and outcome)

Step #6: <u>Match the conditions of your guarantee to the actions that get the best results to get more people to do them.</u>

Pro Tip: Make The Success Activities The Conditions of Your Guarantee

<u>DO NOT DO THIS IF YOU HATE MONEY AND HELPING PEOPLE</u>: As soon as you start getting customers results, note what they did. Then, start guaranteeing new customers those results. But do it on the condition they *do what the best customers did*. The guarantee sells more people. The conditions get them better results. You win. They win.

Action Steps: Figure out what the best people did. Then get everyone to do it. Make your guarantees around the actions that create the most success. More success. More goodwill. More referrals.

190

MAKE FASTER WINS

DAY 1 → DAY 7 > DAY 1 → DAY 100

4. Decrease Time Delay→Make Faster Wins: I define a "win" as any positive experience a customer has. Faster wins increase their perception of speed, increase the likelihood they'll stick, and increase how much they trust you. Triple win. To make wins *feel* faster, we give them wins *more often*.

Let's imagine you have a product that takes a week to deliver. The customer can get one win at the end of that week or win every day with daily progress updates. Same amount of progress, seven times the wins. On top of that, if someone said seven things would happen, and all seven do, I trust them even more. Referring a friend is now lower risk since seven promises were made, and all seven were kept.

Here's five ways I make wins happen faster in the real world:

1. If I have seven small things to deliver, I deliver them at shorter intervals rather than all at once.

2. Updates are wins. If it's a bigger project, I share progress updates as frequently as possible. You can never give someone too much good news. And regular updates, progress or not, is better than leaving your customers hanging.

3. Customers form their lasting impression of a business within the first forty-eight hours after they buy. Force a good impression. Force as many wins as you can in that window. Set many expectations. Meet many expectations. Repeat.

4. They should always know the next time they'll hear from you. I got a slick saying from a public CEO friend of mine - BAMFAM: Book-A-Meeting-From-A-Meeting. Again, never leave a customer in no man's land. They should always know what happens…*next*.

5. Never expect customers to forgive you. Ever. So act like it. For example, you can deliver early, but never late. I add fifty percent to my timelines so I always deliver early. That makes "on time" for me *early* for them.

Action step: Break down outcomes into the smallest possible increment. Communicate as often as reasonable (even if there is no progress, update them). Set timelines with breathing room. Deliver early. More customer wins means more goodwill. And more goodwill means more referrals.

On-Going Value

$....$....$....$....$....

5. **Decrease Effort & Sacrifice → Keep Making Your Stuff Better:** If the customer does less stuff they hate to benefit from your product, you've made it better. If the customer gives up fewer things they love to benefit from your product, you've made it better. And there's no such thing as a perfect product. You can *always* make it better. And the easier you make it for them to benefit, the more goodwill you get, and the more likely they'll refer. Here's my process to keep making my stuff better.

Step #1: Use customer service data, surveys, and reviews to find the most common problem with your product.

Step #2: Figure out your fix. To get a headstart, get feedback from the customers who made your product work for them despite the problem it has.

Step #3: Use that feedback to improve your product.

Step #4: Give the new version to a small group of your (struggling) customers.

Step #5: Get your next round of feedback. If you solved the original problem, then roll it out to all customers. If it didn't, go back to step #2.

Step #6: Move to the next most common problem and repeat the process. Do this until the end of time.

Action Step: Keep making your stuff better. Survey. Make changes. Implement. Measure. Repeat. I run this process every month. Set this as a recurring monthly process. A product that takes less effort and fewer sacrifices means more goodwill. And more goodwill means more referrals.

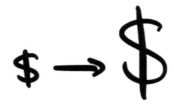

6. **Call To Action→ Tell Them What To Buy Next:** If you have an amazing product, they'll want more. You have to satisfy their desire to buy. If you don't, they'll still buy… but *from someone else*. Don't let that happen. Sell them again. You can either sell them a new thing or more of the thing they just bought. In either case, you'll get even more goodwill and extend the lifetime of the customer. And besides, the more stuff they can buy, the more stuff they can refer their friends to.

For example, in a weight loss company we know, lots of customers referred friends to their first tier product. But, some didn't. A lot of those customers who didn't refer to the first product, when they bought their more expensive thing, referred their friends to that! So you gotta keep selling.

In my experience, people obsess over their front end offers. And that makes sense. But then they neglect the back end *and customers fall off.* And customers that fall off your product are unlikely to refer - so keep selling them so they don't.

Action Step: Treat every customer like it's the first time you've sold them. Make sure your next offer is more compelling than your first. Remind them to buy more after each big win. More things to buy means more opportunities to add even more value. More value means more goodwill. And more goodwill means, you guessed it, more referrals.

<u>One Question to Rule Them All</u>

Let's consolidate these six steps into one thought experiment. I encourage you to try it out with your team. Here it is:

You've lost all your customers but one. The gods of advertising ban you from doing the core four and decree:

    -All customers must come from this one customer.

    -Violate our terms and we will destroy your business, and every other business you start, for eternity.

Tough break. But, the question remains, how would you treat this customer? What would you do to make their experience so valuable they would send all their friends? What kind of results would they need to get? What would their onboarding be? What type of customer would you pick? Think about it. Write it out. *Your business depends on it.* Then…*do it :)*

Start acting like the advertising gods will revoke your core four privileges at any moment. Soon you'll see you have no choice but to start adding more value to get more customer referrals.

Now that we covered that. Do you wanna know how you can get even *more* referrals? →Ask for them.

Referrals: Ask For Them

Do you know why businesses have so few referrals compared to what they could have? They never ask for them. Your customers, like any audience, can only know what to do if you tell them.

Now, I've tried *a lot* of referral strategies. Most failed. And I struggled until I had this epiphany: Asking for referrals only works when you treat it like an offer. *The referrals come when you show the value the customer gets when they refer their friends.* Let me give you two quick case studies to show the power of asking for referrals:

<u>Case Study #1</u>: Dropbox gave free storage to customers *and* free storage to the friends they referred. The referral program went viral and they <u>39 x'd their business in fifteen months.</u>

Get up to 16 GB free space by inviting your friends to Dropbox!

For every friend who joins and installs Dropbox on their computer, we'll give you both 500 MB of bonus space (up to a limit of 16 GB)!
If you need even more space, upgrade your account

0.5GB

16GB

Invite your Gmail contacts   OR   Add names or emails   ✉Send

🔒 We won't store your password and your contacts are secure.

<u>Case Study #2</u>: Paypal gave $10 in credit to customers *and* $10 to the friends they referred. Within two years, the program helped them reach a million users, and six years later, they hit 100 million users. They still use it today.

So how do we harness the same viral growth in our own small businesses? We do what they did. We ask for it.

<u>Seven Ways To *Ask* For Referrals</u>

There are three components to a referral program: how you give the incentive, what you incentivize with, and how you ask. Rather than give you a hundred variations that may or may not work, here are the seven combos that worked best for me:

1) <u>One-Sided Referral Benefit</u>: I'd rather pay customers than a platform any day of the week. Pay your average cost to acquire a customer (CAC) to the referrer or the friend. Make them aware of the incentive.

> Ex: Imagine it costs $200 to get a new customer. Ask the current customer to make an actual three-way introduction to a friend–via call, SMS, or email. Not just a name and number. Also, ask them to do it right when they buy…don't wait. Then, write them a check for $200 when their friend signs up <u>OR</u> give their friend $200 off.

> Ex: This works great for spouses because they both basically get the benefit. Always ask for the spouse & give a household discount.

2) <u>Two-Sided Referral Benefits</u>: This is what Dropbox and PayPal used. We pay our

195

CAC to both parties. Half goes to the referrer (in credit or cash) and half goes to the friend (in credit). This way, they *both* benefit.

> Ex: We sell $500 programs. Our cost to get a customer is $200. For every friend someone refers, we give them $100 cash, and give their friend $100 off signing up. Good for up to 3 friends. This worked really well for my local businesses.

Pro Tip: Run Your Paid Ads For Free

In our service businesses we routinely get an additional 25-30% of sign ups as referrals. *If we asked for a referral right when they signed up.* So if we signed up 100 clients for a promotion, we would usually get another 25-30 clients from referrals. And since we always operate above 3:1 LTGP:CAC, the cash from referrals often covered the cost of the ads (and some). Bingo bango.

---

3) <u>Ask For A Referral Right When They Buy:</u> On the sales contract or checkout page, ask for some names and phone numbers of *people they'd like to do this with*. Show them how *they* will get better results when they do it with a friend.

> Ex: I had a new salesman come into one of my portfolio companies and shatter all the sales records for an upcoming event. We didn't know what was going on. So I hopped on the phone with him - *how are you selling more tickets than everyone else?* He shrugged and said, "I'm doing the same thing as everyone else. I just make sure I ask them who else they'd want to have come with them. Then ask them to introduce me." <u>Half</u> his sales were referrals. So simple, and yet <u>no one does it</u>.

> Scripting example: *People who do our program with someone else tend to get 3x the results. Who else could you do this program with?*

Pro Tip: Not "If" But "Who"

Once someone is a customer, be more direct with your ask. Don't ask *IF* they know someone, ask *WHO* they know.

---

4) <u>Add Referrals As A Negotiation Chip:</u> On top of that, you can ask for referrals as a way to negotiate a lower price. In other words, if someone wants to pay $400 and your price is $500, you can give them the discount *in exchange for* an introduction to three friends. You can ethically charge a different price for the same thing because you changed the terms of the sale.

Ex: "I can't do anything less than $500 down, but if you make a 3-way text introduction to a few of your friends right now, I'd be happy to cut that initiation fee."

And to address the question you didn't ask - if a full-priced customer finds out you gave someone else a discount (which I've had happen), here's all you say: *"Yea - Stacy got $100 off because she referred three friends. I'm happy to give you $100 if you refer me three friends. Who do you have in mind?"* They either back off or they give you three friends. Win win.

5) <u>Referral Events:</u> Where people get points, credits, dollars or even just bragging rights for bringing friends within an explicit time period. Referral events typically last from one to four weeks. Whenever you run one of these events, sell everyone on the benefits of working with others. Use some stats (internal or external) to show high success rates and the selfish benefit to bringing friends. I use names like:

> "Bring-a-friend" Promotion
>
> "Spouse Challenge" Promotion
>
> "Accountability Buddy" Promotion
>
> "Coach Challenge" Promotion where you create teams with your employees and customers. This works well in coaching style businesses.

6) <u>Ongoing Referral Programs</u>: Instead of running a limited duration referral promotion, you talk about the benefits of doing things with others all the time. Think: in your free content, outreach, paid ads, etc. After a buddy did this, he saw a 33% boost in *total* sign ups. For context, he had 1,000,000 customers buy tickets to his virtual event and 250,000 of them were referred…this stuff works.

7) <u>Unlockable Referral Bonuses</u>: Create bonuses for people who 1) refer and 2) leave a testimonial. A few examples: Unlock VIP bonuses, courses, tokens, status, training, merchandise, service levels, premium support, additional hours of service, etc.

Unlockable referral bonuses work well if you don't like paying out cash. The bonuses can also be for *both* parties if you like (since they cost you less than cash). Visit the lead magnet section for some extra inspiration. As always, the more insane you make the offer, the more people will refer. If you want them to refer, make it so good they'd be stupid not to.

You're Only Limited By Your Creativity

Here's what it looks like to combine a few of the strategies above into a killer referral promotion.

Give everyone a gift card for one-third the cost of their program. Tell them they can give it to a friend of theirs if they sign up with them. Give the gift card an expiration date within seven to fourteen days from the date you give it to them→it'll force them to use it. This gives the referrer status when they give it to their friend. Rather than saying "hey join my program for $2000 off" they say, "I got this gift card for $2000. Do you want it? I don't want to waste it." It's seen as a much bigger deal for them and you.

You can still use the three-way introduction with this tactic. Then text a picture of the gift card. Bonus points if you write the friend's name on it before texting the picture. It makes it feel personalized and gives you a legitimate reason for asking for their friend's name (wink).

PS - You can also sell the gift cards at ninety percent off as purchasable gifts (only for friends of customers). The referrer looks like they spent a lot of money, and <u>you get paid to get new customers.</u> I can hardly think of a better way to make money. Again, the only limit is your creativity.

Pro Tip: Match The Thing You Give With The Thing You Sell.

If you don't want to give away money, try to match the referral incentive to the core product you sell. For example, if you have a t-shirt manufacturing company, giving away free t-shirts makes a lot of sense. Because your incentive will attract people who actually want t-shirts. And they're more likely to become paying customers. (Hint: that's why the gift card works so well).

On the other hand, if you give away an amazing limited edition t-shirt for your IT services business, it may or may not attract people who want IT services. So, try to match the thing you give with the thing you sell.

Conclusion

Referrals aren't an advertising method you can "do." It's not one trick or hack (although we learned some of those). *It's a way of doing business.* And it starts with *you*.

After all, referring is always a risk for the customer. They risk *their* goodwill with their friend *in the hopes* of getting more by showing them something cool (your stuff). So customers *only* refer when they think it's very likely their friend will have a good experience. In other words, when the benefits to them personally outweigh the risk of hurting the relationship with their friend. So we add benefits for them and their friends with incentives and we lower the risk by building goodwill (showing we deliver on our promises). And we do that by using the six ways to give your customers more value. Now don't get me wrong, building goodwill does a fantastic job of getting referrals on its own. But if we're smart, which we are, we capitalize on that goodwill, so we can get even more referrals, by using the seven ways to ask for them. Whew!

So give more than you get and you'll never go hungry again. *This is how we treat our customers.* Do this, and you can monetize *goodwill* forever. To keep this in perspective, I always remind myself: *I am compensated tomorrow for the value I provide today.*

Action Items

Figure out your referral percentages and churn percentages to set a baseline. Implement the six "giving value" steps to build goodwill. Then capitalize on that goodwill, using one or more of the seven ways to ask for referrals.

Next Up…

So now we have to figure out how to scale a team. It looks like we'll have to call out potential teammates, show them the value of joining the team, then ask them to join. Wait… that sounds familiar. But seriously, if you really want a $100M leads machine, buckle up. The most valuable chapter in the book is coming up next - *employees*. For real, this isn't a boring chapter, and you're gonna need them if you wanna make the *big money*.

FREE GIFT: BONUS - Customer Referral Frenzy

If you want to know more about ways to use the highest leverage, most profitable way of getting customers, I made a training just for you. You can get it here for free: **Acquisition.com/training/leads**. And as always, you can also scan the QR code below if you hate typing.

#2 Employees

"If you want to go fast, go alone. If you want to go far, go together" - African Proverb

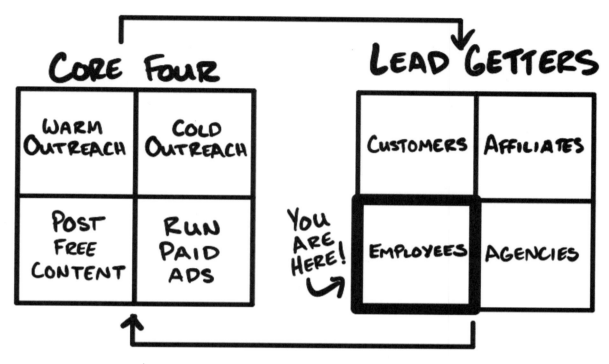

June 2021.

The new sales director piped up, "I know we came in under our goal again, but I don't think we need to change anything, we'll hit it this quarter."

Eyes darted around the room and looked in every direction but mine. The silence was long enough for the executive assistant to mark the topic covered and move on. No wonder we missed our cold outreach goal for the second quarter in a row... nobody challenged the failure. *What, so now we think the third time's a charm?*

"Wait." I said. Now *everyone* looked in my direction. "I'd like to know why we didn't hit this two quarters in a row. I know we can sell–so if we want to make more sales with cold outreach, then we *do* more cold outreach. What's the issue?"

"We lose a rep every four weeks." the sales director said. *Aha.*

"Ok...Why is our churn so high?".

"I was wondering the same thing, but HR says we're actually below industry average churn for this position." He continued, "But, by the time we hire and onboard one, another churns out."

I saw the HR director nodding in agreement. *Getting warmer.*

"OK, so the issue is hiring." I said. "So, what's the hiring situation look like?"

"We hire one out of every four candidates HR pushes to us."

"So if they churn out as fast as we hire them, and you only hire one out of every four, that means you only get like one candidate a week?"

"Yeah, about that" *Almost there.*

"Gotcha" Now I looked at the HR Director, "What's the screening situation look like?"

"We get one qualified candidate per ten screening interviews, give or take." She said.

"So it takes *forty* interviews to get a single, low-skill, frontline worker?"

"I guess so." *Bingo.*

"Alright, we need to change things up." I said. "We're bottlenecked at the one-on-one screening. Start interviewing in groups and look for crazies there. Push everyone else with a good work ethic and basic social skills over to sales. We can teach the rest. Agreed?" The team nodded.

Within six weeks, hiring outpaced churn. Our cold outreach sales increased in lockstep. By the end of the quarter, cold outreach sales had doubled, and made up more than half our total sales.

The issue wasn't our cold outreach method, skills, or offer at all. We just didn't have enough people *doing* cold outreach.

***

If you use the methods in this book, you will see more engaged leads flow into your business. More engaged leads means more customers. But as you grow, so does your workload. In due time, it will take more work than any single person can handle. And you can solve the problem of too much work for one person *by having more people work*. In short, to advertise more, you'll need more workers. And this chapter will show you how employees work, why they make you wealthy, how to get them, and the method I use to turn them into lead-getters.

How Employees Work

Lead-getting employees are people working in your business that you train to get you leads. They get you leads the exact same way you got your own leads in the beginning. They can run ads, they can make and post content, and they can do outreach. They can do any advertising *you train them to do.* So more lead-getting employees means more engaged leads for your business. It also means less work *you* have to do to get the leads. More leads and less work? Sign me up! But wait… Not so fast…

Don't get me wrong—*employees take work.* They just take less time and work than doing everything on your own. In my experience, if you trade forty hours of doing for four hours of managing, you work thirty-six hours less. Brilliant. And the best part is, you can make that trade over and over. You can swap 200 hours of work per week for twenty hours of management. Then, you trade the twenty hours of managing for a manager, who costs you four hours per week to lead. What remains is four hours of work for 200 hours of lead-getting. Boom.

<u>Bottom Line</u>: Employees make a fully functioning enterprise that grows *without you.*

Why Employees Make You Wealthy

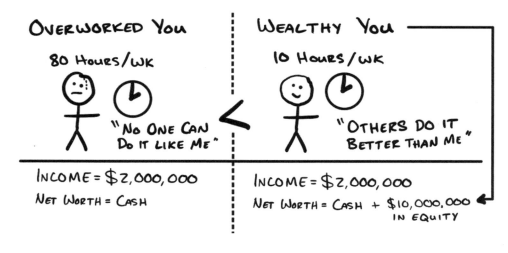

For your business to run without you, other people need to run it.

<u>Scenario #1</u>: Imagine you have a business that makes $5,000,000 per year in revenue and $2,000,000 in profit. And, to make that profit, you have to work around the clock. In this situation, you basically have a high paying job. But let's say you're OK with working all hours and knowing your business would burn down if you took a vacation. Vacations

are for losers anyways (kidding *cough* sort of…). We still have another important thing to look at…

Sure, you make a bit of money, but your business *isn't worth much*. If the business only makes money with you in it, then it's a *bad investment for* anyone *else*. That may not sound like a big deal right now, but let's consider an alternative.

Scenario #2: Your business makes the same $5,000,000 in revenue and $2,000,000 in profit. But there's one big difference: The business runs *without you*. This does two very cool things. One, it turns what used to be a risky job into a valuable asset. And two, it makes you *much* wealthier. Here's how:

First, you get your time back, so you can use that time to invest in your business, buy other businesses, or take your stinkin' vacations. Second, you become much wealthier because your business is now *worth something to someone else*. You turned a *liability* that relied on you into an *asset* you can rely on.

If you have an asset that makes millions of dollars *without you* then that means somebody else could use it to make millions of dollars *without them*. In other words, your business is now a *good investment*. Then investors looking for assets, like <u>Acquisition.com</u> for instance, would buy some or all of it from you. And your $2,000,000 in profit per year, especially if it's climbing, could easily be worth $10,000,000+, *right now*. So your business went from having almost *zero* value to having $10,000,000 of value. So, learning how to get other people to do it for you makes a $10,000,000 difference to your net worth. I'd say it's worth learning how to do it.

Reminder: *You get rich from what you make. You become wealthy from what you own.* And it took me years to realize this because not that long ago…

Everything I Thought I Knew About Employees Was Wrong

Have you ever heard…

> *If you want it done right, you gotta do it yourself.*
>
> *No one can do it like I do it.*
>
> *Nobody can replace me.*

I have. I said all that stuff. I lived all that stuff. For years, every time I hired somebody, I would compare what they could to what I could do. In my head, I felt like it was "me against them." To somehow prove I was the more 'able' one. With my own team! And this belief, this way of "leading" people, never made me more money.

204

For business– "nobody can do it but me" and "if you want something done right you gotta do it yourself" aren't facts... they're false. Somebody did similar stuff before you were around. And somebody will continue doing some version of it after you're gone. In one way or another–everyone is replaceable. It might be by multiple people, technology, or later in time, but *everyone* can be replaced. My suggestion: replace yourself as soon as you can. Then, you can make yourself useful somewhere else. Many other people figured this out. And so can you.

In the early days, whenever I started a business, I could do stuff better than the people I hired. My entire workforce always ended up looking like a ragtag group of misfits who could *kind of* do *one* of the many things I could do. This got me up and running at first, but I fell into the trap of believing I was better than everyone else. I would go back and forth between gloating because I was better than them and complaining because they weren't as good as me. And for whatever reason, it never occurred to me *I was the one* who hired and trained them. Who was I kidding? The reality was twofold: First, I didn't have the skills to train or lead a team properly. Second, I was too poor, and then (when I had a little money) too cheap to hire anyone better. In other words, it was <u>*my*</u> fault they sucked. Oops.

The more I tried to outcompete my employees, the more distracted I became, and the worse my business got. Sure, at the time, *maybe* I could do *anything* better than *any* of my employees. But... I couldn't do *everything* better than *all* my employees. And when I finally realized this, I started adopting better beliefs about talent:

> *'If you want it done right, get someone to spend all their time doing it.'*

> *'If I can do it, someone else can do it better.'*

> *'Everyone is replaceable, especially me.'*

These new beliefs about talent not only made a much healthier culture in my businesses but also came with very profitable side effects. Trusting my employees to succeed made *my* time and attention *far* more valuable. If somebody else can do it, why would I? If somebody else could train them, why would I? If I could learn other stuff to grow the business while my team held the fort down, it makes *way* more sense to do that. So let's do that.

How To Get Employee Leads: The Internal Core Four

Remember the core four? Well, they work for getting employees too. Imagine that. By changing the frame from "letting potential customers know about your stuff" to "letting potential employees know about your stuff" it *immediately* turns into something you already know how to do. But some people also have the opposite problem–they already know how to get employees just fine but still struggle to get customers. *Employees are just other people you let know about your stuff.* So you do the same thing!

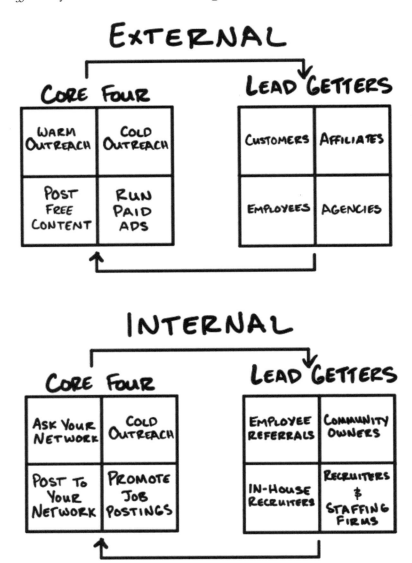

Line up the actions to get employees with the actions to get customers. It's the same stuff!

Customers → Employees

Warm Outreach→Asking Your Network	Customer Referrals→Employee Referrals
Cold Outreach→ Recruiting	Affiliates→ Associations, Guilds, Listservs etc.
Post Content→Posting Job Openings	Agencies→ Staffing firms etc.
Paid Ads→Promoting Job Postings	Employees→Employees (unchanged)

The ways you get employee leads and their lead getters have equivalents to the ways you get customer leads and *their* lead getters. So when you need to get new talent, you just advertise to get it. And when you need more, you do more. And like creating a reliable process to get customers, you can also create a reliable process of getting employees. And you'll need <u>both</u> to scale.

How To Get Employees To Get You Leads

Now you hire someone who costs you money every month. Great. Let's make sure you make it back, *and some* ASAP.

Note–some people looking for work will already know how to get leads. Those people are awesome. You can also count on them to cost more. And if you're starting out, you may not be able to afford them. So, your next best option is to train them. Thankfully, you have an entire book of lead-getting at your fingertips. So the next step is training your employees on how <u>you</u> do those lead-getting activities. I think about and actually approach training with this 3Ds mental model: *document, demonstrate, duplicate*. Here's how it works.

Step One - Document. <u>*You make a checklist.*</u> You already know how to do the thing. Now you just need to write down the steps exactly as you do it. You can also have other trusted observers watch you and document what you do. Bonus points if you record yourself doing the thing multiple ways and in multiple shifts. This way, you can watch yourself *as an observer* rather than breaking your flow by pausing to take notes while you go. Once you've got everything put into the checklist, bust it out on your next work block and *only* follow those steps. Can you do an A+ job *only* following *your* directions *exactly*? If you can, you have the <u>first draft</u> of your checklist for the job.

Step Two - Demonstrate: _You do it in front of them_. Just like your parents taught you how to tie your shoes. You sit down and walk them through the checklist step by step. This may take a while depending on how many steps it takes to complete the thing. If they stop you, or slow you down to understand something, adjust your checklist for that. Now you have the <u>second draft</u> ready for them to try.

Step Three - Duplicate: _They do it in front of you_. Now it's their turn. They follow the same checklist you followed. Except this time, they're the one doing, and you're the one observing. We just want them to _duplicate_ what we did. So if the checklist is right, the outcome will be the same. And if the checklist is off—you'll find out fast! Fix your checklist until it's right. Then, have them follow it until they get it right. And once they nail it, you now have a bonafide lead-getter on your payroll. Congratulations!

Pro Tip: Give Short Windows For People To Prove Themselves.

Most entry level advertising jobs aren't complex. It takes grit more than skill. If you trained someone properly and they're still below expectations three weeks in, cut them.

After you train your first few employees this way, you'll have worked out the kinks for that job and it's pretty smooth sailing from there. At least the training part anyways. Think about it this way, if you vanished tomorrow, could a stranger get the results you get if they only followed your checklist? That's the level of clarity to shoot for.

<u>Some helpful notes on training</u>:

- A helpful way to look at this training style is: _If they get it wrong or get confused then we got it wrong or made it confusing_. If we have to explain what a step means then the step is too complicated. Or, more likely, we tried to put multiple steps into one.

- If they only appear to "get it" after a longish explanation or multiple demonstrations then, again, we've got some work to do. Business owners that ignore this run into chronic training problems. And, word to the wise, you can probably force an inferior checklist to work, but this turns into a _nightmare_ when somebody else takes over your training for you.

- There is a difference between competence and performance. In other words, they can know exactly what to do and *not be that good at it yet*. If that's the case, then your instructions are fine and *they just need practice*. Using an analogy from the fitness world–think "slow then smooth then fast." You don't need to change anything, they just need more reps.

- *Focus on your employee's ability to follow directions more than whether they get the right result.* This is super important because if you train your employees to follow directions then… they will follow directions. And, if they follow directions and get the wrong result… *then you know it's the directions.* That's good. You have a lot more control over that.

- Everytime they do a step successfully–*let them know they did it right.* And if they respond to praise, praise them! And if they goof, that's OK too. That's what training is for. Don't take over for them when they mess up–simply pause, take a step back, and let them try it again. Fast feedback cycles to get people to learn *faster.*

- If they follow your directions *exactly* and get the wrong result–still praise them for following the directions. Praise them, then make the corrections to your checklist on the spot.

- Avoid punishment or penalties of any type for doing stuff wrong during training. As a rule of thumb–reward the good stuff you want them to do more of and they'll do more of it. Learning a new skill is punishing enough, we don't need to add to it.

- It's hard to fix multiple things *when you've never done something before.* Give feedback one step at a time. Give one piece of feedback at a time. Practice until they get it right. Then, move to the next step.

- Whenever there is a major dip from normal performance, retrain the team. They stopped doing an important step in the process (often because they didn't know it was important). Once you figure out the step, reward people for following it going forward.

How to Calculate Returns From Lead-Getting Employees

Excluding the cost of running paid ads, the cost of advertising (outreach, content, etc.) with employees is almost entirely based on the amount of money you pay them to do it. We simplify this by just comparing how much money we spend on payroll to how much money the engaged leads they get bring in:

- Total Payroll / Total Engaged Leads = Cost per engaged lead.

    - Ex: $100,000 / 1000 leads = $100 per engaged lead

- If one out of ten of the engaged leads become customers then our CAC is $1000

    - ($100 per engaged lead) x (10 engaged leads per customer) = $1000 CAC

- If each customer has an LTGP of $4000 then you have an LTGP : CAC of 4:1

    - ($4000 LTGP) / ($1000 CAC) = 4:1

For example: at the time of this writing, I get about 30,000 engaged leads per month at Acquistion.com. I run no paid ads, and do no outreach. But the team responsible for creating the content that generates that interest is about $100,000 per month. This means, it costs me roughly $3.33 per engaged lead ($100,000 / 30,000 leads) in payroll to generate them. We make much more than $3.33 per lead, so we're profitable. You can apply the same math to whatever advertising method you use.

How To Know Which Employees to Focus On To Maximize Returns

Like we learned in Run Paid Ads Part II–if your cost to get a customer is within 3x industry average then you're doing *good enough*. From there, you focus on bumping up your LTGP.

If your CAC is more than 3x industry average then you have a sales problem or an advertising problem. We diagnose this with a single question:

Do my engaged leads have the problem I solve and the money to spend?

- If no, then they're not qualified–that's an advertising problem.

- If yes, then they're qualified and:

    - They're buying but you don't have enough of them–advertising problem.

    - They're qualified but not buying–sales problem.

Don't fire your sales guy if you've got advertising problems. And equally, don't fire your advertising employees if you've got a sales problem. That little question can help you identify which employees to focus on.

But fundamentally, you just need to figure out all *your* costs of getting a customer put together. And as long as they're at least one-third of the profit you make over the lifetime, you're in good shape.

Conclusion

The goal of this chapter was to *shift your perspective*. It's your job to advertise and sell the vision of your company. You advertise it publicly *and* privately to employees *and* customers alike. That's the job. And once you get good at it, you become unstoppable.

I say this because I believe anyone can be taught to do "ground level" jobs for any business– advertising or otherwise. So who you pick is not as important as how you train the ones you do.

Like I've said throughout the book and will say again here—it doesn't take a genius to advertise. I'd even say it hurts. We've got plenty more iron-wills than brainiacs anyways. Remember, this isn't about brains, it's about guts. And although some people might be born geniuses, *nobody* is born with an iron will (after all, we all come out crybabies). All this to say <u>having guts is a skill.</u> And that means *anyone* can have the guts *if they learn how.* So if you have an iron-will, and as an entrepreneur you probably do, it won't take long for you to figure out that you got it from your life experiences. You can pass those experiences on as lessons to anyone who cares enough to listen. Then, they can stand on your shoulders and have a better chance at succeeding in life.

And - you can't really know anything anyway until you train them well and give them a fighting chance to succeed out in the field. Plus, for low level jobs, you'll never have a shortage of labor. Get picky when you have to make massive investments in hyper-specific-multiple-six-figure-C-suite employees. Aka - 'fancy employees.'

I find at this current stage, it's actually a better use of time, to hire and train anyone *willing*. Then, <u>when</u> you find winners, and with this method you will: treat them well, don't burn them out, and give them what they deserve.

In the land of overflowing leads, you'll need allies. Employees are among the most powerful of these allies. We talked about: how they make you wealthy, how they work, how getting them works, how to get them, how to get them getting you leads, how to keep them getting you leads, and how to know you're doing a good job. And once you've built a system for getting people who get you leads (doing the core four on your behalf), you just need to do more.

Author Note: A Word On Fancy Employees

I explicitly left out recruiting director level and up employees because you can easily qualify for Acquisition.com without them. And once you do become a portfolio company, we do it for you.

The Next Lead Getter...

The next stop on our advertising journey leads us to agencies. Yes, you can pay people to shortcut your path. I have paid zillions of dollars to agencies and I believe I've finally *cracked* the code on how to create a win for all parties. For us, so we're not dependent on them forever. For them, so they can make more profit and provide more value to their customers. They've been key to many breakthroughs I've had, so you won't want to skip this next one...

FREE GIFT: BONUS TUTORIAL - Build or Buy - The Talent Roadmap

The longer I do business, the more I ask "who" over what and how. This training may be one of the most tactical and important, because no matter what you want to build, you're gonna need help. Since it's so important, I made a training outlining this content in more depth with some downloads etc. You can watch it free at **Acquisition.com/training/leads**. As always, you can also scan the QR code below if you hate typing.

#3 Agencies

"Everything is for sale"

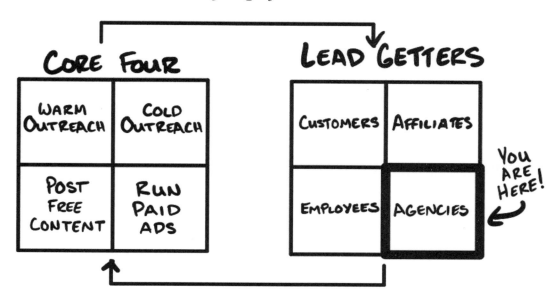

Summer 2016.

I wasn't a tech guy. I was a fitness guy who had learned a few marketing and sales tricks building my gyms. But now I had five, and was launching my sixth. It was time to level up. Facebook had just released some new features: retargeting, interest groups, pixels, etc. And I didn't understand any of it. I bought a few courses but ended up more confused than when I started.

I asked a few friends if they knew anyone who could help. I got two referrals. Both were agencies. I was scared. I had never used one before. I had only ever heard horror stories about advertising agencies. Mostly that they cost a ton and never work. But then I realized that even if they did work, I'd *need* them forever. They'd have my business by the balls! It turns out my expectations weren't far off. They offered to run my ads alright, for an arm and a leg. Money I couldn't justify spending with my low margins. But, then again, my advertising costs were killing me. And at this rate, in a few months, I wouldn't be able to keep my doors open. Stressful.

I refused the first agency because I couldn't afford it at the time. The second call started going the same way. I began to panic. *How am I gonna fix this?* In what felt like a last ditch effort to stay in business, I asked the second agency owner for what I *really* wanted…

"Can you just show me in a few hours how you would run ads on my account?"

"No." He fired back. "My time's not for sale."

Worried but still hopeful…"What sort of arrangement could we come to?"

He thought for a moment. Then his eyebrow shot up and a smirk appeared. "Fine. $750 an hour." *Gulp.* His intimidation tactic worked. But at least I knew his time was for sale... so I wanted to find out more.

"And for $750 per hour *you* will sit down with *me* and show *me* how *you* would run *my* ads?"

"Yes."

"And, I'd be the one doing everything? Like, you'll walk me through what to do and look over my shoulder as I do it, then you'll explain why you do it that way?"

"Yea"

"And you're confident you can make my ads more profitable? …and show me the more advanced stuff too, right?"

"Yea. I mean. If you wanna pay me $750 an hour, we can do whatever you want. It's your money" He said, half laughing. It sounded more like *It's your funeral.*

I paused. "Alright. I'll do it. We'll meet one hour a week. You give me homework and I'll study between calls. Fair enough?"

"Works for me. But you gotta pay for the first four hours up front"

So that's what I did. I placed a three thousand dollar bet on this guy's word that he knew what he was doing. *Yikes.* But, every week thereafter, I showed up. And like a good student, I came with notes and questions ready. I also recorded and rewatched every call because I didn't want to miss anything.

The first two calls, he took the wheel and I watched. Calls three and four, he put me in the driver's seat. By calls five and six, it clicked. I got how he made decisions and what data he tracked. At seven and eight, I realized I didn't need his help anymore. I had learned how to run paid ads, at least on Facebook, like a pro. And, if I had to make a guess, it was because I learned it…from a pro.

In this chapter, we explore a not-so-obvious-but-much-better-way to use agencies to get more leads. Let's get crankin'.

How Agencies Want You To Think They Work

Advertising agencies are lead-getting service businesses. You pay them to run paid ads, do outreach, or package and distribute content.

For example, let's say you want to post free video content. But, you know nothing about making video content or how to distribute it. You'd need to learn how to pick video topics, record videos, edit videos, make thumbnail images, and write headlines. Or, you'd need to hire the people who do. Enter the agency. They say they've hired and trained people to do that stuff already. So they promise faster, better, and more cost-efficient results than you could get on your own. And as soon as I had enough money, it felt compelling enough.

After my first experience with an agency, that I mentioned earlier and went quite well, I decided to use more. But my experience with the next ten plus agencies was *different* because I used them 'the right way.' Each went something like this:

Step 1: They got me excited about all the new leads they would bring.

Step 2: I'd go through an onboarding process that felt valuable (and sometimes was).

Step 3: They assigned their "best" senior rep to my account.

Step 4: I saw some results.

Step 5: They moved my senior rep to the newest customer...

Step 6: A junior rep starts managing my account. My results suffered.

Step 7: I complained.

Step 8: The senior rep would come back once in a while to make me feel better.

Step 9: Results still suffered. And I'd eventually cancel.

Step 10: I'd search for another agency and repeat the cycle of insanity.

Step 11: *For the zillionth time*–Start wondering why I wasn't getting results like the first time.

To be clear, like the introduction to this chapter shows, agencies *can* play a valuable role in business growth. But not the way *they* want you to. I don't want anyone else falling into the same trap. In fact, I hope all the money I wasted goes towards paying down your ignorance tax too. So keep reading.

It's frankly ridiculous that it took me so many years to figure out that I actually used an agency the *right* way…the *first* time! But now, after playing their game so many times, I feel I cracked the "how to use an agency" code. And it doesn't come from playing their game *at all*. It comes from playing a different one. And this chapter breaks it all down in three steps:

1. Hiring an agency versus doing it yourself

2. How I use agencies now. And how you can, too.

3. How to pick the right agency

Hiring An Agency Versus Doing It Yourself

First, let's get this out of the way. Good agencies cost money. So if you have no money, then agencies are out of the question. You've gotta learn through trial and error. And that's no big deal. *We all start that way.* But if you do have some money, I suggest using agencies for two things: learning new methods and learning new platforms.

If I want to learn new ways to do content, outreach, or paid ads, then I hire agencies offering new ways to do them. They've already made the big mistakes. So instead of wasting time figuring it out myself, I skip straight to the 'make money' part. I like the 'make money' part.

I also use agencies when I want to start advertising on a platform I don't understand. I make money faster because they do the early setup and maintenance for me and because I get them to teach me how to do it.

Hiring an agency is all about investing in important skills you can't really learn anywhere else. That is, unless you go through *all* the trial and error to learn it yourself. And if you did, you lose the time, and attention you could have used to learn the other important stuff that scales your business. And scaling your business is the whole point.

Action Step: As soon as you have enough money for a good agency, start poking around. If you follow the rest of the steps in this chapter, you'll make it all back… and then some.

How I Use Agencies Now. And How You Can Too.

I've become a little more sophisticated than the story I told at the beginning. Here's how I use agencies now. Rather than believe the lie that "I'll never have to learn this stuff because they can do it," I start every agency relationship with a purpose and a deadline to fulfill it. I open by saying:

"I want to do what you do in my business, but I don't know how. I'd like to work with you for 6 months so I can learn how you do it. Plus, I'll pay extra for you to break down why you make the decisions you do and the steps you take to make them. Then, after I get a good idea of how it all works, I'll start training my team on it. And once they can do it well enough, I'd like to change to a lower cost consulting arrangement. This way, you can still help us if we run into problems. Are you opposed to this?"

In my experience, most agencies are *not* opposed to this. And if it doesn't work for them, that's perfectly fine. Just move on to the next agency. But, before you start kicking everyone to the curb, be willing to negotiate. At some price, it's worth it for both of you. Viva capitalism!

This is how I use agencies now. Like when I wanted to learn YouTube, I actually hired *two* agencies. The first, I hired to keep me committed to making videos while they did some legwork on the platform itself. The second I hired (at 4x the price) to really teach us the in-depth ideas behind making the best content possible. And once our videos beat their videos, we dropped down to consulting only.

I've used this method again and again. I hire one "good enough" agency to learn the ropes of a new platform. Then, I hire a more elite agency to learn how to maximize it–*and I cannot recommend this strategy enough.*

If you are upfront about your intentions and the agency agrees, you get the best of both worlds. You get better short-term results because they (probably) know more than you. And, you get better long-term results because you learn how to do it yourself or your team learns to do it for you. *You also spend the maximum amount of time with their best reps.*

Remember, you only get a *fraction* of the agency's attention, so results get worse whenever they get new clients. Meanwhile, your team gets better and better because they stay focused on you full-time. So compare your team's results to the agency's until you beat them. Then, cancel the relationship and put the money into scaling everything you just learned.

Action Step: When you find an agency to work with (next step) set terms with them and deadlines for yourself. Use the template above as your guide. And feel OK with negotiating a bit to make it work.

To be clear, I still own equity in an agency software, ALAN. So I'm not against agencies. I just share how I've had success with them. Are there massive companies that use huge ad agencies? Sure. But they're not who I'm writing for. For most people, spending $10,000, $50,000, or $100,000 on an agency is a significant cost. So, this is how I've gotten the best return from working with them. Also - some people never want to learn - and for those people - agencies are great. I personally always want to learn, which is why I use agencies this way.

How to Pick The Right Agency

After working with tons of bad agencies, and a handful of good ones, I created a list of what all the good ones had in common. Now it isn't the last word on what makes a good agency, but it is useful stuff that's worked for me.

Here's what I look for:

1) Somebody I know got good results working with them. If you only know about an agency from their paid ads or cold outreach… they probably aren't as good as the ones who rely solely on word of mouth (and the best ones do).

2) Prominent companies got good results working with them. I may not know the companies personally, but if I recognize them, it's a good sign.

3) A waiting list. When demand for a service exceeds the supply, they are probably pretty good.

4) A clear sales process that makes a point to set <u>realistic</u> expectations. No funny business.

5) No short term hacks. They keep the talk on long term strategy. They also give clear timelines for setup, scaling, and results.

6) They tell me exactly what they need from me, when they need it, and how they use it.

7) *They* suggest a regular schedule of meetings and offer several ways to update me on their progress.

8) They give updates in simple terms and have clear ways to track so I know how costs compare with results.

9) They make a good offer:

   a. <u>Dream outcome</u>: is what they promise what I want?

   b. <u>Perceived likelihood of achievement</u>: how many other people like me have they gotten there?

   c. <u>Time delay</u>: how long will it take?

   d. <u>Effort and sacrifice</u>: what do they require me to do when working with them? What will I have to give up? Can I stick with those for a long time?

10) They are expensive. All good agencies are expensive… but not all expensive agencies are good. So talk with as many as it takes. And use this list as a guide to find the good ones.

>   …if an agency checks those boxes, they're worth considering.

Pro Tip: Talk To More Agencies To Be A Better Customer

Being an informed customer *helps everyone*. So, before you buy, get informed. Talk to five or ten agencies to learn how they work. At first - you'll learn a bunch of new stuff. But over time, the difference between the better ones and the worse ones becomes obvious. *Now*, you can make an informed decision.

If the agency doesn't meet my needs, but I like the people, I'll ask them to refer me to another agency. A good agency offering a one specialty will send you to other good agencies who offer the one you want. Those are some of my favorite referrals.

Action step: Even if an agency agrees to your terms, talk with a few more before you make a decision. Compare them using the checklist above, and then pick the best one for you.

Conclusion

Even though this isn't the "traditional" agency model, *both* businesses benefit. They get a customer they otherwise wouldn't have. And we get a money-making skill for life. In the story at the beginning of the chapter - it cost me eight hours and $6000 to learn a skill that's *made me millions*. Does that seem worth it to you? It better.

And to make this agency method work at scale, you have to count on a good amount of time where you pay the agency and your team *to do the same stuff*. You've gotta give yourself some breathing room to get results from the agency, learn what they do, *and* train your team on it... all at once. Yes, it costs a lot of money. And yes, it's totally worth it when you get it right.

And get it right you can. After agencies put a low level employee on my account for the millionth time, it finally clicked. This can't be *that* hard. At first, it took about a year to get my team better than an agency. As I got better, it went down to ten months, then eight. And now, I've got it down. I can get my team as good or better than the agency in less than six months or less. And every time I want to learn a new method or platform, I repeat the process.

The better you get, the cheaper it becomes, and the more money you make. Funny, that sounds a lot like advertising.

Next Steps:

1) Decide if using an agency makes sense for you right now.
2) Talk to a lot of agencies to get a feel for the market. Don't be cheap.
3) Use the agreement framework I outlined.
4) Set a clear deadline to force you (and your team) to learn the skills.
5) Use both teams until yours beats theirs regularly.
6) Switch to discounted consulting until you feel like you're teaching them instead of them teaching you...then cut 'em loose.

Now that we know how to profit from the high risk world of agencies, we explore the lead-getter that's made me the most money. We recruit an army of businesses who can get us even more leads - *affiliates*.

FREE GIFT: What To Look For in An Agency Checklist

If you want to know the best way to use agencies, rather than being used by them, I made a free training for you. You can watch it free at: **Acquisition.com/training/leads**. It has swipe files and some other goodies. As always, you can also scan the QR code below if you hate typing.

#4 Affiliates and Partners

"Nothing makes friends like money"

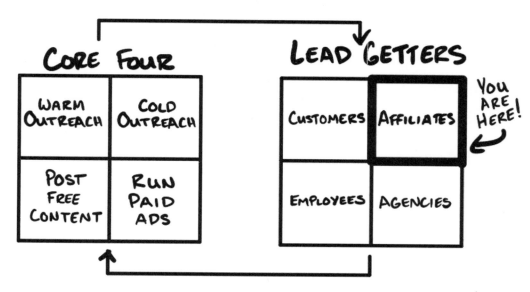

December 1st, 2018

I had no idea how the Prestige Labs launch would go. I had no idea if our clients would like it. I had no idea if the technology we built would work. I had no idea if payouts would happen on time. I had no idea if our warehouse would mess up orders.

But I did know over a year of preparation went into this launch. We put everything we had into creating a top-tier product. We spent over $1,000,000 custom-building affiliate software and training. And - we bought $3,000,000 in inventory for sales that may never happen. It took *every* business skill I had to make Prestige Labs real. And, in just a few hours, we would roll it out to our gym owner affiliates. I felt like a kid on Christmas Eve. And if it didn't work, *it wouldn't be for lack of effort.*

Author Note: The Game Podcast Episode 98 "I Remember"

If you want to go back in time, you can hear 'young me' talk about my thoughts/concerns the night before the launch. You can be right there with me. It's episode 98 on my podcast <u>The Game with Alex Hormozi</u> titled "I Remember." This is before I knew the success it would become. To find it, just go wherever you listen to podcasts and search "Alex Hormozi" and it'll come up.

The Game w/ Alex Hormozi
Alex Hormozi

Launch day…

I finished the two-hour presentation soaked in sweat. *It's done.*

I 'sold' the opportunity to sell my supplement line at their gyms. I would *train* the new affiliates to promote Prestige Labs at their gyms. So, for this to work, they would have to go through the training *and* use it. But, if they did, everyone would profit. I had no idea if it would work.

Three weeks later…

We made $150,000 in *total* sales. Meanwhile, $3,000,000 worth of product sat in an air-conditioned warehouse… *It didn't work.*

At this rate, including operating costs and affiliate payouts, it would take five years to *break even*. Even if we could stick it out, our premium product would expire well before then. We were all but screwed. I felt miserable. It was terrible. *Who am I to think we would sell all that stuff? I just wasted MILLIONS. How could I be so stupid?*

But…on the fourth week…something wild happened…

BOOM! $100,000 on Monday.

BOOM! $110,000 on Tuesday

BOOM! $92,000 on Wednesday.

We did over $450,000 in sales the fourth week *alone*. The trend continued. $429,000…$383,000…$411,000…$452,000. We averaged more than 300 orders per day across 400+ active affiliates. Orders just kept coming in. Check out the snapshot of our internal report below. It shows, from left to right, revenue by _week_. I couldn't believe the results. Sometimes, I still can't.

Gross Revenue	$429,112	$383,717	$411,848	$404,838	$452,204
Net Revenue	$407,164	$358,073	$391,197	$384,119	$429,982
Refunds	$21,948	$25,644	$20,651	$20,719	$22,222
Count of Orders	2266	2052	2084	2124	2367
Average Order Size	$189	$187	$198	$191	$191
Active Affiliates	428	409	416	437	444

The best part is, *I didn't advertise or sell any of the products at all.* No paid ads. No sales team. Nothing. The affiliates did everything–and the affiliate machine I built still prints money to this day. So if that sounds like something you're interested in, hang tight, because I'm gonna show you exactly how I built it.

How Affiliates Work

An **affiliate** is a lead-getter. They are an independent business that tells their audience to buy *your* stuff. Affiliates seem like referrals on the outside, but are much different under the hood. First, they have their own businesses and do their own advertising. Second, they agree to offer *your* stuff to *their* engaged leads in exchange for money, free stuff, or both.

Now, you get affiliates by advertising and then making them offers *just like you would customers.* But, affiliates demand a unique type of offer. Instead of offering your product, you offer a fast, simple, and easy way to make commissions promoting it. And that can mean literally millions of engaged leads to your business. So this makes affiliates one of the highest-leverage lead-getters out there.

225

Why You Want An Affiliate Army

Each affiliate you get adds another *stream* of leads and customers. So recruiting, activating, then integrating with an army of affiliates causes crazy scaling, fast. That's good. We want that.

Compare these two scenarios:

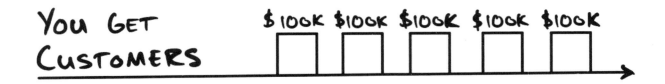

Scenario #1: You sell ten *customers* per month worth $10,000 each. Your business caps at $100,000 per month. In twelve months you've made 1.2 million. Assuming no other advertising, your business *plateaus*. Low-Leverage.

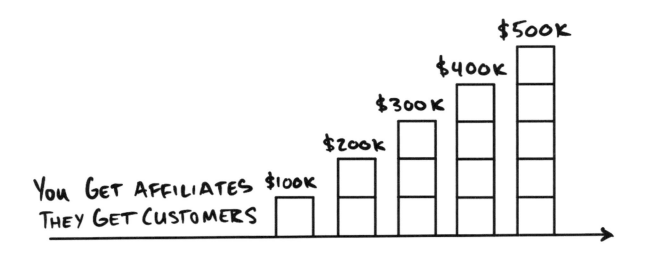

Scenario #2: For the same effort, you sell ten *affiliates* per month. Each month, those affiliates bring you *one* of those $10,000 customers. Now, every single month you add an *extra* $100,000 in revenue. In twelve months you've made *7.8 million*. And it grows *every month thereafter*. Same work, more money. High-Leverage.

Let's use ALAN, my software company I grew with affiliates, to show how this works in the real world:

ALAN grew with three levels of affiliates:

1) Agency super-affiliates who brought agency leads

2) Agencies who brought local business leads

3) Local businesses who brought end consumer leads

One super-affiliate added ten agencies per month. The ten agencies brought in a combined fifty or so local businesses per month. Those local businesses brought in a combined 2500 leads per month. ALAN worked those leads for about $5 a pop. A cool $12,500 *per month.*

But it didn't stop there. Each super-affiliate brought in *more* agencies who brought in *more* local businesses who brought *more* leads every month after that. So every super-affiliate we signed on brought in $12,500 the first month, $25,000 the second, $37,500 the third, and so on. With only a few agency super-affiliates, we scaled to $1,700,000 per month within six months of launching. *That's* why you want an affiliate army. So let's build one.

How To Build An Affiliate Army in Six Steps

Affiliates are among the most advanced ways to get engaged leads. First, you have to convince them to advertise someone else's stuff. Second, you have to convince them to advertise *your* stuff. Third, you have to *keep them advertising* to make them a long-term lead source. It seems like a lot. And it is. But, I have good news…

I've built two companies with affiliates: ALAN and Prestige Labs. Together, they have done more than $75,000,000 in revenue from over 5000+ affiliates. And the affiliate strategies I share worked for me. So they can work for you. I'll break down each step.

Step 1: Find Your Ideal Affiliates

Step 2: Make Them an Offer

Step 3: Qualify Them

Step 4: Figure Out What To Pay Them

Step 5: Get Them Advertising

Step 6: Keep Them Advertising

That's it. Let's dive in.

Step 1: Find Your Ideal Affiliate

The ideal affiliate has a business with a warm audience full of people like your customers. Start making a list of those businesses. If none come to mind, answer these questions about your best customers:

What do they buy? → *Who provides that stuff?*

Where do they go? → *What businesses are in those surrounding areas?*

What do they like to do? → *Who provides those services?*

If direct to consumer–the employers of your consumers could make great affiliates:

What types of businesses do they work for? What kinds of jobs do they have?

In a nutshell… *Who's got my leads!?*

For example, when I started ALAN, agency owners were my ideal affiliate. So I made a list of 200 products and services *for agencies* and the businesses that delivered them. After a little bit of work I realized they fit pretty neatly into categories: **softwares, products, equipment, services, groups they belong to, and events they attended**. Every time I create a new affiliate "hit list" I start with these categories. Note: If you find a business that falls into multiple categories, there's a high chance they've got lots of good leads for you and that they'd make a great affiliate.

Now that I knew the businesses that had my leads I knew exactly where to put my advertising efforts. It wasn't fancy, so don't overthink it.

Action Step: Make a sheet with each of these questions and categories. Search online to fill it in. If you struggle, call up your customers and ask them! End result: Create a lead list of your highest potential affiliates.

Step 2: Make Them An Offer

We make the affiliate-offer and advertise it the same way we would any other offer. We call out our audience, show our value elements, and then call them to action. But affiliates will only sign up with us if we give them a strong reason. Thankfully, it's pretty simple. Since affiliates are businesses, or start a business by signing up, *you offer them a new way to make money.* We'll start with the callout.

<u>Call out:</u>

Call outs for potential affiliates often include:

- The affiliate business owners themselves - *ATTENTION SPA OWNERS*

- The affiliate's customers - *Do you work with busy professionals who spend all day in meetings?*

- Results the affiliate businesses promise - *To the heroes who heal the stress of others...*

- Products and services the affiliates deliver - *If you sell lotions or scented oils this is for you...*

- To our own customers - *Do you know anyone who owns a spa?*

Now that we can grab a potential affiliate's attention - let's make it worth their while...

<u>Elements Of Value</u>

There's an unlimited number of ways to show value, but all money making offers follow a similar structure. That's good news, we don't need to reinvent the wheel. Most affiliate money making offers show value like this:

Make more money from your current customers and get more leads than your current offer (<u>dream outcome</u>)...with a high chance of working since your customers already want the product (<u>perceived likelihood of achievement</u>)...without needing to build, deliver, or provide customer support for the product yourself (<u>effort and sacrifice</u>)...so you can start selling it tomorrow (<u>time delay</u>).

Action Step: Explore the different value elements and fill in the blanks. I won't go deeper on this since we've covered it already. You simply need to make *affiliates* the customer you're advertising to.

Now that we've got the potential affiliate interested in our offer, let's qualify them.

Step 3: Qualify Them

Potential affiliates become actual affiliates when they understand and agree to your terms. And - just like customers - we want to get them their first win as fast as possible. So we setup our terms to force them to win as fast as possible.

I do that by getting them to invest. I prefer they invest their time, their money, *and* in the product itself. Any can work. But, nine times out of ten, *if they pay, they'll pay attention.*

229

Here are the two ways I get my affiliates invested and winning: make them a customer, and make them an expert. Let's dive into each.

Way #1: Make Them A Customer: Make them buy and preferably use the product to keep affiliate status. This is the lowest barrier investment that's worked for me. I've found the more money an affiliate invests in your product, the more money they make. This should make sense. If they don't believe in your stuff enough to buy it, they probably shouldn't sell it. You can tell them I said so.

> **Pro Tip: Bulk Purchases**
>
> If you need to make more money per affiliate, you can require them to buy in bulk. This was huge for Prestige Labs affiliate success. Once they bought a big package up front they started following through and winning. The bigger investment ultimately made them (and us) more money. If you have physical products, then try bulk purchases. If your company has a line of products, like Prestige Labs does, then toy around with big bundles.
>
> Here's how you phrase the offer: *"So you want anything extra or just go with the <u>minimum order?</u>"* By presenting a minimum purchase, they will at least buy that. And more often than you think–they'll buy *more than* the minimum. Badaboom.

Way #2: Make Them An Expert: I make them pay for the onboarding and training that certifies them as a product expert. If you have them buy a product to become an affiliate, you can have them use that as credit towards a certification. As in, the certification *comes with* the products they bought. Now, aside from actually making the affiliate useful, certifying them does two things. First, it covers some of the costs of advertising. Second, it means I can afford proper onboarding and training of every. single. affiliate.

How much do I charge? I recommend 10-20% of what the average active affiliate makes in the first twelve months. So if your average affiliate makes $40,000 per year selling your stuff, then charge $4000-$8000 to onboard and train them. Too low, and you won't get them invested. Too high and you won't get enough affiliates. I found 10-20% maximizes the number of people who become *active* affiliates. If you're just getting started and have physical products then use the bulk purchasing strategy from the pro tip. Otherwise, you can use the strategy from the warm reachout chapter and raise the minimum investment every 5 sign ups until you hit the sweet spot.

Action Step: Make your affiliates customers, experts, or both (my favorite way). If you don't get enough people to start, lower the commitment. If you don't get enough people to follow through, raise it.

Step 4: Figure Out What To Pay Them

The first biggest problem to solve with affiliates is getting them bought in. But the second biggest problem is how to *keep them bought in*. And no matter how you slice it, keeping your affiliates bought in depends on how you reward them for advertising your stuff. I prefer to reward people that do things I like with money and free stuff, especially if they make me money first. So let's talk about that.

When I figure out ways to pay affiliates I look at two basic things:

1. What they get paid for
2. How much they get paid

1. *What* They Get Paid For

Before I do any affiliate payout money math I ask myself a simple question. What *exactly* do I want the affiliate to do? Once I figure that out, *that* is what I pay them for. Then, more often than not, how much they get paid and how often they get paid nearly solve themselves. I pay affiliates for two basic things: new customers, and repeat customers. Over time, if you track your metrics better, you can pay them for steps *before* someone becomes a customer. Like for the lead magnets downloaded, appointments set, or anything else you know reliably turns into sales for you.

2. *How Much* They Get Paid

I suggest paying affiliates based on your maximum allowable cost to acquire a customer (CAC).

Example: choosing your maximum allowable CAC. Let's say we sell a single-use product for $200 and it costs $40 to fulfill. This gives us $160 to pay the affiliate *and* run the business. If we want an LTGP:CAC ratio of 3:1 then three parts goes to the business–$120. And one part, *$40,* goes to the affiliate. This means we will pay up to $40 for an affiliate to get a new customer.

But here's where things get interesting. I used to give away the farm (the whole CAC). I suppose I still do, but I've gotten pickier about who I give it to. Not all affiliates are created equal. So, I suggest having a three-tier payout structure. Using the example above, with a $40 maximum allowable CAC, a three-tier payout structure might look something like this:

- Tier 1: 25% CAC = $10 Payout - Anyone who agrees to my initial terms qualifies.
  - Example: They sign up and buy products or a certification.
- Tier 2: 50% CAC = $20 Payout - Once they activate.

- Example: *actually finishing the certification they bought*, doing a specific number of posts and outreach, doing a launch, etc.

- This gives them a nice reward (twice the pay) for activating.

- Tier 3: 100% CAC = $40 Payout - Once they <u>sustain</u> a level of performance.

  - Example: They maintain five customers per month on subscription.

This tiered method also has a hidden and very profitable side effect. The <u>average</u> payout is *much less* than your maximum allowable CAC. This means if we leave the maximum payouts for top affiliates, then we get to keep the "leftover" profit. We can use the leftover money to run huge contests, advertise to get more affiliates, incentivize rising stars, etc. Or, I suppose, we can just plain pocket it.

For example, if 20% of sales come from tier 1, 20% from tier 2, and 60% from tier 3, your blended payout is $30 instead of your maximum allowable CAC of $40. This means your LTGP : CAC ratio just improved from 3:1 to 4:1. And often, cutting marketing costs by 33% can translate into 10% to 20% more net profit at the end of the year. A massive jump.

Pro Tip: Pay With Product If Possible "Sell 3 Get It Free"

Everyone likes free stuff. Often, more than what it would cost them to get it. Rewarding performance with product is a cheap *and* effective way to keep them winning. They value it at retail, but it only costs you - your cost. A nice arbitrage of value.

Set sales tiers and bonus your affiliates with product or credit toward the retail cost. At lower tiers, you can even compensate *exclusively* with free stuff. For example: If your affiliates send you tons of massage clients, it's totally acceptable to reward your affiliates with free massages. At low volume, a massage is often worth more to them than sending them a check for $30 (your cost). But as affiliates send you more customers, they'll usually opt for more money. After all, cashing in 100 massages becomes unrealistic.

At Prestige Labs, I offered anyone who sold more than three packages per month a free $200 bundle of their choosing. This also made every affiliate a sponsored athlete. They got free products for life as long as they kept three clients per month buying. I called it "Sell three to get it free."

Action step: Figure out what you want to pay your affiliates for so that you can plan out how much to pay them, with what, and how often.

Step 5: Get Them Advertising - Launch

Like referrers, how much value affiliates get from you determines how much they advertise your stuff. So, *treat them like customers.* Give them something good, fast. And nothing does that for affiliates like big launches and lots of cash.

Here's how launches work:

Affiliates advertise your lead magnet or core offer to their audience *before they can buy it.* They post. They do warm outreach. They run paid ads. They may even do cold outreach. They do as much advertising as they can until the day of launch. When the product is available, they sell it to all the engaged leads they assembled. Some sell one-on-one, some pitch to the whole group. And others simply make the product available.

So if you're gonna do launches to activate your affiliates, which you should, you may as well do them right. I use the whisper-tease-shout method. I can't remember where I first heard this, but the name stuck. Let's launch.

Before we get launching, remember: *good launches have the work done ahead of time.* So do all the work for them. Then, they can plug and play. Let's break down each launch phase. And, I'll give an example of my book launch to drive each point home. Note: this is how you launch *anything,* not just affiliates. I put it in the affiliates section because I haven't found a better way to activate affiliates than launches.

Whisper: *Think "Call Outs."* Like an ad, the key to the whisper phase is *curiosity.* Keep the product itself mysterious and hint at how big of a deal it is. Keep whispers short. And bonus points if you show behind the scenes of making your product.

If you have something in the works, you can start the whisper phase a few years out. The further out you start whispering, the bigger deal it becomes to your audience. We start this early because, the longer something appears to take, the more an audience will value it. For example, all other things being equal, an audience will value a product that took ten years to make more than one that took ten days. So - *show your work.*

Remember: curiosity comes from wanting to know what happens *next.* So embed questions about the product in their minds. We need to tell them about something they want to know more about, then say…*not yet.*

For example during the whisper phase of my book launch: I posted content, reached out to friends, emailed my list, and told potential affiliates about major updates to the book. I showed what draft I was on. I took pictures behind the scenes of me printing out drafts. I showed the many versions of the frameworks I drew. I shared videos of myself editing the book early in the morning and late at night, etc…all of it made <u>people who want leads</u> get curious and *pay attention.*

Action Step: Start whispering every four to six weeks until you get sixty days out. Then whisper every two to three weeks until you get thirty days out. Then, start teasing…

Tease: *Think "Elements Of Value."* It's time to start satisfying all the curiosity you created during the whisper phase. Reveal your product, make the date of the launch public, and start <u>showing</u> the elements of value. Use the What-Who-When Framework from the paid ads chapter.

For example during my book launch, the tease phase: I was more specific and revealed more "hard" information about the book. I started advertising how the book satisfied the dream outcome of limitless leads. Of doing less work, and getting it done faster than they could imagine. I also showed dozens of examples using the book to its potential.

Action Step: Start teasing once per week until fourteen days out. Then tease twice per week until three days out. Three days out, it's time to shout from the rooftops.

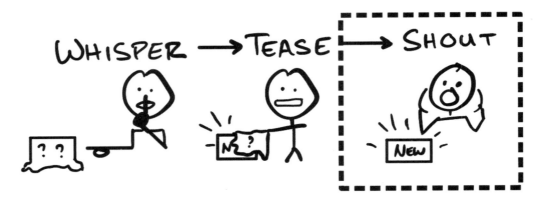

Shout: *Think "Call to Action."* Give specific actions for the audience to take when the product launches. Now you start pounding the audience with bonuses, scarcity, urgency, and guarantees around being "the first ones." You shout to get as many people exposed to your offer as you can.

For example during my book launch, the shout phase: I gave specific calls to action. Short, sweet, clear reminders to register for the book launch. I reminded everyone of the exclusive bonuses only for people who bought during the launch.

Action Step: Shout at least twice a day starting three days out. On the day of, start shouting every few hours until two hours out. Then shout every thirty minutes until you launch the product.

Pro Tip: Movie Releases

The best real world example of whisper-tease-shout is movie releases. They do five second trailers a year out. Then a thirty second ninety days out. Then longer trailers as the date approaches. They drive curiosity, then interest, then action.

Action Step: Get your affiliates to launch. Set them up with everything they need to do the whisper-tease-shout right. They do the advertising. You get the engaged leads. *Everyone* gets paid.

Step 6: Keep Them Advertising

The strategy we use to *start* them advertising differs from the one we use to *keep* them advertising. In an ideal world, you sell an affiliate once and they send engaged leads for life. Integration gets us there.

I've got three ways you can integrate your product into their offer. I order these from easiest to hardest. First, you can get them to *give away your lead magnet* with every purchase of their stuff. Second, you can get them to *sell your lead magnet separately* to their audience. Third, you can get them to directly *sell your core offer*.

They give away your lead magnet for free, which makes their core offer more valuable for no extra cost. Then, you upsell your core offer and every offer thereafter.

1) Affiliates Give Your Lead Magnet Away When Somebody Buys Their Stuff. The idea here is for your lead magnet to make the affiliate's offer more valuable. This allows them to charge more for it *and* get more leads than they could without it. Remember, the best lead magnets give away a free trial or sample of your thing, reveal a problem, or offer a single step of a multi-step solution. Here are examples of each:

Samples And Trials: Say I sell massages and recruit the personal training studio next door as an affiliate. Now, everyone who buys personal training from them gets a free massage from me. The personal training studio now has a stronger offer they can charge more for *and* we get more massage leads. Everybody wins.

Reveal a Problem: Instead of giving a free massage, we offer a free or discounted posture assessment with every training package they sell. Assessments and discounts add less value to the affiliate's offer, but some people will still do it. And to be clear, after assessing the customer, you make them an offer to solve the problems you revealed.

<u>One Step In A Multi-Step Process</u>: Say you have a three-part treatment plan. Massage, stretching, and adjustments. People getting enough value from one step will fear missing out on the rest of the steps. So the more they think the other steps will help solve their larger problem, the more likely they are to buy them. Your affiliate would give away step one of your multi-step process for free. You'd upsell the leads from there.

<u>What I did.</u> We'd get gym affiliates to give away a free nutrition consult to every new member. Then, we'd upsell our products at the consult. They can market that they have nutrition consults included to get more leads and they could charge more for the added value. And we get the opportunity to sell those leads. Everybody wins.

Pro Tip: White Label Lead Magnets

One of my favorite strategies is to let them use the lead magnets I've already made for my audience, *for theirs.* Just make sure your affiliates agree with how you give value *and* understand your call to action. At most, a few tweaks in the copy will make your lead magnet work for them. For example, for gyms, I made white-labeled (no logo) meal plans, grocery lists, and food prep instructions. I gave them to the gyms to use as lead magnets *for their customers.* All they had to do was slap their logo on it - and boom - their audience got to benefit from all my work *instantly*. And, we *both* got more leads.

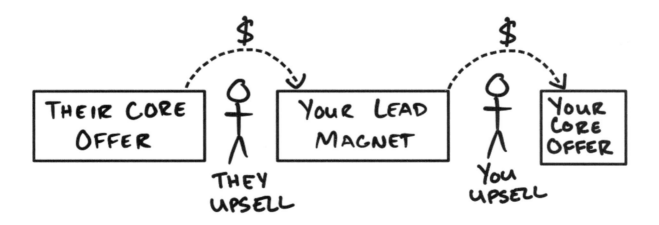

They sell their core offer. Then, they upsell your lead magnet. Then, you upsell your core offer and every offer thereafter.

2) Affiliates Sell Your Lead Magnet. Basically, the affiliate can sell anything of yours that turns their customers into your customers. It could be a book, an event, a service, software, a sample product, etc. Also, giving affiliates all the cash from selling a lead magnet *you fulfill* becomes all profit and no work for them—an attractive proposition for any business. Your money comes by selling your main thing for more than it cost you to deliver your lead magnet. And if you do it this way, you don't need to split any money with them on your core offer. Another win-win.

Example: They sell each of those things we gave away for free in the step above. They sell your massage at a discounted price. They sell your assessment (which you could do 1-1 or in a group format like a workshop). They sell part one of your multi-step solution.

What I did. The gyms would sell a nutrition consult with us and keep the money. They'd maybe charge $99 or $199 to sell an hour of our time. If we were clever, we'd let them keep all the money. If we do, they'll send us even more leads. Then, we'd upsell our products during the consult.

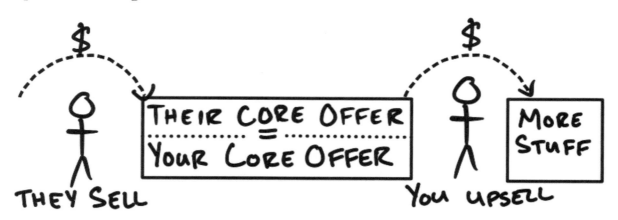

…then you split the money. Either you split the upfront cash, all cash for a certain period of time, or all cash forever. I prefer to pay forever so my affiliates stay motivated to keep my customers forever. And, I never cap payouts.

3) Affiliates Sell Your Core Offer. An affiliate sells your core offer directly to their customers and adds another source of income without extra work. For some affiliates, this is their entire source of income! Many companies offer this structure as either a new business opportunity or a bolt-on to the affiliate's existing business. Either way, anything you sell, they can sell. When you do it this way, the affiliate will get a higher percentage of your lifetime gross profit - but - you won't have to do anything but deliver.

Example: They sell your entire massage package. They sell your entire program or services. They bundle their services with your paid services and charge an even higher price.

What I did. We taught gyms to hold nutrition consultations with white labeled products. Then we taught them to upsell our supplements right to their members and we split the money.

All three strategies work. They're just different. After testing, we continue to do Strategy 1 (twice per year as a big event) and Strategy 3 on an ongoing basis. That being said, many similar businesses in our portfolio use Strategy 2. I'm just sharing what worked for us.

Bottom Line: Integration is the long term strategy for using affiliates to get enduring lead flow. Treat affiliates like customers. Make your offer make sense for their business. Make it so good they'd feel stupid saying no.

Action Step: Integrate with your affiliates by choosing whether you want them to give your lead magnet away, to sell your lead magnet, or to sell your core offer directly.

Those are the six steps to recruiting an affiliate army. Now that we covered that, let me give you three real-life case studies to drive this home.

Three Case Studies You Can Model

Service Business Case Study #1: National Tax Preparation Services

My friend's $50M business prepares LLCs, bank accounts, and articles of incorporation. He focuses on people starting businesses for the first time. But, he doesn't try to compete with Legalzoom. Instead, he built it partnering with people who train new entrepreneurs. His strategy is simple: help those people sell more of their stuff by also selling his stuff. So, he offers every affiliate's customer a free LLC setup. Remember learning about the "high cost lead magnet" from Section II? This is one of those.

Launch: He does a big blast off seminar to his affiliates' audiences to kick things off. People happily take him up on his free LLC offer. That's his lead magnet.

Integrate: Once affiliates see the success of the launch, they integrate his lead magnet into their core offer. Then, my friend's team gets on the phone with the *customers his affiliates bring him for free*. Here's how he makes his money. He sells them what they'll need next. The services they'll need to start their business: bookkeeping, tax preparation, etc.

He hasn't spent a dollar on paid ads. His true advertising costs are two things. One, delivering his free lead magnet (the LLC setup). And two, paying a percentage of every first sale to the affiliates that sent them. That's it. And everybody wins.

Physical Products Case Study #2: Prestige Labs, my supplement company

We sell gym owners at Gym Launch and train them how to advertise and sell their gym memberships. Prestige Labs has a line of supplements for active adults. This makes Gym Launch a perfect affiliate for Prestige Labs. It has a community of gym owners that also have active adult customers. So when Gym Launch sells a new gym owner, they introduce the new gym owners to Prestige Labs. Then the Prestige Labs team follows the "launch then integrate" strategy above. (We really do this).

Launch: We give the gym owners advertising materials so they can re-engage their current and former customers. We focus on warm outreach and posting free content for a free 28 day challenge. When they come in for the free challenge, gym owners sell them supplements to use with the program. The gym owner gets more customers. They make money. We make money. Everyone wins.

Integrate: After the launch, we teach them to sell supplements to every <u>new</u> gym member. So when new clients buy a membership package, the gym owner sets up a nutrition orientation. At the nutrition orientation, the gym owner sells them $50-$1000 of supplements. So if a gym signs up twenty clients per month, and gets seventy percent of them to buy supplements, we get fourteen new customers per month per gym. It doesn't sound like much, but when you multiply 4000 gyms x 14 new sales per month x $200 average order = a lot of money every month.

Local Business Case Study #3: Chiropractors

Chiropractors want new patients. And a portfolio company of ours teaches them to use an affiliate strategy to get them. Their model is simple: go to high volume businesses that have people that are in need of adjustments. A gym fits the bill nicely. Here's what they do.

Launch: They get the gym owner to promote a three hour workshop where they show correct exercises and posture to get more from their workouts. The gym owner promotes the workshop for free *or* sells the workshop for $29-$99 per person. The chiropractor splits the money with the gym owner. Hint: if you give the affiliate (gym owner in this case) 100%

of the money, they'll want to do it more. So if a gym gets thirty people to show up for $99, they make $2970 profit for zero work besides a few emails and posts. At the workshop the chiropractor soft pitches their services and gets a bucket of new patients. Easy peasy lemon squeezy.

Integrate: Long term, the chiropractor convinces the gym owner to include one to two adjustments with every new membership the gym signs up. This increases the value of the gym membership compared to the guy down the street. And, it shows the gym prioritizes its members health and safety (a big concern for beginners). Win win. Now, every new gym member becomes a lead for the chiropractor to follow up with. They repeat this process with thirty gyms, and get more patients than they can handle.

Pro Tip: Employees Are Leads Too

Companies that hire a lot of people make great affiliates. This is HUGE for direct to consumer businesses and *wildly* underused.

<u>Example</u>: Every new hire at a company gets a free massage in their new employee packet. Or, you can give free massages to their employees at lunch. It's free. It's easy. And lots of companies want to provide more value to their teams. They get free value, you get free leads. And since they're probably not in the same business as you, there's no risk of you 'competing' with theirs. So employers can be among the easiest affiliates to integrate with.

Costs and Returns

"Affiliates can't work for my business" the loser said.
"I have to make affiliates work for my business" the winner said.
Be a winner.

When calculating returns with other methods, we compared lifetime gross profit (LTGP) with cost to acquire a customer (CAC). So we spend money to get customers and the customers, in a profitable business, give us *more* money back. Affiliates work differently.

We spend money to get affiliates, sure. But we don't really make much back *from* affiliates themselves. Instead, the money we spend to get an affiliate comes back *from the customers they bring us.* So to calculate returns, we compare how much it costs us to get an affiliate with the gross profit of *all* the customers they send to our business.

Example:

Let's say we own a widget company that grows with affiliates.

- It costs us $4000 in advertising to get an affiliate. CAC = $4000

- Our average affiliate sells $10,000 in widgets per month and stays for 12 months.

    ○ ($10,000 per month) x (12 months) = $120,000 total sales

- The widgets have 75% gross margins. In other words, they cost 25% of retail price to make.

    ○ ($120,000 total sales) x (25% cost of goods) = $30,000 total cost of goods

    ○ ($120,000 total sales) - ($30,000 total cost of goods) = $90,000 in gross profit from all the customers the affiliate brings

- We pay affiliates 40% of the gross profit:

    ○ ($90,000 gross profit) x (40% payout) = $36,000 to the affiliate as payment.

- Here's the gross profit we have left after cost of goods and payouts:

    ○ ($120,000 total) - ($30,000 costs) - ($36,000 payouts) = $54,000 leftover

- Let's find our affiliate LTGP to CAC ratio:

    ○ ($54,000 gross profit left) / ($4000 to get an affiliate) = 12.5 : 1

        …Not too shabby.

If you recall from earlier, we need to be *at least* at 3:1 to have a decent business. Like the example, we want the ratio even higher than that (5:1, 10:1+). Now, if we had these numbers, we'd just do *more*. But, if your actual LTGP : CAC is less than 3, here are the three ways to improve it:

1) Lower CAC: We get affiliates *for less* (by improving our ads, offer, and sales process).

2) Increase LTGP & Decrease CAC: Get more to *activate* (by creating a launch process).

3) Increase LTGP: We make them *worth more* (by improving our integration process).

With affiliates, you now have at least two layers of customers. Your customers, and the people who get you customers. And if you've got super-affiliates you add a third, the people who get you the people who get you customers! This adds complexity, but if you can manage it, it's worth it.

Now that you understand how to use affiliates to advertise, and how to make them more profitable– let's bring it all home.

Conclusion

Like referrals, affiliates aren't an advertising method you can 'do.' They're people who advertise your stuff to benefit you both. You do the core four to get them, and if you want them to love you, then you *treat them like customers*. Because in a lot of ways, *they are*. And if you deliver more value to them than it costs them to get it (especially hidden costs), they'll get you more leads than you can handle.

And like we learned earlier, <u>there are two ways to create a compounding business. You can find more people that never stop buying your stuff *or* you can find more people who never stop selling it for you.</u> Referrals are the former. Affiliates are the ladder.

In theory, once you build an affiliate army, you never need to advertise again. They keep getting you leads month after month. The main reason - it makes sense for them. The way you do business, your leadership, and the value of your product all come into play. You are only as good as the goodwill you have with your affiliate partners. Arrange it right and you should both be better off from the relationship. They should be able to spend more to acquire customers through a more compelling offer, higher profits, or both. And, in return, you get more engaged leads. So why doesn't everyone do this? They don't know it's possible. They don't know how. Or, they don't want to. Simple as that. Hopefully we solved all three of those issues at once.

Remember, *advertising always works*, it's only a matter of efficiency. So once you start, keep going until it works.

Action Steps

Advertise your affiliate offer until you get ten to twenty affiliates. Get results with those affiliates and use their feedback to work the kinks out of your offer, terms, launches, and integration strategy. Then, scale like crazy by turning their results into your first batch of affiliate lead magnets.

FREE GIFT: Build Your Affiliate Army BONUS

As you can see - I am a big fan of building affiliate programs when they're done right. To help you 'do it right' on your first try, I made an in depth video training for you. You can get it free at: **Acquisition.com/training/leads**. And as always, you can also scan the QR code below if you hate typing.

Section IV Conclusion: Get Lead Getters

"The last skill you ever need to learn is how to get other people to do everything you need for you."

We do the core four to get engaged leads: warm outreach, post content, cold outreach, and paid ads. And we use them to get two types of engaged leads: the ones that become customers, or the ones we turn into lead getters. Lead getters come in four flavors: Referrers, Employees, Agencies, and Affiliates. Each have key strengths:

- Customer referrals have the biggest potential for low-cost exponential growth.

- Employees have your *direct* influence and run your business on your behalf.

- Agencies teach skills you keep forever and can transfer to your team.

- Affiliates, once you get them going, can operate entirely on their own.

You can either do the advertising or other people can. And there are more "other people" than there are of you. *You get more leads for the work you do when you have help.* So if you want to get a ton of leads, this is the way.

Maybe your head is officially spinning. Now that you understand these advertising methods, you see leads everywhere you look. *We have so many ways to grow!* And you'd be right. But...you don't know which one to focus on.

Any or all of these lead methods can underpin a successful lead-getting strategy, and I put them in the order of what happens naturally. If you start on your own, you tend to get your first referrals before you start building a big team. And when you start building a big team (employees) you'll probably start looking for professional help (agencies). And only when a business owner has a handle on managing people inside of their business do they tend to get the guts to try and manage people outside their business (affiliates). In any case, you have to forget the idea that everything is going to work out the first time.

If you think you're going to become a millionaire the first year you go out on your own, you're probably wrong. It's very unlikely. And an obsession with "getting rich quick" will likely ensure it never happens. People try shortcuts for a decade until they realize they should have picked a strategy and stuck with it for a decade. If you do that, success is inevitable. Once you find something that works for you—*stick to what you pick.* Those are the best words of encouragement I can offer. The longer you play the game, the better you will get, and the more success you will have. *Just don't quit or switch methods after seeing a few losses.* It's normal to lose in the beginning. In fact, I *expect* to crack a new lead source in three to six months (and this isn't my first rodeo). So if your expectations are *faster* than that, do you think your expectations are reasonable?

We covered a lot here. This section was how you scale: you get other people to help you. They are the missing link. Each has their own strategy and best practices. Use what applies to you now.

This leads us to Section V: Get Started. I want to put everything together for you in a nice bow so you know *exactly what to do next*. Together, we'll eliminate leads as the bottleneck in your business forever. Onwards!

Section V: Get Started

"It's not the end. It's not even the beginning of the end. But it is, perhaps, the end of the beginning"

-Winston Churchill

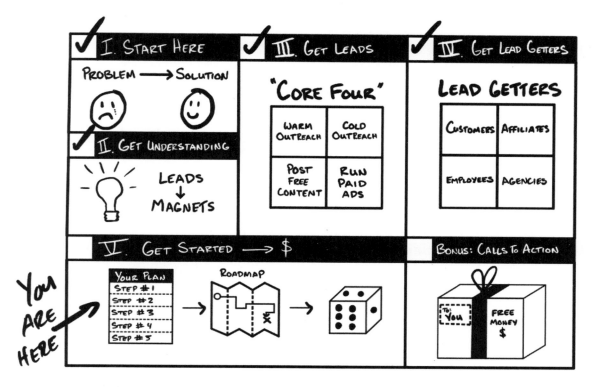

June 2017. Three months after we lost it all, again, and switched Gym Launch to licensing.

"Hey Leila, what do you make of this?" I asked.

"What's up?"

I gave her my phone.

> *Mr. and Mrs. Hormozi, we cordially invite you to a private event for entrepreneurs earning eight figures and up. Let me know if you're interested.*

"Seems cool" she said. "...but we're not making eight figures?"

I pretended not to hear her. "You wanna go?"

"Sure. Is it included in our mentorship dues?"

"One sec, I'll ask"

An email response came a moment later:

> *No, this is an additional fee. It is a two-day event limited to ten people at a private resort.*

"Nope" I said.

"Huh. Can we afford to go?" *Ouch.*

"Who cares? We can't afford not to go."

10 days, a long flight, and a short drive later…

We made it. The "cool kids" meet up. I had one goal, to add as much value as I could to everyone else in the room. But the moment I walked in, I knew I was out of my league. I recognized almost everyone there. They were famous in the advertising world. They all spoke at huge events. Signed autographs. Made millions. Then, there was me. I wasn't an eight-figure entrepreneur. I was a kid from Baltimore just paying to breathe everyone else's air.

Once everyone settled we had a short housekeeping discussion and then got down to business. This way of doing things was a sharp contrast to the big stages, booming sound systems, flashing lights, and other theatrics that "real" events have.

The first speaker was ready to go. He had a 'man bun' and loose yoga-ish clothing. He looked like a hippie. But then, he opened with how he was *only* doing $3,000,000 per month…*is this for real!?* I felt like a fraud. The numbers he shared with such a casual attitude blew my mind. *How is this possible?*

He continued on with his talk using all sorts of business, advertising, and tech jargon. He pointed to dizzying charts and graphs. I came here to learn more about advertising but felt dumber by the second. I recognized enough of the words to realize I knew nothing useful about them. His presentation went *way* over my head. I started sweating bullets. Leila grabbed my hand. We both felt stressed and out of our depths.

He finished and finally opened up for Q&A. *Excellent.* But the questions were still at the same level as his presentation. *Nope, I'm still doomed.* Then, an awkward voice cracked. "So uhh… What courses are you taking to learn all this stuff?" *Now we're talking.* I leaned in. Pen in hand. His answer changed my life:

"At this point, I don't expect to learn anything new from courses. I have to learn by doing. And I 'do' by spending a percentage of my revenue to test new campaigns, new channels, new pages, or just plain crazy ideas. And I learn something every time I test, so the money is well spent. Whenever one of these tests is a winner, and *some* are, it's a big deal. I learn something amazing and make far more money than I spent. It raises the bar for my business and, more importantly, myself. So whether it's 1%, 5%, or 10%, set *some percentage of your advertising budget* aside to try new things without expecting a return. Consider it an investment in your education."

I felt chills go through me like some judgment demon left my body. He gave me permission to fail.

None of this is magic. If he can do this, so can I.

***

The next week, I *tripled* my advertising budget. Yes, it was a bit aggressive. But my mindset had completely changed. I'd either make more, or get better:

Our business went from $400,000 in June to $780,000 in July. From there, my cost to get customers went up too high. So I tried new audiences. Most failed. Then, a hit. Boom, we cruised past $1M to $1.2M to $1.5M per month.

Then, I realized we didn't follow up with our engaged leads… at all. We tested email. Didn't work. We tested phone calls. Nothin'. Then I tried text blasts. Wham, we zoomed to $1.8M the next month.

From there, we tested paid ads like crazy. We made way more of them *and* put more focus on their production value. Boom. We cruised past $2.5M per month.

Then, we launched our affiliate program and stacked another $1.5M per month *on top*. That took us past $4m per month. Years later, our portfolio now does more than $16,000,000 per month.

So test until you find something that works. Take massive action. Stay focused. Double down on it until it breaks. Then test until you find the next thing that works, and double down on *that*. Taking these leaps are the only way to unlock the business you want and the life that comes with it. And maybe, slay your judgment demon too.

So from now on…

You either win or you learn.

The End of the Beginning

Your speed to making big money depends on how fast you learn the skills to making big money. Getting more engaged leads with the skills of advertising, is a great start to making more money. In fact, if you make *any* amount of money, more engaged leads will make you even more. And, sadly, *those skills take time to learn.* So I share my experiences to shave *years* off your time. To shorten the gap between no money and mo' money. It's time to make it happen.

Outline Of The "Get Started" Section

This final section has three chapters. They are short and sweet, just like our time together.

<u>In the first chapter</u>, Advertising in real life– I'll lay out my one big advertising rule. Then, I'll give you my personal one-page advertising plan you can use to get more engaged leads, *today.*

<u>In the next chapter</u>, Putting It all Together– I'll lay out the roadmap to scale from your first few leads all the way to your *$100M Leads* machine.

<u>Finally</u>, A Decade In Page–I'll distill everything we learned into bullets to show how far we've come in our time together. Then, to send you on your way, I'll share a parable that has gotten me through even my hardest times.

Advertising in Real Life: Open To Goal

If some is good, more is better.

June 2014.

When I launched my first gym, I used the same paid ads I used at Sam's gym from way back. And they worked, for a while. Over time, the costs started creeping up. I got less leads for the same money. But, I still needed more customers. I wasn't sure what to do.

I talked to a mentor who ran a chain of tanning salons for some advice. He said "before all this fancy internet stuff, flyers crushed for us, you should try those." So, try them we did. We printed 300. Over the next day, we put them on cars in areas close to the gym. A day passed. Nothing. The next day, the phone rang. *Finally!*

"Hey, you put a flyer on my car–" My heart raced. *It worked!*

"–Yes, yes I did! How can I–?" But before I could finish, he interrupted right back.

"–yea, you scratched my Mercedes…" *Crap.* "…you're gonna need to pay for–" I panicked and hung up the phone. He called back. I let it ring. He never called again. That was the only call I got from the flyers. No leads. Nothing.

Universe: 1. Alex: 0.

A few weeks later

I sat in the lobby of my gym *waiting for customers to fall into my lap*. Feeling bored, and a bit frustrated, I called the mentor with the 'bright idea' to put out flyers.

"Hey Alex - how's it going?"

"Uh, not too good."

"Why what's up?"

"We put out the flyers like you said."

"Oh yea, how many leads you get from 'em?"

"None."

"Hmm…that's odd." He paused. "What was your test size?"

"What do you mean?"

"You know, how many did you put out?"

"I put out 300." I said in a resentful tone.

"Shoot, you only put out 300? Hard to know if anything works with such a small number…I test with 5000. Then when we find a winner, we put out 5000 per day, every day, for a month…"

Five thousand? He *tests* with almost seventeen times more than my entire "campaign." And he does it in a <u>single day</u>. I felt like the person who says exercise doesn't work after going to the gym one time. And I *hate* that person.

"…I mean what kind of response did you think you were gonna get?" he chuckled. "If we get half a percent, that's decent. If we get one percent, that's a winner. With 300 flyers, half a percent would be like one and a half people. That makes it pretty hard to know if you got a winner or not."

I had nothing to say. He was right. *I felt like a fool.*

I doubt he remembers the call. But, it stuck with me. I promised myself I would *never* let effort be the reason *anything* didn't work for me. It could be something else. The offer. The copy. The image. The targeting. The media. The platform. The position of the moon. But *not. my. effort.*

Those 300 measly flyers taught me a mondo lesson. I did the right stuff, but I didn't do it enough times. I lacked what can be described in a single word: volume.

Neil Strauss once said "Success comes down to doing the obvious thing for an uncommonly long period of time without convincing yourself you're smarter than you are." The right action in the wrong amount still fails. Most people, myself included, *stop too soon*. We don't do *enough*.

Most people dramatically underestimate the volume it takes to make advertising work. They're not doing half as much or a third as much as is required. In fact, they're doing dramatically less. I was doing 1/1500th the level of effort required to make a flyer campaign work–*I just didn't know it*.

I hear this all the time. "Alex, I reached out to 100 people over the last six weeks, I only got one customer, it doesn't work." Response: "You did 1/42 of the amount of work required. It was 100 per day, not 100 over time."

Most people do not get that advertising is an inputs and outputs game. To them, outputs appear out of their control. Their low effort inputs get them their low and unreliable output of engaged leads. We're ending that now. You input advertising effort. Your output is engaged leads. Period. Now, we are crystal clear on the stuff you do (the core four). And like we learned when maximizing the core four–You just gotta put in *more* and do it *better* than before. We started with the rule of 100–but when you make that the norm, you're ready to take it to the next level with…

Rule of 100 on Steroids–Open To Goal

A very successful gym chain allowed their sales managers to make their own schedules. But there was a catch–they had to sign up five new members per day *no matter what*. So if they did it by lunch, they could cut out early. But if it took 18 hours, so be it. They called this type of work schedule 'open-to-goal'.

I've found that elite entrepreneurs and salespeople across industries do some variation of 'open to goal'. This is because it's like the rule of 100… but for the big kids. You don't just commit to doing something a specific number of times… you commit to the work until you hit a specific number of outcomes–no matter what. So it means you unlock a whole new level of effort you never even realized you had. It might mean only doing something fifty times to get the desired result. Or, like the flyers, five thousand times, every day, for *years*.

If you want to take your advertising to the next level - <u>work until the job is done.</u> Give up the idea of 'doing your best.' Instead, do what is required. And sometimes that means your best just needs to get better.

How I Make Open To Goal Work For Myself

If I had to pick the three habits that best served me in my life - they would be:

    1) <u>Waking up early (4-5 am)</u>–Pro tip, this actually means *going to bed early…*

    2) <u>Getting right to work</u>–No rituals. No routines. I drink coffee and get to work.

    3) <u>No meetings until noon</u>–No interruptions. Nothing. Fully focused work time.

To be clear, I don't think there's any magic to waking up early. But I do think there's magic in a long stretch of uninterrupted work immediately after a long stretch uninterrupted sleep. After all, it's the most productive hours in a row of the most productive work I can do… with nothing getting in my way… Every. Single. Day. How can you lose?

And since I have a good idea of what I can do in a day, I set my daily goal accordingly. Then, only after my dedicated block of work–do I go put out fires, talk to humans, and deal with the other day to day stuff.

Waking up early, getting right to work, and working 8 hours straight has been my highest ROI "habit stack." By a longshot. If you choose to try it, I hope it serves you as well as it has served me (or better). And for those of you thinking "Wait! That's more than twelve hours of work a day!" You're right. I'm playing to win. But if it overwhelms you at first, I get it. Just throttle it back a few hours and then work your way up. Some days it's tough, but I always like to remind myself:

"Do more than they do, and you will have more than they have."

Alex Hormozi ✔
@AlexHormozi

Whenever I get to a low point where I think "why do I even bother?"

I just try to remind myself "this is where most people stop, and this is why they don't win."

Since my job is usually to "get more customers" in most of my companies, advertising is what I focus on. This book, for example, was written exclusively in that open to goal time block. Why? Because it's an asset that can bring me more companies.

So, if you're gonna follow my high ROI habit stack, then you're gonna want a clear action plan for that time. This is the simplest advertising plan I can give you.

One Page Advertising Checklist

Step #1: Pick The Type Of Engaged Lead To Get: Customers, Affiliates, Employees, or Agencies

Step #2: Pick Rule of 100 or Open To Goal. Commit To Your Daily Advertising Actions

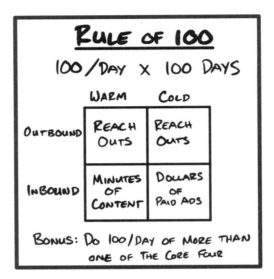

Step #3: Fill Out The Advertising Checklist For That Daily Action

	Advertising Daily Checklist
Who:	You
What:	Your Offer or Lead Magnet
Where:	Platform
To Whom:	Audience/List
When:	First 8 Hours
Why:	Get X Engaged Leads or Lead Getters
How:	Warm/Cold Outreach, Content, Ads
How Much:	100 or Until you hit your goal
How Many:	# of Follow Ups/ Times Retargeted
How Long:	100 Days or Until you hit your goal

Step #4: Do this daily action until you have enough money to afford paying someone else to do it.

Step #5: When you do, go back to step 1. Make employees your new target lead type. And repeat steps 1-4 until you have the help you need. Then, scale again.

Conclusion

Lots of pages. So many ideas. We're almost at the end. But, you don't have any more leads. What gives? Answer: Reading doesn't get people interested in the stuff you sell… *advertising does.* If you're not telling anyone about the stuff you sell, then you aren't getting anyone interested in the stuff you sell. Period.

This chapter laid out the plan to advertise in the simplest way I could:

- Work 'open to goal.'

- Structure your day to make open to goal possible.

- Create *and* commit to that goal with the one page advertising checklist.

Many skip planning, or worse, they write a one hundred page plan that never gets used. So skip the atrocious waste of time that is writing pages of baloney. Harness the power of laying out your action steps on a *single page.* It leaves little room for excuses, distractions, and delusions. You either did the stuff or you didn't. You can fill out your one page advertising checklist in about five minutes. And once the naked truth stares back at you, all you have left is to *do it.*

FREE GIFT: Downloadable Advertising Checklist

You can watch an added training and download this checklist to fill out for yourself at **Acquisition.com/training/leads**. As always, you can also scan the QR code below if you hate typing.

The Roadmap - Putting it All Together

Zero to $100,000,000

"A leader must aim high, see big, judge widely, thus setting himself apart from the ordinary people who debate in narrow confines."

- Charles de Gaulle,

French President During World War II

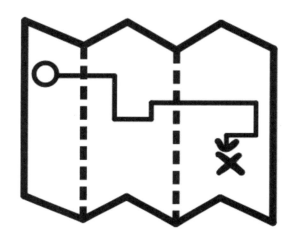

To get to where you want to go, it pays to know what lies ahead. So in this chapter, I describe the phases you will go through as you scale your advertising. Acquisition.com uses this roadmap to scale our portfolio companies from a few million a year, all the way to $100,000,000+. These levels will help you identify where you are on the advertising totem pole so you know what to do to get to the next level.

Level 1: *Your friends know about the stuff you sell.* To start getting engaged leads, you make one offer, to one avatar, on one platform. The moment you get engaged leads, is the moment you can start making money. For me, this started with reaching out to *everyone* I knew.

<u>Primary Action</u>: Warm outreach.

Level 2: *You <u>consistently</u> let <u>everyone you know</u> about the stuff you sell.* You know the exact inputs to get an engaged lead with your chosen advertising method. And, by scaling those inputs, you get *consistent* customers with it. But the consistent customers come from maximizing your personal work capacity. For me, on top of warm reach outs, I maximized my personal work capacity with paid aids, using a case study as my lead magnet. But looking back, I wish I would have started with posting free content. So I suggest that.

<u>Primary Actions:</u> Do as much warm outreach and post as much content as you can *consistently*.

Level 3: *You get employees to help you do more advertising.* You've maxed your personal advertising inputs, but not the platform. And if you want more engaged leads that can only mean one thing. Doing more. For me, I hired a videographer and a media buyer to take most of the paid ads work off my plate.

<u>Primary Action:</u> You hire people to advertise profitably on your behalf.

Level 4: *Your product is good enough to get consistent referrals.* You continue building goodwill and shoot for getting 25% or more of your customers from referrals. Now, you've set yourself up to ramp your advertising again. But to make that work, you have to get more serious about hiring a team to make it happen.

This is when I realized that my ads were shut off but I was still getting referrals every week. So, I doubled down on referrals. I built goodwill using customer feedback to update my product every two weeks. I also started a strong referral program with big incentives at the same time.

<u>Primary Actions:</u> Focus on your product until you get consistent referrals then go back to scaling your advertising with a bigger team. This is where most people mess up. They let their product slip and never recover.

Level 5: *You advertise in more places in more ways with more people.* First, you expand to new audiences on your best platform. Then, you make ads with all placements and media types the platform supports. And, after your team can get consistent results, you expand your team again to add: *another platform, lead-getter, or core four activity*.

For me, I hit two birds with one stone. I expanded my paid ads to include potential affiliates. And this paved the way for my affiliate programs.

<u>Primary Action:</u> Advertise profitably using at least two methods on multiple platforms.

Level 6: *You hire killers.* Your executives grow departments specific to an advertising method or platform without you. And you're not looking for potential. You're looking for experienced leaders specializing in exactly what you want. We capped here.

It took me three years to figure out two things. One, that I needed veteran executives with experience suited to my problems. And two, that they needed stronger incentives. But by the time I realized this, I sold those companies. Once I started Acquisition.com I realized the power of expanding the pie to get more of the right people invested in winning. This is how we crossed $100M+ then $200M+ in portfolio revenue and beyond.

<u>Primary Action</u>: Get battle-hardened executives and department heads to take over new advertising activities and channels.

Pro Tip: Hire Experience, Not Potential.

I tried cold reach outs twice before it worked the third time. The main difference: the person I hired to run it. First, I tried someone external with experience - that failed. Then I tried internally with no experience - that failed. Then finally, I hired internally *with* experience - that worked. Since it's a people heavy, operationally complex machine, the person you hire to manage the team matters a lot. Pick experience. They should know *more* than you do. <u>If you're not learning from them in the interview, you've got the wrong person.</u>

Level 7: I'll come back and edit this chapter once I cross a billion. I promise, I'll send the lessons as soon as I have them. You have my word.

<u>Last Points</u>: I know this looks clean. But it never is. Real business is *messy*. It takes *a lot* to find what audiences, lead magnets, methods, and platforms work best. And you can only find out what works if you try. So you have to try a lot of different things, a lot of different ways, for a long enough time to know for sure.

Nobody can ever know the absolute best thing to do. But I do know this: the more you advertise, the more people find out about the stuff you sell. The more people who know about the stuff you sell, the more people will buy it. This is the key to the *$100M Leads* Machine.

Let's look into your future. Your business makes $100,000,000+ annual revenue. It's great to have a clear picture of what the $100M machine looks like. Let's have a look, shall we? First and foremost, your advertising fires on all cylinders…

- Your media team scales tons of free content, in all media types, on many platforms.

- You regularly make offers to your warm audience to get more customers or affiliates.

- Your ravenous audience makes *anything* you launch *immediately* profitable.

- You have teams running and scaling profitable paid ads across multiple platforms.

- Your cold outreach team gets you more customers.

- You have an affiliate manager launching and integrating all new affiliates.

- You have recruiters *and* recruiting agencies bringing in more lead getters.

- Your product is so good that a third of your customers bring you more customers.

- Your executive team drives all this growth without you.

- And…*you have more engaged leads than you can possibly handle.*

How long does this take? For business owners who know what to do–anywhere from five to ten years. Building something great, even if you know exactly what to do, takes time. And so many like to trumpet "overnight success," but looking behind the curtain tells a different story. It took my wife and I *more than ten years of our best effort,* to cross the first

$100M in net worth. So the bigger your goals, the longer your time horizons need to be. You want to play games where if you wait, you win.

Alex Hormozi ✓
@AlexHormozi

Entrepreneurship isn't for the faint of heart.

The load is heavy and the road is long.

FREE GIFT: BONUS TUTORIAL - Scaling from $0 to $100M+

Sometimes it's useful to hear a narrative of what each stage is like. If you know what comes next, you can start preparing for it today. I recorded a free tutorial where I help you identify where you are at, and what comes next so you can win. You can grab the tutorial free at, you guessed it, **Acquisition.com/training/leads**. As always, you can also scan the QR code below if you hate typing.

A Decade in a Page

"Simplicity is the ultimate sophistication" - Leonardo Da Vinci

We've covered a lot. And I think organizing what we learned into one place helps it sink in. So I made this "back of the napkin" list of what we've covered and why.

1) How to define a lead from this point forward. Now you know what you're after: engaged leads, not just leads.

2) How to turn leads into engaged leads with an offer or lead magnet. And, how to make them.

3) The *Core Four* - the only four ways we can let people know about the stuff we sell.

   a) How to reach out to people who know us: *ask them if they know anybody*

   b) How to post publicly: *hook, retain, reward. Give until they ask.*

   c) How to reach out to strangers: *lists, personalization, big fast value, volume*

   d) How to run paid ads to strangers: *targeting, callouts, What-Who-Whens, CTAs, client financed acquisition*

4) Maximizing the Core Four: *More Better New*

   a) What keeps us from doing what I'm currently doing at ten times the volume? Then solving for that.

   b) Finding the constraint in our advertising. Then testing until it frees the constraint. Then doing *more* until it gets constrained again.

5) The Four Lead Getters: *Customers, Employees, Agencies, and Affiliates*

   a) How to get customers to refer other customers

   b) How to get employees to scale your advertising without you

   c) How to get an agency to teach you new skills

   d) How to get affiliates launched and integrated

6) When advertising in the real world: *The Rule of 100 and Open to Goal*

   a) The five step one-page advertising plan to get more leads *today*.

7) The seven levels of advertisers and the *$100M leads* machine in action.

As I promised in the beginning, the result of these bullets is more, better, cheaper, reliable engaged leads. I hope this book provides you utility. I hope as a result of reading this you know how to get more leads than you currently are. And I hope I unmasked the mystery behind lead getting.

Also, since you are one of the few who actually finish what you start, I want to leave you with a parting gift: a fable that has gotten me through my hardest times.

The Many Sided Die

Imagine you and a friend play a dice-rolling game. You are each given one die. One of the die has 20 sides. The other has 200. On each die, only one side is green. And the rest, are red.

The point of the game is simple: *Roll green as many times as you can.*

The rules of the game are as follows:

- *You can't see how many sides you have. You can only see if you roll red or green.*

- *If you roll green—One of your red sides turns green, and you get to roll again.*

- *If you roll red—Nothing happens, and you get to roll again.*

- *The game ends when you stop rolling. And if you stop rolling, you lose.*

<u>What do you do?</u>

You roll. When you roll red, you pick up the die and roll again. When others roll green, you pick up your die and roll again. When you roll green, you pick up the die and roll again. You keep telling yourself one thing. "The more I roll, the more greens I get." At first, you roll green once in a while. But as more red sides turn green, the greens happen more. With enough rolls, hitting green becomes the rule rather than the exception.

<u>What does your friend do?</u>

He rolls a few times and hits red each time. He sees you roll a green and complains that you *must* have a die with fewer sides. He reasons, it's the *only* way you could have rolled green before him. And although you did, you also rolled many more times. So which is it?

In either case, he rolls a few more times in frustration and hits a green. But then he complains about how long it took. He's spent more time watching you and complaining than actually playing. Meanwhile, you've hit your green streak. *It's so much easier for you*, he tells himself. *You get greens every time! This game is rigged, so what's the point?* He quits.

***

So who got the die with 20 sides? Who got the die with 200 sides? If you get the game then you see, once you roll enough times, <u>*the die you're given doesn't matter.*</u>

- Die with fewer sides might roll green sooner.

- Die with more sides might roll green later.

- But, a die with a green side *always* has a chance of rolling green… *if you roll it.*

- Every die hits its green streak when rolled enough times.

All of us get a many-sided die. And looking at the other players, you have no idea if it's their 100th roll or their 100,000th. You don't know how "good" other players are when they start, you can only see how well they do *now*. But, if you understand the game, you also know *it doesn't matter.*

A few begin playing early. Others begin much later. The rest sit on the sidelines complaining about how lucky the players are. I guess so, but they're luckier because they play. And when they hit red, which they do, they didn't quit. They rolled again.

Learning to advertise is a lot like the game of the many sided die. You do not know if it will work until you try. And when you start advertising, you will probably hit red on your first rolls. But if you try enough times *you will hit green*. And *when* it works, you have a better chance of getting it to work *again*. The more you do it, the easier it gets. You begin to understand the game. No matter how many players there are or the number of sides on the die you're given, you start to see the only two guarantees:

1) The more times you roll, the better you get.

2) If you quit, you lose

So here's my final promise:

<u>You cannot lose if you do not quit.</u>

Free Goodies: Calls To Action

If it's free, it's for me!

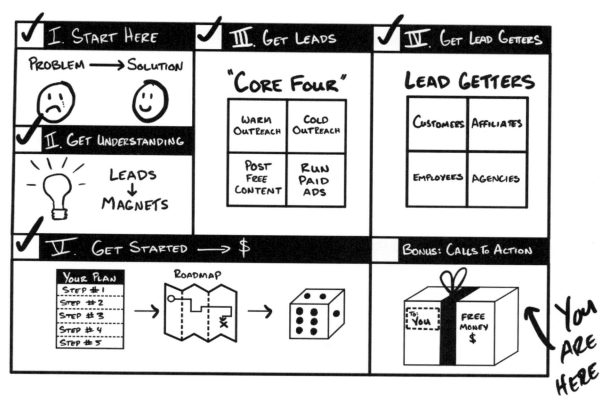

I'm gonna give you a bunch of free stuff in a second - so stay tuned.

Dr. Kashey (my editor) and I spent over 3,500 hours on this book. We wrote 650+ pages and 19 drafts with varying frames, themes, and points of focus. But ultimately, the changes left only the most distilled 'need to knows' inside. We went through 127 pages of hand drawn models to carve out the few that made it into the book. All that to say - I hope this work results in you growing the business of your dreams.

When I look back on my life these books will be among the things I am most proud of. I wouldn't be able to write as fervently if I didn't think people would read it. And as much as I strive to be the man who would work as hard if nobody cared, I am not there yet. Your support and positivity make a difference for me. So thank you from the bottom of my heart for allowing me to do the work I find meaningful. I am forever grateful.

If you are new to #mozination, welcome. We believe in big ambitions, and matching our ambitions with giving and patience. And I have a personal goal in that spirit of giving: *to die with nothing left to give.*

So if you're still with me, thank you. I want to provide some more goodies.

1) **If you're struggling to figure out <u>who</u> to sell to,** I released a chapter called "Your First Avatar" between this book and the last. Think of it like a 'single' from a music album. You can get it for free at **Acquisition.com/avatar.** Just pop in your email and we'll send it over.

2) **If you're struggling to figure out <u>what</u> to sell**, you can go to Amazon or wherever you buy books and search "Alex Hormozi" and $100M Offers. It should get you on the right path. The digital version is available for sale at the cheapest price that the platform would let me make it and still list it as a book.

3) **If you're struggling with getting people to buy, my next book will be on persuasion and sales.** It may or may not be out by the time you read this. It'll either be called $100M Sales *or* Persuasion. I haven't decided yet. But if you search my name you can look for any other books that may be out by the time you read this.

4) **If you want a job at Acquisition.com** or in one of our portfolio companies - we love hiring from #mozination. We love doing this because we've found our best returns investing in great people. Go to **Acquisition.com/careers/open-jobs**, and you can see all the job openings across all our companies and our portfolio.

5) **If your company is over $1M in EBITDA (profit)**, we'd love to invest in your business to help you scale. It brings so much pleasure to know our portfolio companies have grown much bigger and faster than mine *because they avoided the mistakes I made.* If you want us to take a look under the hood and see if we can help go to **Acquisition.com**. Sending your info is fast and easy.

6) To get the **free book downloads and video trainings** that come with this book, go to **Acquisition.com/training/leads**.

7) **If you like listening to podcasts and want to hear more**, my podcast at the time of this writing is top 5 in entrepreneurship and top 15 in business in the US. You can get there by searching "Alex Hormozi" wherever you listen. Or, by going to **Acquisition.com/podcast**. I share useful and interesting stories, valuable lessons, and the essential mental models I rely on every day.

8) **If you like to watch videos,** we put a lot of resources into our free training, available for everyone. We intend on making it better than any paid stuff out there, and let you decide if we succeeded. You can find our videos on YouTube or wherever you watch videos by searching "Alex Hormozi".

9) **And if you like short form videos,** check out the bite sized content we pump out on the daily at **Acquisition.com/media**. You'll see all the places we post and you can pick the ones you like the most.

And last, thank you again. Please be one of those givers and **share this with other entrepreneurs by leaving a review.** It would mean the world to me. I'm sending you business building vibes from my desk. I spend a lot of time there, so it's a lot of vibes. May your desire be greater than your obstacles.

Hope to meet you and your company soon. Ad astra.

Alex Hormozi, Founder, Acquisition.com